Counseling and Advice Giving in Pastoral Care

Bernard D. Green, S.D.S.

Religious Education Division
Wm. C. Brown Company Publishers
Dubuque, Iowa

ISBN 0-697-02276-5

10 9 8 7 6 5 4 3 2 1

Dedication

To my parents who showed me that the wisdom of "ordinary" people can be quite extraordinary and should never be underestimated.

"And it is also said," answered Frodo: *"Go not to the Elves for counsel, for they will say both no and yes."*
"Is it indeed?" laughed Gildor. *"Elves seldom give unguarded advice, for advice is a dangerous gift, even from the wise to the wise, and all counsel may run ill. But what would you? You have not told me all concerning yourself; and how then shall I choose better than you?"* (J. R. R. Tolkein. Lord of the Rings. Boston: Houghton, Mifflin, 1965, p. 93)

Contents

Preface

Occasionally in the news we hear rather disturbing reports of people suing counselors and ministers for giving them wrongful advice. While these suits seem mostly to have failed, the very fact of this development is in itself disturbing, since it may inhibit many ministers from taking their counseling role seriously. Nevertheless it does challenge us to take a serious look at the place of advice giving in counseling. It is on this that I would like to reflect. The questions we are concerned with are: is advice-giving to be equated with pastoral counseling or is there a difference between them? If there is a difference, what role, if any, does advice giving play in pastoral counseling?

To begin with we will look at advice giving and counseling in general, to see whether we can formulate an understanding of the essential dimensions of advice giving and to what extent modern counseling practice supports its use and why. Out of our discussion, we will formulate an understanding of the place of advice giving in the counseling process. Then we will examine the issue in terms of pastoral counseling, paying attention to the theological issues involved. This process will afford us an opportunity to explore several important themes in pastoral counseling, particularly those concerned with the tension between the individual and the community. This, in itself, is an instance of a deeper tension today between two basic frames of reference current in the wider cultural environment: the tension between the subjective and the objective approaches to understanding reality. Since this tension is so crucial to understanding the value and limitations on advice giving, it will be explored in some depth, and its implications for the practice of counseling as a whole will be examined.

The aim of this work then is to be able to see the nature and use of advice giving in a clearer light, both as to its possibilities as a way of helping another, and also its limitations. In doing so we should be able to highlight more clearly the principles involved in a genuinely helping relationship and so meet the challenge posed to us by current lawsuits. It is then an opportunity to look more deeply at the factors that we need to be aware of if we wish to really be of assistance to others in their emotional, social and spiritual confusions.

In light of this, the reader will find that the material is dealt with in a somewhat polarized way, with various extremes contrasted with one another. This is a methodological choice to help highlight the principles. It is not meant to be an accurate description of the normal situation in which the counselor will find himself. On the whole, the counselor will not be dealing with extremes but with ordinary situations which will not clearly illustrate either ends of the spectrum. But by looking at the extremes we will be able to illustrate more clearly those principles which are relevant to all counseling situations and thus help the counselor recognize and assess their presence in a given situation.

In looking at these principles, we will also have to be quite "radical" in the sense of getting down to and exposing the roots of the attitudes and tendencies to which we are referring. While this, on occasion, might seem like taking a sledgehammer to crack a nut, it again has importance in the elucidation of the principles involved. We are not concerned with simply giving rules of thumb, since these tend to come out of general and uncritically accepted assumptions derived from a particular cultural situation. While such rules of thumb undoubtedly have their own limited value, our present situation requires that we go deeper, particularly in the area of pastoral ministry which deals with people at the core of their being. Today, in the area of human technology, there are certain fundamental and far-reaching perspectives and dynamics involved which need to be raised to consciousness and critiqued in the light of the gospel to which we are committed. More than ever, Christians today need to be able to distinguish the principles out of which they are being called to live from those which are present and operative in the world at large, not simply to denounce or reject them, but also to be able to learn and benefit from them. It is possible to reach through to these assumptions through an examination of what is involved in giving advice, and I have taken the opportunity of doing so. So while these sections might at first glance seem unnecessarily complex and deep in dealing with the topic at hand, I think they will help us to see more clearly the issues involved and help us to formulate the principles on a sounder basis.

This essay will be concerned with much wider issues than those involved with simply avoiding malpractice suits and the legal issues involved. A discussion of the value and limitation of advice giving in counseling might help us reduce the possibly negative effects of using it in our ministerial work. The discussion will also help us take a fresh look at the principles that should inform our pastoral practice, thus rendering us more effective in this important ministry.

Acknowledgments

I would like to acknowledge my indebtedness to some of the people who have helped me with the development of this book. In the first place, Father Charles A. Curran, late Professor of Research in Human Relations at Loyola University, Chicago. Although I never personally had the privilege of meeting Fr. Curran before his untimely death in 1978, his works have had an enormous influence on my thinking about and my practice of counseling and education. Anyone familiar with his work through the many workshops that he presented around the country to clergy, religious, and laypeople will recognize his presence at many points in this work. With regard to this, I would like to make it clear that, apart from one reference only, when Father Curran is mentioned as a resource, it is the above Father Charles A. Curran, the psychologist, who is being referred to and not Father Charles E. Curran, the moral theologian.

Like so many other people, both in and out of Church circles in the United States, I came to the work of Father Curran through the Counseling-Learning Institutes. In their workshops, the training of people in interpersonal communication, counseling, and homiletic skills, and through their continuing research into the psychological dynamics of education, especially in the area of language learning, they carry on the work which Father Curran inaugurated. It was through the patient willingness on the part of the staff to discuss the various aspects of this topic with me and their encouragement to persevere with the writing of it, that it has now come to the point of publication.

In particular, I would like to mention Father Roland Janisse who gave of his time unstintingly to do some very essential editorial work and so prevented the grammar and the language from being too barbarous. Father Daniel Tranel who spent long hours with me discussing some of its central ideas, helping me to sort out what was significant and what was not; and Dr. Jennybelle Rardin who constantly encouraged me through the difficult parts, always willing to try to understand my convoluted attempts to express what were only vaguely sensed and inadequately formulated opinions. While I hope they feel that their efforts were rewarded by the final result, needless to say, in the last analysis, I alone am responsible for what is presented here, both for the positions taken and their mode of presentation.

However, this work would not have been undertaken in the first place had it not been for queries from my students at Sacred Heart School of Theology as to the value of advice giving. I owe them a debt of thanks for stimulating me to think about it. The faculty, too, helped enormously in the beginning by being willing to spend an afternoon discussing the concepts. My own community also, the Society of the Divine Savior, deserves recognition for their continuous support of me in this project. This includes not only my superiors who encouraged me to publish but also those with whom I have lived over the last four years, for their willingness to put up with my frequently "antisocial" behavior as I spent long hours in front of the computer. Even when I was with them physically, I was very often mentally in some other realm, pondering and worrying over some aspect or other. And to all my other friends who may have felt neglected during the writing of this book, thanks for your forebearance and patience.

Introduction: the Equivalence

For many who wish to do pastoral counseling, whether clergy or laity, especially those who have not been through a formal counseling program, advice giving and counseling are often perceived to be synonymous. People take for granted that the role of the counselor is essentially one of imparting information. This notion is drawn either from their education or reflection, based on their personal life experience, on how best to solve a particular problem or difficulty. It might be called the prescriptive approach to counseling: It either offers a way of acting that the person had not previously thought about, or prescribes more effective ways of acting than those hitherto used by the client.

This generally held view is sustained by the widespread tendency in popular psychology, especially in the self-help newspaper columns. These popularizers offer advice for the solving of every conceivable psychological and social difficulty that people may have. Given this widespread practice, it is hardly surprising that as Lawrence M. Brammer and Everett L. Shostrom observe,

> In the thinking of the man on the street, counseling and psychotherapy are almost synonymous with giving advice (Therapeutic Psychology. Englewood Cliffs, N.J.: Prentice-Hall 1960, p. 269).

The acceptance of counseling and advice as synonymous terms has deep roots in our culture. Historically, a counselor helps the ruler to grasp the complex dimensions of situations so that he can make the best possible decisions. The counselor provides those in authority with information and perspectives and suggests how best to proceed.

This historical background is still enshrined in the definition of counseling given in the Webster Collegiate Dictionary, for instance, where it is described as "advice given especially as a result of consultation." Advice is defined as "a recommendation regarding a decision or course of action."

Still actively present today, this usage is incorporated by religious orders in their organizational structures, with General Superiors and Provincials all having their bodies of counselors. The President, too, and other governmental leaders have their special *counselors* to advise them. In the practice of law, we retain the term *counselor-at-law* for one who advises regarding the best way to proceed in a lawsuit. More generally, we continually use the expression, *to seek somebody's counsel* when we need advice over some matter or other.

Because counseling and guidance are often considered virtually identical, it is entirely understandable if a person sees professional counseling as consisting of expert guidance in providing the best way to act in his difficulties. However, if one goes to a counselor simply expecting this sort of service, she is likely, in many instances, to be rather surprised to find that the *counselor* is reluctant to give such clear information and directions. The reason for this is that there are many in counseling circles today who strongly question the value of giving advice in the realm of personal difficulties and even view it with great caution. These practitioners do not see themselves as essentially advice givers and, contrary to popular usage, may find this activity disadvantageous to the client.

How widespread is this attitude? Even Allen Ivey and Lynn Simek-Downing, who agree that counseling does have a directive function, say this of advice giving:

Most of our life is spent in expression of content or in hearing others express content . . . [i.e. as to what to do]. It is perhaps natural therefore that counseling and therapy tend to down-play this skill which people have developed more extensively than they need (Ivey, Counseling and Psychotherapy. *Englewood Cliffs, N.J.: Prentice-Hall, 1980).*

Their concern about advice giving is that it is an overused way of helping people. Advice giving tends to be a rather facile and unthinking substitute for real thought and in-depth consideration of a person's difficulties and, as such, is more a way of satisfying the person's view of himself as a helper than in fact as an expression of any real commitment to be helpful.

Reflecting this concern, Brammer and Shostrom believe that:

The WEIGHT of counselor opinion, however, seems to be against the use of straight, opinionated advice. It certainly has gross limitations for extended psychotherapeutic types of counseling (op. cit., p. 271).

Although there is a tendency to equate the two terms in the popular mind, in the field of professional *counseling,* they are not considered to simply synonymous. Indeed, in some forms of *counseling,* advice giving plays so little a part in what goes on that it might be legitimate to question whether it should still be called *counseling.* By continuing to use the word *counseling* to describe what they do, practitioners who downplay the role of advice giving run the risk of confusing people as to what counseling is, since, given their background of expectations, clients do come to them expecting definite information and expert direction as to what to do.

This confusion then leaves us with some important questions. How widespread is advice giving in modern counseling? Do modern psychotherapeutic thinking and practice promote advice giving or even the equivalence between advice giving and counseling? If counseling, as such, is not to be equated with advice giving, what then is *counseling?* If advice giving in counseling is not seen in a favorable light, why isn't it? Is there anything intrinsic about giving advice that has caused this uneasiness, apart from the possible lawsuits mentioned in the Preface? Are there good reasons for seeing advice giving as less than helpful and therefore to be used only with caution and in particular circumstances? Can we formulate an understanding of the helping process that, while minimizing advice giving, enables us to still see it as *counseling* without doing violence to the word?

In Part I we will seek to answer some of these questions. First, we will consider the intrinsic components of advice giving and their relationship to the various schools of counseling to see what levels of importance are given to advice giving and why. We will explore in some depth the role that the explanation of the dynamics of human functioning, especially as based on psychological research, might play in counseling practice in contrast to what might be called clarification of the unique inner life of the individual. Is counseling most effectively based on the one or the other? Finally, we will seek to formulate some basic understanding of the dynamics of effective counseling and assess the role that advice giving might play in it.

Part I Advice Giving in Modern Counseling Practice

1 Subjective and Objective Approaches to Counseling

Advice Giving: A Paradigm

Before we can decide whether therapeutic counseling can legitimately be viewed as advice giving or be able to assess to what extent advice giving is a valid aspect of the helping process, we need to discern the contours of what is involved in giving advice.

On the assumption that the giving of advice is a time-honored activity in human affairs, and that it has its own intrinsic rationale and validity, what are the presuppositions upon which it is based? There would seem to be four such pre-suppositions.

The first presupposition is that the counselor is able to identify accurately with the client's situation. It assumes that in its essential and significant outlines the counselor shares with the client a common understanding of his or her sit-uation. Either they share in the same situation, i.e., they are both concerned about a situation in which they are both involved (such as an advisor to a president), or they have shared in a similar situation as one person might advise another about, for example, climbing a mountain. The ability to give advice would seem, in the first presupposition, to depend on the degree of commonality between one set of experiences — that of the counselor, with another — that of the client.

The second assumption would be that the counselor has access to perti-nent data the client needs in order to make a more informed decision as to what to do. This assumption rests, then, on the counselor's ability in some respect or other to understand the situation of the client better than the client. This expertise might derive either from superior knowledge about the situation, because, either from education or experience, he is more familiar with its content and dynamics than the client, or from the fact that he can see the situation more clearly, i.e., has access to more data about it because he lacks the confusions and tunnel vision caused by emotional involvement.

The third assumption is that he or she shares with the client the same un-derstanding of what would constitute a desirable or undesirable outcome to the situation. In other words, the counselor needs to be able to share the same value system, at least with regards to the particular situation involved. If the client does not have a real sense that he or she and the counselor share the same value system and hence can agree on the goals to be achieved and the means whereby they are to be achieved, the client is likely to be prevented from acting on any suggestions or directions given.

The final and most important assumption would be that the counselor is confident that the other is willing and able to take responsibility for any actions he or she does actually take. This would seem to be implicit in the status of a counselor as one who is employed by another. It is the client who is the authority figure, employing the counselor for help in a particular area for which the client has primary responsibility. The client needs assistance in order to carry out that responsibility and seeks those whom he feels are able to render that assistance.

It is this which distinguishes advice from a command. Advice is a recommendation; it leaves the final decision up to the client; and in that decision the client assumes personal responsibility for the outcomes.

On this paradigm, the counselor as advice giver is essentially a servant, a sort of auxiliary brain, an extension of the client's own review and decision-making process: He understands the client's situation, offers him information about it that the client could not otherwise have and so enables him or her to see it more objectively. The counselor suggests lines of action that will produce agreed upon outcomes, but does so on the understanding that the final decisions as to what can and should be done will be made by the client.

Generally, we can say that advice giving is a legitimate activity in and of itself when (1) the counselor is able to understand the situation of the client more objectively than the client; (2) he has expertise in the area in question, i.e., understands its dynamics and is able to function therein better than the client; (3) the counselor is able to agree with the client on the goals to be achieved and the legitimacy of the means to achieve them; and (4) the counselor is confident that the client is able to take personal responsibility for acting on the advice.

This analysis offers us a paradigm against which we can assess how well modern therapeutic counseling can or ought to be considered as synonymous with the giving of advice. Following from this, the analysis indicates to what extent counseling psychology backs up or reinforces the general notion that helping a person in psychological and social difficulties is primarily a matter of offering information and direction. We need to ask to what extent the counselor is seen as: (1) possessing an area of expertise over the data of the client's situation that the client himself does not have, such that the counselor has a more accurate understanding of it than the client has; (2) being able to share in the meaning structures and value system of the client to the extent that they are able to be in agreement as to what is pertinent and what is not; and (3) essentially a servant to the client, ready to structure the relationship around the belief that the client has the ability to take responsibility for what he does with any advice that may be given.

Application of the Paradigm
to Modern Psychotherapy

It is, in fact, questionable whether what is called therapeutic counseling today in any of its forms fits this paradigm or is capable of doing so with any exactness. This will become clearer as we examine each of these dimensions in turn.

The Expertise of the Counselor

We might begin by asking why go to a counselor? What is it that people are seeking when they come for psychological counseling? Generally speaking we might say that people seek counseling because they do not understand what is going on in their lives and the reasons they cannot meet those basic needs or achieve emotional well-being and satisfaction in their living. They are confused, anxious and dispirited and wish to get some sort of understanding of what is wrong and what they might do about it. Their area of concern, then, is usually their emotional relationships with themselves and with others. This is then rather a vague and undifferentiated area of concern. Even though the *presenting* problem might seem clear-cut enough (e.g., *Why do I keep falling out with my boy or girl friend? What shall I do about my failing grades?*) and might seem to be a simple act of asking for specific information about a specific practical problem. It is in fact usually more: an expression of inner confusion as to why the person is not achieving some real and desired satisfaction in relationships and activities. The assumption is therefore that when a person comes to a counselor his or her concern is personal integration, both internally and externally, and the achievement of a sense of satisfaction with who they are and how they are living.

Against this background, is the therapeutic counselor in a position to give advice? Does the therapeutic counselor have the expertise concerning the client's situation which the latter needs in order to be able to function more adequately? Counseling theory is divided over the answer to this question. Basically, there are two frameworks of counseling theory. Patterson calls them the *manipulative* and the *understanding* approaches, Combs would refer to them as *closed* and *open* systems; they might also be referred to as the *objective* and the *subjective* approaches, or as Joseph Rychlak calls them, the *extraspective* and the *introspective*. (See Rychlak, *Discovering Free-will and Personal Responsibility*. New York: Oxford University Press, 1979.) The former objective is closely allied with advice giving or the giving of information about the client's situation and what to do about it; the latter objective would avoid this.

1. The Objectivist Approach

In the objectivist approach the counselor's expertise is seen as being based on his scientific knowledge of the intrapersonal and interpersonal dynamics of human functioning. As Frederick Harper puts it:

> *Counselors must understand that the interpersonal art of applying counseling skills and resources is based on the scientific study and understanding of human behavior. . . . Counseling theory offers a conceptualised framework for exploring client behavior and charting steps for helping the client to improve behavior or resolve problems. Traditional counseling theories are founded upon principles of personality theory and principles of psychology in general* ("Counseling and Biological Psychology," Counseling and Human Development, *December 1985: p. 4).*

Knowledge of these principles is seen as putting the counselor in the position of being able to understand better than the client the psychological forces operating in a situation, and hence he is more competent than the client to say what can be done to improve it. His ability comes out of a body of *scientific* knowledge which allows him to better interpret the data of the client's experiencing and elucidate its *real* meaning. This knowledge is based on an analysis of the client's situation in terms of some explanatory framework which the counselor believes is the most comprehensive and accurate available. Possession of this framework of knowledge enables the counselor to accurately interpret what is going on and make suggestions as to what to do about the client's situation in order to achieve optimal results.

The general assumption on which this is based is derived from a view of reality as objectively given, stable in its essential reality and governed by discernable regularities or *laws* which are capable of being discovered through the use of the *scientific* method. Psychology based on this perspective seeks to find those laws which are of general applicability and able to account for the specific events of human behavior. In this it shares the same perspective as that of the physical sciences, particularly in its classical form, which postulated that any given state in nature was the result of a previous state and could be completely explained in terms of it; discovery of the forces operating in the prior state would theoretically enable us to predict with accuracy the consequent state. In principle it was felt that all reality was capable of being explained from careful observations and classifications of the data. Through experimentation and isolation of the causal variables, the hope was that we could bring these variables increasingly under rational control.

The Objectivist Approach in Psychology

Psychology, then, in the objectivist framework, is viewed as an empirical science, concerned with discovering the objective laws and principles that govern human behavior. It seeks to codify and describe how the different elements of the human reality interact to produce particular results in the hope that it can formulate a body of normative knowledge. It also devises effective techniques which will enable us to understand completely what is going on and hence both predict and control the outcome. Offer and Daniel Melvin Sabshin articulate the hope that lies behind the search for an objective scientific understanding of human reality, in particular as it relates to the study of normality, in these words:

> *In our opinion, a theory concerning normal human development has tremendous appeal for the following reasons: first it will make sense of our personal lives. We will know what to expect in each stage and we will be better prepared for potential crises. Furthermore, it will enable us to better understand our children and our parents and to help them when necessary. We will also know when someone deviates from the normal pattern; in other words, we will recognize when he or she needs outside, professional help in order to get back on track. We will also know when the outside help is sufficient and we can continue to develop by ourselves. A theory will also allow us to optimally control our future and permit us to make better decisions concerning ourselves, our families, and our friends. In short it will, or should, make us feel better (Normality and the Life Cycle. New York: Basic Books, 1984, pp. 393–94).*

The core aim of this approach to psychology is a comprehensive, empirically based, and scientifically verified explanation of human dynamics which enables us to control and predict human functioning. In their discussion of research into interpersonal relations, the authors of *Interpersonal Dynamics* indicate the influence of this perspective in social psychology when they write:

> *Today in the social sciences, two languages compete for primacy: the language of the "game" and the language of the "myth." Game languages follow the model of the physical sciences by defining all terms*

5

operationally and in formal terms. . . . Analysis of social interaction is made in terms of moves and countermoves. . . . In all these fields the trend toward miniature systems is indicative of the model of the tight situation, rigidly defined, where individuals can be assumed to conform to a set of rules which can be completely specified (Warren G. Bennis, et al. Interpersonal Dynamics. *Homewood, Ill.: Dorsey Press, 1968, p. 16).*

This normative knowledge which will give us hard data about human functioning on a par with that offered by the mathematical, *hard* sciences is what society generally expects of psychology. Industry, politics, and allied fields all look to psychology as a science for advice on how best to format and present products and programs so that they have the best chance for acceptance by the public at large. In an article in *Newsweek,* there was a report on a series of computer programs which is now available to help people do this. It illustrates the understanding of psychology that I am referring to. It reports:

the first such project, a program . . . called Sales Edge, *designed to give salespeople a detailed strategy for manipulating customers into buying through a matching up of the psychological characteristics of both parties. . . . Johnson's (the originator) initial emphasis will be business users (high need achiever males, somewhat cynical) but in the long run he foresees life strategy programs for pepping up a marriage or encouraging an underachiever child. And recreation strategy will mean computerized help for coaches who want to motivate football teams in the manner of Knute Rockne or tennis players seeking customerized psyche-out ploys against their opponents ("Selling Psych-out Software,"* Newsweek, January 16, 1984).

This, then, is the sort of knowledge the public expects from psychology today. A glance over the shelves of any bookstore will reveal that there are numerous writers in psychology who are willing to try to meet this expectation for advice on how to achieve a wide variety of life goals. They all largely operate out of this objectivist approach, offering a body of normative knowledge about human dynamics and a variety of *proven, effective, simple,* and *fast* techniques by which to mold and determine the dynamics of human situations to achieve optimum results.

The Objectivist Approach in Counseling

In those schools of psychotherapy which operate out of this perspective, the counselor is likewise seen as the expert on the dynamics of the person's situation and what to do about it in order to achieve the best outcome. At present the objectivist approach is most clearly dominant in what is called the medical model of therapy, with its notion of mental illness, and its corresponding notion of *cure.* But its influence is more generally reflected in the use of the word *treatment.* Treatment implies diagnosis of a particular disorder, a knowledge of what needs to be done to eradicate the disorder, and the ability on the part of the counselor to deliver the right treatment. The model itself requires that we look at psychological difficulties on the basis of specific treatments for specific difficulties, as these are determined by the experts to be based upon the objective knowledge of the nature of mental illness. Many institutions that provide mental health services expect that their counselors be able to set up specific treatment programs for the variety of psychological ills that people bring to them.

Psychiatry, especially, in which this model is best exemplified, shares much of the aura of medicine in which the doctor is the expert in what is going on inside the patient and is able to tell him what to do in order to put it right and achieve full health again. This approach is being reinforced with the increasing knowledge of the value of drugs in the amelioration of certain conditions. With the spectacular results being attained in our knowledge of brain functioning through neurological research, there seems to be an increasing movement in psychiatry to a predominantly biochemical understanding of mental illness in which mental *sickness* is seen to be *caused by* an underlying chemical imbalance or deficiency in the brain. Morton Reiser describes this movement thus:

> Students and clinicians alike turn increasingly to reductionist science, understandably hoping that it will ultimately render clinical science more effective and clinical art unnecessary. Nowhere is this more true than in psychiatry. For a time after World War II, psychoanalysis was regarded as holding promise not only of advancing our understanding of mental illness, including etiology and pathogenesis, but also of providing a scientific psychological basis for the clinical art of nonpsychiatric medical practice, as well as of psychiatry itself. Progress during the past thirty years, in the neurosciences, especially neurobiology, is now overshadowing clinical psychodynamic considerations in the clinical area (Reiser. Mind, Brain, Body. New York: Basic Books, 1984).

This, however, is a recent phenomenon. In the beginning, the practice of psychiatry drew its techniques for treatment mainly from the more purely *psychological* fields of psychoanalysis and behaviorism and, despite the fact that the use of drugs is becoming more central, many psychiatrists would still generally want to combine the use of drugs with psychotherapy, usually but not exclusively, of the behaviorist or psychoanalytic varieties.

The alliance with these particular forms of psychotherapy is understandable since both schools operate out of the same objectivist framework. In classical psychoanalysis the determinants of behavior are considered to lie in the dynamic tension between certain internal biological forces operating in the unconscious and the external world which thwarts their satisfaction. This leads to their repression and consequent distortion through the operation of defense mechanisms. This process is usually linked to specific childhood events, education, and traumas. The analyst is seen as the expert on the unconscious processes operating in the client and interprets for the client what his real situation is. Through various techniques such as catharsis (the release of blocked emotional energy) and abreaction (the reexperiencing of the original trauma), he seeks to alter the internal stimuli which is producing the undesired behavior. The object-relations school of psychoanalysis has moved away from the emphasis on drives to a more phenomenological analysis of perceptual and emotional structures, which, though derived from childhood, are still operational in the present. Both schools still follow the objectivist's main metapsychological framework. Weiner describes present psychoanalytic perspectives as resting on three foundations:

First dynamic approaches are based on inferred processes. Behavior is explained in terms of underlying aspects of personality structure and dynamics that are considered to account for it. . . . Second, dynamic approaches stress intellectual processes . . . [such that] success in dynamically oriented psychotherapy is expected to depend on how extensively a person can gain understanding and impose reason on emotion. . . . Thirdly, dynamic approaches emphasize historical processes. Psychological difficulties are believed to originate in prior life experiences that have burdened a person with unresolved conflicts and mal-adaptive coping styles (Michel Hersen, Alan E. Kazdin, Alan Bellack, eds. Clinical Psychology Handbook. New York: Pergamon Press, 1983, p. 22).

Hence, Ivey and Simek-Downing explain the task of psychodynamic therapists thus:

Psychodynamic counseling has been described as an "uncovering therapy," in that the techniques and theory are focused on discovering the underlying unconscious processes governing behavior. Once these unconscious processes are discovered in their full complexity, the individual is believed able to reconstruct her or his complete personality (op. cit., p. 194).

Diagnosis and information giving as well as therapist directed treatment programs are intrinsic to this approach, since, as Jacob Arlow explains, from the psychoanalytic point of view, it is believed that

As far as the individual is concerned, the sources of his neurotic illness and suffering are by their very nature unknowable (Raymond Corsini, ed., Current Psychotherapies. Itasca, IL: F. E. Peacock, 1979).

The patient, then, is heavily dependent upon the therapist for explanation and direction. Out of his metapsychological theory, as it is called, the analyst interprets the *true* meaning of the patient's behavior or condition about which he himself is totaly unaware. He then informs the patient of these connections, particularly those concerning his past, especially as they relate to what is going on in the present in the relationship between himself and the patient. He then directs the patient as to what must be done if his condition is to be improved. In general, counseling, influenced by this psychodynamic understanding, as Combs et al. say, demands of helpers that they:

be expert diagnosticians, who know at any moment precisely what is going on and where events must be channeled next (Arthur Combs, ed. Helping Relationships. Boston: Allyn and Bacon, 1978, p. 105).

Behaviorism, too, is part of this same approach. In behaviorism, however, the determining stimuli are in the environment. The person is seen mainly as a stimulus-response loop in which, through learning, certain stimuli have come to be linked together and produce certain behavioral responses which at least at one time brought certain rewards which reinforced their practice. One changes the situation by changing the behavioral response to the stimuli. In behavioristic therapies the therapist is seen as the expert, both on what reinforcement dynamics are present in the client's behavior, and on how to modify or change or reinforce behavioral responses, depending on what is desired. He informs the client of what these are and guides and monitors his progress in changing them.

In the objectivist framework, then, the counselor, out of his knowledge of psychology, is presumed to be the expert in the particular behavioral or developmental dynamics that might be operating in any particular situation. He is able to explain these to the client and, on the basis of this normative knowledge to prescribe what to do in order to achieve the best possible outcome. From this point of view, counseling is essentially an educative process in which advice is generally expected to play an intrinsic part: The therapist gives the client information about himself and advises him as to what he might do to improve his situation.

We can see the influence of this framework in counseling generally in such writers as Gerhard Egan when, for instance, in his discussion of how psychopathology models can distort our listening to a client, he says:

> For instance, being able to listen to what clients have to say through the filters of a developmental model — one that deals with the normative stages, tasks and crises of the entire life span — can help counter bias introduced by listening through abnormal-behavior models (The Skilled Helper. *Belmont, CA: Brooks/Cole, 1982, p. 73).*

Here the studies done in developmental psychology are given the status of an objective norm. The person is located in this framework, and his behavior and mental condition are analyzed in terms of its concepts, and his or her behavior is predicted out of it. And, although Egan gives strict guidelines on the use of interpretation and advice giving, nevertheless the pressure from within this framework is to ultimately prescribe behavioral responses to help the person weather the situation and move on fruitfully to the *next* stage. In one example of this approach a minister advised a wife whose husband was having an affair with a younger woman to be patient and understanding with him *because he was going through a mid-life crisis.* The person's situation was diagnosed in terms of a certain framework of psychology. On the basis of that diagnosis, advice was given how best to achieve the optimum results — *the survival of the marriage.*

The objectivist approach, then, is based on the belief that it is possible for us to gain a secure and certain understanding of that COMMON HUMAN NATURE which we all share in such a way that knowledge of it enables one person to accurately know the situation of another and so direct her as to how to improve it.

2. The Subjectivist Approach

In recent years, however, the objectivist approach has come under severe criticism from the subjectivist position which charges it with subordinating the individual to abstractions and of reducing him or her to the level of an object. The human person from this perspective is seen neither as governed from behind by physiological or biological causality nor as simply a result of external pressures and forces, and therefore cannot simply be reduced to their interplay. He is viewed also as the result of the unique and individual way in which the various elements that go to make up personal history and circumstances are construed, especially those concerning the future and what is perceived as being ideal and hence most significant, in terms of realizing fulfillment. The result is that in a fundamental sense each person is seen as living in a world of their own, which in its particular gestalt of meanings and values, cannot be reduced to general categories. Since the individual person is seen as the originating source of that gestalt, it cannot as such be known by anyone other than the self and therefore cannot be subordinated to the *knowledge and expertise of another*. Hubert B. Urban details the central emphasis of this subjectivist perspective thus:

> *An additional characteristic appears to be a common disposition to seek ways to take into account the enormous complexity that any given human person appears to represent. The observation is repeatedly made that individuals retain an exceedingly large number of different and changing intentions, values, patterns and styles of behaving and that these can be manifested in a great variety of ways depending on the person's circumstance and the nature of the environmental context within which he or she is functioning (Urban.* Clinical Psychology Handbook, *p. 164).*

Since the human person is viewed as intrinsically involved in the creation of his world, he cannot be considered merely an object which is simply acted upon either by internal or external forces which can be *figured out* and changed from the outside. In his dreams, hopes, and desires, he is a causal agent in the construction of his world both internally and externally, and in that causal activity there is a certain freedom of creativity which introduces into personal life an intrinsic unpredictability. Change in the structure and meaning of that world and hence the behavioral patterns that result from it, is ultimately dependent on the subject and is primarily his or her responsibility. The emphasis in the subjectivist approach is not upon explanation but clarification — the clarification of the unique phenomenology of the world as perceived by the individual.

The influence of this *subjective* perspective in the counseling world is making itself felt in the existentialist/humanistic/phenomenological schools of psychotherapy. Although it is present in a wide variety of forms, undoubtedly the most influential on counseling theory in America has been that stemming from the Rogerian school. Between these schools and the *scientific-objectivist* schools there seems at the moment to be a huge gap. Urban has likened it to the gap between the sciences and humanities referred to by C. P. Snow as two distinct cultures (Urban. *Clinical Psychology Handbook*, p. 156). The difference might be summed up by saying that this approach is centered on the UNIQUENESS OF THE PERSON rather than on the commonality of human nature.

In counseling this emphasis on the unique subject shows itself in the belief that the locus of expertise in the world of the client in terms of its meaning, values, and possibilities is seen as belonging, not to the counselor, but to the client. The counselor is essentially ignorant of the particular gestalt of meanings and possibilities open to the client. Each individual that comes to him is seen as a potential source for the counselor of new data that will revise any abstract understanding he or she may have learned or formulated about the essential dynamics of human behavior. Since only the client is sufficiently present to that world at any one time, only he or she is able to say what should be or can be done within it. The counselor stands outside of that world and at best can only gain an approximate understanding of what it is like and what it means.

Furthermore, whether the counselor is able to get a real understanding of that world of the client, is seen as depending, not on detached observation and categorization or diagnosis, but on the capacity of the client to actually touch and articulate those present meanings and so really reveal himself to the counselor. This constitutes the process of therapy, and its success essentially depends on the quality of the relationship between the client and the counselor, especially on the level of trust that develops between them. It also depends on the counselor's ability to really be open and present to the uniqueness of the client as well as his willingness to grope with him or her for articulation of that content. It is in the process of that articulation that the inner meaning-world of the client begins to change. As it emerges, it is critiqued, its inadequacies are recognized, and a clearer view of the self and its situation is developed.

The capacity of the counselor to help the other bring order and meaning into his world is seen as depending on a radically different type of relationship than that advocated by the objectivist approach. He is no longer a simple observer who dispassionately analyzes the client's inner and outer situation, and interprets it from within an objective, *scientific framework;* instead he is an active participant who through his relationship actually brings about change in that situation. The world of the other is not a static reality which can be tabulated in terms of impersonal causal connections, but one which is continually being created out of the intrinsic personal freedom of the individual. Hence, it is always changing as the person changes his perceptions and beliefs about it and what he sees as its possibilities for him or her. The counselor is not the master of this change and its direction, but its servant. He is the catalyst who makes possible change and growth through his relationship with the client. But the form and direction of that growth and development is dictated by the client's individual perception of what is desirable, necessary, and possible at this moment.

From this perspective, if the counselor has an area of expertise which the client needs, it is not in terms of cognitive content but of process. The counselor's skills are oriented to enabling the client to clarify for himself what his situation is thus making it possible for him to determine for himself what he should or should not do about it. Neither his level of knowledge of the psychological dynamics nor his social status and authority is any longer the primary qualification for being a counselor; rather, the level of his or her ability to enable the client to discover for himself the relevant factors in his situation and how best to deal with them is now important. This depends far more on the quality of the relationship that the counselor has to offer than on the level of his theoretical knowledge of human dynamics. It was this development which opened up the field of counseling to nonprofessionals, i.e., to those without academic degrees in psychology, as well as to what is called peer counseling.

Conclusion

It is obvious that in this understanding of counseling, advice giving as a requirement of the counselor does not play any real part. For those who do counseling out of this framework, the commonly accepted understanding of what the word *counseling* means simply does not fit, and, given the background of expectations on the part of clients today, it can cause a certain amount of initial confusion as to what the process is about. Although it is generally accepted that both forms of helping have the right to use the word, its use to cover both approaches does in fact mask over what are two fundamentally different approaches. From the point of view of expertise, the objectivist approach, on the surface, is much closer to the popular meaning of the term *counseling* as advice giving. If the subjectivist approach is to be called counseling also, then it would have to be on a different basis, one that is very much out of line with the popular understanding of the term. In fact, Charles A. Curran has made out a case for limiting the use of the word to the more subjectivist approach and labeling the former approach *guidance.* He does so on the basis of a more original use of the word in which the virtue of counsel primarily relates to the individual seeking help. The individual in coming for help is in a process of *taking counsel with him- or herself,* i.e., the client is seeking to sort out his or her inner confusions and difficulties in order to determine what best to do to achieve their fulfillment in some way or other. The process of counseling is primarily an internal process of surveying all the various factors in one's situation, both internal and external, in order to achieve a better self-understanding with a view to making the best decision as to what to do. It is primarily a process of self-advisement. The one who assists in the process is called a counselor because he or she participates and makes possible this *taking counsel with oneself* (see *Counseling in Catholic Life and Education.* New York: Macmillan, 1964).

For Curran, then, counseling is advice giving but primarily the self-advisement, generated from within the client by the process of *taking counsel* with another. He would further label the sort of advice giving that is equated with *counseling* in the popular sense as guidance, i.e., the bringing to bear on the particular difficulties the client is in all the knowledge that the counselor has, drawn from education or experience. He would clearly distinguish these two approaches because he sees them as two fundamentally different processes, requiring different skills on the part of the person helping. They can be treated as distinct operations or combined in the same helping process, depending upon the expertise of the person helping. On the other hand, William Clebsch and Charles Jaekle would subsume both processes under the title of guidance. They write:

> *Fundamentally, the guiding ministry assumes that useful wisdom, which edifies and illuminates the meaning and direction of a person's life, can be made available within the framework of the helping act. This wisdom may be thought of as having its origin from within the troubled person himself, from the experience of the counselor, from the common values regnant in their mutually shared culture, from a superior wisdom available to the counselor, or even from a body of truth or knowledge independent of the counselor and counselee. In any case, the wisdom must be fashioned or shaped to the immediate circumstances of the troubled person that it may be appropriated and used in the context of the particular trouble at hand* (Pastoral Care in Historical Perspective. *New York: Jason Aronson, 1983, p. 50).*

Whereas Curran would see these two as essentially different processes, utilizing different skills, Clebsch and Jaekle would put them on a continuum, with advice giving, or what they call *inductive guidance* on one end and listening, or *eductive guidance* on the other (cf. p. 50). They would define the two modes thus:

> *Guidance commonly employs two identifiable modes. Eductive guidance tends to draw out of the individual's own experiences and values the criteria and resources for such decisions, while inductive guidance tends to lead the individual to adopt an apriori set of values and criteria by which to make his decision. Perhaps the most familiar modern form of eductive guidance is that commonly known as* client-centered therapy, *while inductive guidance classically appeals to the long tradition of Christian moral theology and causistry (Clebsch and Jaekle, op. cit., p. 9).*

Howard Clinebell in his work *Basic Types of Pastoral Care and Counseling* holds to the distinction between the two processes but calls the helping process that utilizes both as educative counseling. He describes it thus:

> *Educative counseling shares the common elements of all pastoral counseling described in chapter four. It becomes educative as it moves towards three goals: (1) discovering what facts, concepts, values, beliefs, skills, guidance or advice are needed by persons in coping with their problems; (2) communicating these directly or helping persons discover them (eg. through reading); (3) helping persons utilize this information to understand their situation, make wise decisions, or handle problems constructively (London: SCM Press, 1984, p. 325).*

Given the very different processes involved, there does appear to be a need to label them differently. To call both processes either guidance or counseling would seem to confuse the issue. Despite the fact that generally the objectivist approach would seem to have the better popular claim to the title, it would in fact seem to be more correct to follow Curran in this. He restricts the word *counseling* to the self-advisement process and *guidance* to the education process. On the one hand, this would enable us to retain a distinction between them based on the different dynamics involved. On the other, it would help us to link up modern counseling tradition with the more historical notion of the virtue of counsel which has importance in Christian moral tradition. However, the word *counseling* used to encompass both approaches and for the time being, that is how we will continue to use the term. We will, however, use the distinction between counseling and guidance when we come to discuss the role of advice giving in the overall *helping* process.

Counseling and Values

The second dimension in our paradigm is the sharing of a common world of meaning and values, especially with regard to those overall life goals that dictate what is most desirable to pursue and what is not. For advice giving to be possible and effective, both parties must be able to agree, at least in general terms, on a vision of what real fulfillment might be and hence on the meaning and significance of the data of experience and what ought to be pursued. Here, too, we find a difference between what we have called the objectivist and subjectivist positions.

1. The Objectivist Approach

The *objectivist* approach tends to operate out of the perspective that it is possible to have definite, objective, behavioral content goals which are deemed to be most humanly desirable and that psychological science is capable of saying what these are. This perspective is implicit in the objectivist attempt to gain a comprehensive understanding of human reality. It includes not simply what is but what can and ought to be. He or she believes that it is possible for psychology to say what is healthy or correct or growth-producing in terms of human well-being and happiness. This objectivist framework has been clearly expressed by Wolff who, according to Offer and Sabshin, believes that:

> *If mental health is a reality, then psychiatrists should be the judges of matters pertaining thereto, for they are the most knowledgeable people in this area. In fact, just such a trend has developed. With regards to juvenile delinquency, certain forms of adult crime, aspects of education, and so forth, we have begun to treat the issues as amenable to expert judgement, like questions of fluoridation, inoculation and so forth (op. cit., p. 385).*

Perhaps the most prominent exponent of this position in psychology is B. F. Skinner who, out of his belief that all behavior is environmentally conditioned, advocates a society totally controlled by behaviorist techniques, in which the behavioral ideals have been clearly and scientifically worked out and the population has been behaviorally conditioned to realize them.

In clinical psychology, there are three main ways of conceptualizing these goals. The first concept is that of normality as health, with health being defined rather negatively as the absence of obvious pathologies (as defined in the official catalog of the American Psychological Association, the DSM 111). This concept is found in its clearest form in the *medical model* of psychiatry. Offer and Sabshin describe it thus:

> *This definition of normality seems to correlate with the activity of the model of the doctor who attempts to free patients from grossly observable symptoms. To this physician, the lack of unfavorable symptoms indicates health (Normality and the Life Cycle. New York: Basic Books 1984, p. xii).*

The goals of therapy here are usually directed to the elimination of the pathologies.

The second is the normality-as-average approach. Here the goals are the generally accepted ways of functioning and behaving which are acceptable to the social and cultural and moral community at large, and these are determined by surveys and statistical research. These goals, then, tend to incorporate not only what constitutes psychological health but also what would often be considered the community's moral and social values. Here the main aim of the therapeutic work is adjustment or helping the individual to fit into and adapt to the behavioral expectations of his social environment. This is especially true in institutional work, i.e., where counseling enables clients to adjust to the goals of the institution or the society at large which supports them. Out of this perspective, courts, for instance, will often make it a condition of sentencing that the person *go for counseling.*

Usually, because these goals have the official sanction of society and are bound up with community health policies and insurance, they are simply assumed by the counselor to be shared by the client. Since sanity is largely dependent on community validation, the mental health professional is seen as the agent of the community in that validation. This approach, then, rests upon the accepted fact that people today do look to the mental-health professional to discover what is normal and rational, what is mentally and emotionally healthy and unhealthy, what is behaviorally ideal, and what is not.

However, implicit in the objectivist approach is the belief that where discrepancies exist between the client and the counselor about what might be desirable attitudes and behavior, the views of the counselor can take precedence so that it is permissible for the counselor to try to persuade or manipulate the client without his explicit knowledge into adopting these views for *his own good.* This is particularly true in institutional or general community work. People are referred to specific counselors, perhaps by the courts or educational authorities, in order that they might be persuaded or motivated to bring their lives in some way into line with the psychiatric and community norms of healthy, acceptable behavior, and the mental health professional is expected to produce the desired results.

From this perspective, we often find that the counselor uses his authority to secure for the client desirable life goals which are commonly accepted by the culture. In this the therapist is much more explicitly acting out of the third way of conceptualizing ideal life goals, that of the myth. This is a basic symbolic formulation of what ideally constitutes human fulfillment and hence what sort of lifestyle and activities are most valued. Offer and Sabshin call it *normality as utopia* and describe it thus:

> *Normality as utopia, [a view] most widely held by psychoanalysts, conceives of normality as that harmonious and optimal blending of the diverse elements of mental apparatus that culminates in optimal functioning, or self-actualization (op. cit., p. xii).*

This approach can be found even in what are commonly called the humanistic schools of psychology and counseling which explicitly avoid the pathology and statistical–average approach to discerning normality. It is a much more explicitly philosophical and imaginative discernment of what the ideal person and lifestyle are like. It is objectivist in that out of the philosophical framework the client is implicitly or explicitly oriented toward actualizing a particular counselor-approved self-structure and behavioral pattern.

In the more *scientific* and *medical* forms of psychotherapy, this mode of determining the normal and the healthy, while generally formulated on the basis of specific behaviors, is usually more implicit than explicit. It is a sort of invisible center around which behavior is judged to be pathological or not. It remains implicit because generally it reflects the *myths* dominant in the culture. The DSM 111 itself is built around such a center, though this is not spelled out.

Being a rather implicit and general philosophically based norm, it leaves room for the therapist's own idiosyncratic understanding of what constitutes its concrete realization and in this can lead to a clash between the counselor's and client's value systems. This clash shows itself most clearly in the area of religious values. C. A. Patterson relates an instance of this:

> *Ginsburg mentions an analyst who was dissatisfied with a patient at the end of analysis because she still attended church. Church attendance was not a value for him — in fact the goal of this particular analysis was the severing of religious ties* (Counseling and Psychotherapy. New York: Harper and Bros., 1959).

Robert Lovinger shows how, because of counselor and psychotherapeutic training, this discrepancy between the personal values of the client and counselor, particularly in the area of religion and morality, can easily occur. He writes:

> *It might be concluded from the above that religious feelings and values are more important to many patients than to most psychotherapists . . . the academic study of religion is rarely an aspect of the therapist's training and the overall attitudinal matrix of a psychology-oriented education tends to foster a negative attitude toward religion* (Working with Religious Issues in Therapy. New York: Aronson, Inc., 1984, p. 3).

With regards to *expertise* there is a correlation between the *objectivist* approach and the paradigm that we have set up relative to the meaning of *counseling*. In this there is obviously a real discrepancy between the objectivist approach and our paradigm. Whereas in the folk usage the counselor was very much the servant of the authority in his decision-making process and was relied upon because he shared in that authority's goals and consequent value system, the counselor in the psychological realm, operating out of an objectivist perspective, tends to become the source and arbiter of the values one should espouse and live by. He views it as part of his or her expertise and responsibility to seek to influence the client in some way to adopt and live these goals and values himself. He seeks then not simply to advise but also to pressure and even manipulate. In this he is expected to know something about, and be skillful in, the use of the various reinforcement techniques and strategies developed by the behaviorist schools. It is on the basis of this *expertise* that social agencies and institutions refer people for counseling: They are sent not simply to get advice but to have their goals and values altered to fit more closely those held by society.

2. The Subjectivist Position

Exponents of this perspective tend to view the matter of goals and values differently and on the whole tend to emphasize the relativity of explicit behavioral ideals. They would emphasize, as Offer and Sabshin put it, that:

> *Normality is, in part, a cultural construct, based on social consensus. . . . These norms are fluctuant; they change from one social setting to another and over time (op. cit., p. 374).*

As many would see it, to a great extent, pathologies gain their status as deviations not from objective data, but from the commonly accepted goals of the society in which they are formulated. They highlight the fact that what is pathological in one society may very well not be considered so in another; that in different and older cultures what is commonly seen as pathological in modern society was very often seen as a divine possession to be highly respected and valued. They would point out that the list of pathologies that the Western world, particularly the United States, has formulated is itself a subject of controversy at least on some points, e.g., homosexuality or promiscuity. The DSM 111 was the subject of much debate before it was adopted, and many would still argue about the status of many of the items included as pathological. Furthermore, as Richard Farson has pointed out, pathologies themselves change their content and form from age to age. He writes:

> *Our knowledge about such phenomena as social roles, customs, elite groups, and values becomes obsolete in a few years, not simply because we know how to measure or investigate them, but because life itself has changed them; behaviors have changed; the structure has crumbled, and looking back, we see only the residue of what we believed to be firm knowledge. . . . The psychopathologies of one era give way to quite different manifestations in a later time* (Science and Human Affairs. *Palo Alto, CA: Science and Behavior Books, 1965, p. 3).*

Because they emphasize the normality–as–myth perspective the subjectivist approach tends very strongly toward leaving the decisions regarding values in the hands of the client. In this it tends more clearly than the objectivist approach to democratize the counseling process, maximizing the freedom of individual choice as to behavior and lifestyle; moreover it emphasizes that the ultimate authority in what is right or appropriate to do within the world of meaning and values that they live in is primarily the client and not the counselor. The tendency here again is away from directiveness and advice giving.

Because these more subjectivist approaches do not lay emphasis on particular content goals, they are not primarily concerned about the difference in overt value systems. As such they do not ask of the counselor that he take on or agree with the value system of the client or try to replace it with his own. He is called upon to respect the client's values, even where they are very different from his own. His role again is to facilitate the process of value clarification and assessment, to enable the client to become more conscious of the value confusion and tension that might exist in his life and so become more capable of deciding for himself what values he wishes to realize.

This does not mean, however, that among subjectively oriented counselors there are no normative values operating. The counselor in this framework works out of what we have called *normality as ideal,* in that it looks not to what is average or communally acceptable but to a more philosophically intuited sense of the *best.* Despite the fact that many in the humanistically oriented framework have often turned this ideal into an objectively delineated set of behaviors, and hence have become objectivist in their approach, in the more serious and consistent of these approaches, the emphasis in therapeutic treatment is usually shifted from content to process. The reason for this is the belief that if one relates to the client in a certain way then the client will of his or her own accord move toward a positive socialized ideal, and there is no need to manipulate the client to do so. The normative value operating here is that of client self-determination based upon an understanding of the human person as a dynamic striving to realize a certain self-structure that is inherent in human beings. If one provides the right nurturing environment then this inner nature will begin to emerge of its own accord. The ideal is that which emerges from the process, and because it is part of man's essential being, this self, is positive in its wishes and desires and tends toward certain universal values. Thus Eugene Gendlin claims that:

> The experiential process we have described seems regularly to arrive at certain values. While these are phrased and represented in many different ways, they are universal process values found in the basically common biological and interpersonal organization of human organisms ("Values and the Process of Experiencing," The Goals of Psychotherapy. Alvin Mahrer, ed. New York: Appleton-Century–Crofts, p. 198).

From this point of view the expertise of the counselor is seen as lying, not in superior knowledge of psychology and human dynamics and therefore of what ought to be done or pursued, but in his skill in aiding the client's own evaluative and decision-making process. By relating to the client out of a belief in his or her ability to achieve personal competence to live his or her own life according to positive values, it is considered that the counselor will evoke this competence in the client. This view of the ideal means that the counselor's values tend to govern, not so much the direction they wish the client to take, but more what the counselor is willing to do for the client. This includes the type of relationship and help he or she is prepared to offer, and it is expected that at the beginning of counseling, the counselor should outline something of the methodological values that he is operating out of and hence give the client the chance to decide whether or not he shares them. In this, generally speaking, the subjectivist approach is much closer than the objectivist to the paradigm we have offered.

3. Conclusion

In both forms, then, the helping process has gone beyond what we have delineated as the advice-giving mode. On the one hand, there is a tendency to subordinate the client to the goals and values of the counselor given a normative status. The overall goal of counseling here is that of adjustment to socially and scientifically acceptable norms somewhat external to the client in the sense that they derive primarily from others and not from himself. On the other hand, in the subjectivist approach, it is not seen as essential that the client and counselor share the same overt value system, except perhaps with regard to the process itself.

The Capacity for Responsibility

The third dimension of our paradigm assumes that the client is capable of weighing and deciding the value of the advice given and therefore he is personally responsible for what he does with it. Here there seems to be a great deal of confusion and diversity in the field of psychotherapy. To help clarify the situation here, some would make a distinction between psychotherapy and counseling. They would assign to the former the realm of severe internal personality problems where the person is severely impaired in his of her ability to respond rationally and responsibly to the situations they are in. To the latter they would assign relationships in which the person is considered to be internally integrated but confused as to how to act in terms of specific situations (see Patterson. *Counseling and Psychotherapy: Theory and Practice*. New York: Harper and Bros., 1959, p. 5). In this latter situation, counseling is divided up in terms of the external realm with which it deals, educational, vocational, etc. The counselors who function in these areas are very often called guidance counselors. They assume the client's capacity to judge the value of the advice given and own responsibility for the consequences of acting on it. Guidance counselors, therefore, function more closely in terms of the paradigm we have outlined; they offer information to another out of their area of expertise and recommend courses of action. They are most prominent in the educational field.

1. The Objectivist Position

But this is a restricted area and, as we have seen, the term *counseling* is used in a much broader sense to encompass internal personality difficulties and more general life problems. And here, too, there is a division between the objectivist and subjectivist approaches. Although both would see it as a major part of their work to develop the capacity to act differently and more productively in the future, there is a tendency on the part of the objectivist approach, at least theoretically, to underplay the capacity for personal responsibility. This latter approach is more deterministic in its view of human nature, seeing present situations as *caused* by a prior condition over which the person has little knowledge or control. The person, then, is seen as capable of acting differently in the present and future only if in some way this prior situation is altered and its influence on the present is eradicated. In psychoanalysis these determining factors located in the past are blocked from consciousness by the operation of defense mechanisms of which the person is unaware. He is unable to grow out of these determining influences without the expert help of the therapist who raises these things to consciousness. Despite emphasis upon rational knowledge of those influences, these defense mechanisms tend to underplay, at least theoretically, the freedom and responsibility that conscious knowledge usually implies.

In behaviorism the determining forces are located in the interplay between the internal structure of the person and the external world in which he operates. Even less than psychoanalysis does behaviorism support the idea of personal responsibility. The person acts differently only because he or she responds to different reinforcements or stimuli. Both, then, because of their more mechanistic views of human dynamics, tend to underplay personal responsibility for the way one is and for what one does. Altering the way the person is and the way he behaves is largely the responsibility of the skill of the therapist, and the client is seen as dependent on the counselor or therapist and his skills.

In both perspectives the client does not understand the real reasons for the way in which she is acting and is radically dependent upon the counselor or therapist to show her. She is seen to be lacking the ability to be responsible for what she does, somewhat in the same way as we would view the behavior of a child.

This way of seeing client responsibility in Wisconsin is now written into its laws. Commenting on the recent statutes governing sexual relationships between therapist and client, Patricia Wolleat writes:

> Lack of a requirement of consent places sexual exploitation by the therapist on the same footing as the statutory assault laws relating to children. The law has stepped in to protect a person presumed incapable of giving consent by holding the perpetrator strictly accountable. The patient or client in therapy is treated as one incapable of consenting to sexual activity with the therapist because of the nature of psychotherapy. Psychotherapy is a setting where power inequities, client vulnerability, and client dependence on the therapist may so predispose the client to follow the directives of the therapist that the client is unable to make competent judgements about the conduct of the therapist or to communicate unwillingness to participate in sexual activity ("Sexual Exploitation by Therapist: Implications of the New Law for Counselors," The Wisconsin Counselor. Winter 1985, p. 4).

In this view of the capacity of the client to act responsibly on any advice that is given, the objectivist approach is out of line with the paradigm we have offered.

2. The Subjectivist Perspective

However, those who espouse the more subjectivist approach point out that, despite the theory, in practice there seems to be in the objectivist position both a great deal of reliance on the ability of the clients to do what they are rationally advised to do, and an assumption that somehow the clients are responsible for their own growth process and change.

Subjectivist approaches, however, tend to make explicit the belief that ultimately the client bears a real measure of responsibility for his own situation and hence for what he does in his life. Counselors of this persuasion may well recognize in many clients that their capacity to be responsible for themselves is at the moment weak or uncertain, nevertheless they would see themselves as relating to the person in such a way that they enhance and strengthen the core capacity that is already there in his or her potentiality as a human being. In their emphasis on the intrinsic creative freedom of the person, they would say that in some way the person is responsible for his or her own sickness, or at least for its continuance. They reject the idea that a person is a prisoner of either his past or his present situation, and emphasize the possibility of creatively changing the meaning of his experiencing and the personal responsibility to do so. The work of the counselor here is in strengthening that innate capacity, but the actual responsibility for change is the client's, not the counselor's.

3. Comparison of the Two Approaches

While the objectivist approaches would seem to tend, on the one hand, to support advice giving, theoretically they seem to underplay the capacity of the person to act out of that personal responsibility which makes advice giving effective. The subjectivist approaches, which would downplay the role of advice giving, support the possibility and importance of personal responsibility.

Porter writes on the different implications for therapy of the external and internal frames of reference thus:

A second reason why it is important for us to be able to distinguish between the internal and external reference frames arises out of the fact that the two hypotheses discussed in the preceding paragraph do exist and their implications for counselor conduct are markedly different. To the extent that the hypothesis of the essential impotence of the client in the face of his defense is valid, the emphasis upon an external reference frame, upon not accepting at face value the client's view, upon seeing through the client, becomes of importance. To the extent that the hypothesis of the essential ability of the client to reduce his own defense and to achieve new and more complete meanings is valid, the emphasis upon the internal reference frame, what the client sees the situation to be, becomes of importance (Introduction to Therapeutic Counseling. *Boston: Houghton Mifflin, 1950, p. 62).*

Conclusion: Relevance to Pastoral Counseling

What we call counseling today evidently is not a homogeneous field: It covers very different types of operation, none of which clearly coincide with the paradigm we have outlined. Some assume a field of expertise with regard to content; others would not. Some would assume a field of common values or subordinate the client to their own set of behavioral norms; others would avoid that. In some, advice giving would be intrinsic to the process of therapy; in others, it would be largely excluded. To use the word *counseling* today as a way of describing the service that is offered people does not immediately tell what it is we are prepared to do for them or how we will relate to them. This vagueness extends to pastoral counseling, too, which has always made use of existing forms from outside its own specific discipline in order to carry on its ministry. For instance, Clinebell in an earlier edition of his influential work, *Basic Types of Pastoral Counseling* (1966) gives six different forms that are commonly used which include the highly directive forms as well as what we have called the subjective modes. In this he mirrors the general situation in pastoral counseling today, a situation which in one form or another has always prevailed through its history. In their exposition of pastoral care down through the ages, Clebsch and Jaekle show how with regard to the particular function of guidance, practice has oscillated between an objectivist framework and a subjectivist one. Comparing the Middle Ages with today, they write:

. . . guidance in the Middle Ages was mainly inductive, [objectivist], but in modern America it is largely eductive [subjectivist]. In the early Middle Ages, it became necessary to convince persons in rather uncivilized circumstances that certain acts were wrong or hurtful while other deeds were right or helpful. In our own times of cultural pluralism and individualized values, the eductive mode has come to dominate the pastoral guiding function in a remarkable way (Pastoral Care in Historical Perspective. *New York: Aronson, 1983, p. 12).*

Clinebell, in a recent edition of his book *Basic Types of Pastoral Care and Counseling* (London: SCM Press, 1984), has sought to integrate the objectivist and subjectivist modes into a unified pattern and indicate where each is most effective. One can agree or disagree with the resulting synthesis, but Clinebell has raised what is a common task in the field of counseling today, whether secular or pastoral: that of seeking a synthesis between the subjective and objective approaches. The very confusion in the field is an impetus to seek a point of integration at a higher level. In order to be able to decide what role, if any, advice giving has in pastoral counseling, we need to look at what is emerging in this synthesis and see what part advice giving plays in it.

The Movement Toward a Synthesis

To what extent counselors see advice giving as an essential part of their service depends largely on which theoretical framework they have adopted. If they operate out of an *objectivist* framework, then advice giving is likely to form a large part of their way of helping; but, if they espouse the more *subjectivist* position, then advice giving will be considerably less.

At the present moment, opinion is divided as to which frame of reference is more dominant in counseling. Patterson summed up the situation as of a few years ago, thus:

> *Currently in the field of counseling and psychotherapy, the trend towards manipulation does not appear to the writer to be as strong as the trend towards the understanding approach (Patterson. Counseling and Psychotherapy. New York: Harper & Bros., 1959).*

As we have seen, in terms of pastoral counseling, Clebsch and Jaekle hold something of the same point of view, believing that the most dominant form is that of *eductive counseling,* as they call it.

There is certainly some warrant for this assessment of the current situation: there is an increasing cross-fertilization process going on in psychotherapeutic theory and research that is gradually blurring the boundaries between the two approaches and producing a new synthesis. Marvin R. Goldfried and Wendy Padawar report that:

> *In a survey of clinical psychologists within the United States, Garfield and Kurst (1976) have found a very strong trend in the direction of greater eclecticism, in that approximately 55% of the respondents depicted their theoretical orientation as one that drew from several different sources ("Current Status and Future Directions in Psychotherapy," Converging Themes in Psychotherapy. Goldfried, ed. New York: Springer, 1982, p. 11).*

Sheldon Korchin in his review of the history of clinical psychology writes:

> *Moreover, serious question is being raised as to whether all therapies are effective in terms of properties they have in common rather than in terms of those qualities that distinguish them. . . . With this recognition, there has been serious movement towards reapproachment among contending therapeutic systems, with the possibility that the overall effectiveness of therapy can be increased by including elements from different systems (Clinical Psychology Handbook, p. 18).*

Rather than look for this synthesis at the level of theory, researchers have found it more fruitful to look at what counselors and therapists say they actually do. This is a significant movement in that it is a movement toward an analysis of what is actually taking place in experience; it is looking to the inner grammar of the actual human endeavor of seeking to be of help to another, rather than simply deducing directions out of a preestablished theory. It is seeking to discover the inner logic and structure of the actual experience and the discipline that it un-consciously imposes on those involved in order for them to be fruitful. Those in the actual experiential situation are in fact implicitly present to that logic, and that situation will to some extent structure what they actually do in accordance with it, irrespective of what their theory simply dictates that they do. There is nothing absolute about this, though, since theoretical convictions as to the correct way will also affect what is done and how it is done. Even though looking at actual practice may reveal factors that are important this does not obviate the necessity of seeking a theoretical justification.

In this new synthesis the *understanding* or subjectivist approach which em-phasizes the uniqueness of the subject and his or her own capacity to decide which is the best way forward holds an important position. The Goldfried and Padawer chapter "Current Status and Future Directions in Psychotherapy" indi-cates this when they detail some of the common elements that are currently found in the actual practice of psychotherapy in contrast to what the theory would demand. We can summarize these commonalities thus:

> *(1) Expectations that therapy will succeed. The placebo factor as it is called. (2) A particular quality of therapeutic relationship characterised by warmth and understanding. (3) Obtaining an external perspective on oneself and the world through disinterested feedback. (4) Corrective experiences in which the client learns more appro-priate behavior. (5) Continued reality testing in which attempts to be and behave differently are monitored and critiqued (op. cit., pp. 15– 19).*

Goldfried and Padawer go on to describe the quality of relationship which they found to be characteristic of therapists as being . . .

> *one whereby a warm, understanding and nurturing therapist wins the trust and respect of the patient or client. This in itself is believed to have a beneficial effect, as it is relatively rare for people to experience interactions with others in our society who are willing to listen sym-pathetically. But the therapeutic relationship can offer more than this, in that it provides an important context in which change may occur. . . . While the therapist may serve as a significant other during the process of encouraging individuals to feel, think, and behave dif-ferently, the primary objective is to have them reach a point of greater autonomy and self-mastery (ibid., p. 16).*

A common feature then of modern day counseling, from the point of view of practice rather than simply theory, is the quality of the intersubjective rela-tionship and the experience of being accepted and understood which leads to the enhancement of that personal responsibility and freedom which characterizes subjectivity. At the same time we see, in this Goldfried and Padawer quotation, the *objectivist* background in the *encouragement to think, feel, and behave differently.* Encouragement in specific directions implies approval on the part of the counselor of those directions. Presumably the same encouragement would be withheld from those thoughts, feelings, and behaviors which were not approved by the counselor. As we shall see, this background is still very strong in the eclectic approaches to counseling.

The Recognition of Subjectivity

However, among dynamically oriented psychotherapists there is an increasing acceptance that it is essential that the unique subjectivity of the client be taken into account in such a way that education about processes and causal relations must be subordinated to the capacity of the client to benefit from knowing them. Korchin writes of this:

> *However fascinating knowledge is in its own right, it is sought by the clinician in order to better help the lot of the patient. Furthermore, the clinical approach is necessarily personalogical, for the clinician must deal with the individual lives in their complexity as patients struggle to adapt and grow. Processes in the person or in the environment, in his physiological nature or his social situation, are most relevant as they come to have meaning for the particular person (In* Clinical Psychology Handbook. *New York: Pergamon Press, 1983, p. 16).*

In this there is a subordination of *objective* knowledge to the unique subjectivity of the client, in that just what is offered in terms of explanation and behavioral change is subordinated to the capacity of the client to own it and hence integrate it into his or her meaning and value system. The unique patterning of meaning and value that constitutes the client's world is acknowledged and made paramount.

This is clearly reflected in Lawrence Hedges' explanation of modern psychoanalytic thought when he writes:

> *The use of the natural science model for psychoanalytic investigation has gradually given way to thinking of psychoanalysis in the context of an interpretive discipline involving the systematic study of introspective and interactional experience. What has lacked clarification so far is a crucial notion stemming from Mahler's developmental approach: that each person coming for treatment lives a UNIQUE patterning of self and other experience characteristic of a certain phase of emotional development [my emphasis] (*Listening Perspectives in Psychoanalysis. *New York: Jason Aronson, 1983, p. 13).*

Here it is recognized that the uniqueness of the subject and his perceptual world as well as the developmental *causes* of his situation need to be taken into account in the treatment process. Hedges further emphasizes that the main instrument in the *cure* is the empathic ability of the analyst in the immediate relationship, rather than his ability to give intellectual interpretations of what is going on with the client. This is becoming increasingly advocated in the object-relations school of psychoanalysis.

This same emphasis is surfacing even among behaviorally oriented therapists, where again, we find the same recognition of the centrality of the unique subjectivity of the client if treatment is to be successful. Weiner comments thus:

> In therapy, many behaviorally oriented clinicians have begun in recent years to recognize the role of client attitudes and the treatment relationship in fostering and sustaining desired behavior change. As perceived by these clinicians, maximally effective treatment occurs only when clients understand the manner in which reinforcement contingencies have determined and can modify their behavior; when they develop improved internal capacities for self-control and self-determination; and when they hold a positive view of the helping relationship (Clinical Psychology Handbook, p. 27).

With this the movement is away from the more manipulative tendencies which were explicitly advocated by behaviorism. Ivey and Simek-Downing comment:

> There have been times in the past where behavior therapists were more concerned with producing change in the client, as they defined the need (sometimes even without client awareness), than in meeting immediate concerns important to the client. The movement in behavioral counseling has been distinctly away from such manipulation, to the point that client involvement is now virtually an axiom in any behavioral change program (Counseling and Psychotherapy. Englewood Cliffs, N.J.: Prentice-Hall, 1980, p. 226).

The Bias Toward Objectivism

With this attempt to integrate the subjective and objective approaches, the place that advice giving has in counseling is changing, and generally more precise guidelines are now offered for its use. These include the suggestion that advice should be kept more to the latter end of the treatment program, after a period of self-exploration and clarification of goals has taken place.

However, while there is undoubtedly a move toward a reconciliation of the objective and subjective approaches which would alter the role of advice giving in the counseling process, in general the bias would still seem to be toward the objectivist approach in which counselor expertise and guidance are predominant. The subjectivist position has had some real modifying influences, but the framework overall remains essentially objectivist. So at the moment we cannot really claim a reconciliation between the two perspectives; at most there is an uneasy partnership, with the subjectivist perspective in the junior position.

The Problem-Answer Paradigm

The paramount influence of the belief that it is possible to construct a normative picture of the dynamics of human functioning shows itself generally in the prevalent tendency to interpret human difficulties in living in terms of *problems. What is the problem?* is an almost universal way of responding to a person's request for help. Attempts to respond inevitably focus on finding *an answer* to *the problem,* with the burden of finding that answer usually being placed on the *expert.*

So, although it can be understood in a personalist sense, generally the paradigm which lies behind the use of this framework is that of mathematics and technology in which the goal to be achieved is clear, but in some way or other there is a blockage to realizing it. This barrier is the *problem* and the *answer* is that which eliminates the barrier. As in the popular understanding of mathematics, what is sought in this paradigm is *the answer,* the one solution which fits exactly and effectively eliminates the problem. Combs, *et al.,* describe this framework thus:

> *In a closed system of thinking outcomes are known in advance. . . . Problems have clear beginnings and ends, and goals can be stated as oughts and* should*s. Objectives can often be expressed in terms of specific acts or behaviors and subject to precise methods of measurement and assessment* (Helping Relationships. *Boston: Allyn and Bacon, 1978, p. 103).*

Translated to the counseling situation, it becomes necessary for the counselor to discover and catagorize the *real* problem, understood from within some normative framework and then to dig into the client's life to discover *the cause* of the problem. Armed, then, with what he considers to be relevant information, he seeks to devise a solution that will eliminate the problem. A recent work on developmental psychology illustrates this framework very clearly. N. Golan summarizes:

> *Next we presented a series of developmental and psychosocial bridging intervals in the adult life-cycle and tried to sketch out the various phases in each process which must be passed through in order to return to stable functioning, as well as the tasks which must be carried out in order to effect such change* (Passing through Transition. *New York: The Free Press, 1981, p. 239).*

The *shoulds* and *oughts* in this closed system derive from a confidence that the research has enabled the author to get a clear picture of the whole. It presumes a capacity to conceptualize definitively the whole field of operations, the end to be attained, the relationships between the various factors involved, the modes of operation of the various forces within the field and, hence, the things or actions that must take place to realize the positive result. It is not surprising, then, that when it comes to describing therapeutic activity in helping a person through these transitions, the author is able to tie her approach to that of the *problem-solving* approach to counseling. Hence, she can write:

> *Diagnosis, according to Perlman, is aimed at identifying and explaining the nature of the person's problem, appraising it within the framework of specific intentions and goals, and using that appraisal as the guide for further action. As treatment progresses, the bits of evidence gathered from the client shape the caseworker's judgment of how fast to move, what supports and services seemed called for, and what parts of the applicant's problems need priority consideration. Therapeutic techniques vary according to the person, his particular problem, his conception of what he wants, and the caseworker's treatment style (ibid., p. 263).*

The similarity to what goes on in the realm of physical medicine is apparent here. Psychotherapies which operate out of this paradigm are largely oriented toward discovering the precise *problem* which constitutes the barrier to the achievement of desired goals, the validity of which is judged by the theoretical framework of the counselor. The counselor, out of that superior understanding of the client's situation and its causes, is in clear charge of deciding what must be done, when, and how. To help the client do this many counselors will use a variety of testing instruments such as the Minnesota Multiphasic Personality Inventory (MMPI) or the older Rorschach inkblot tests to aid in diagnosing what is going on in the person, where the blockages are, and what sort of treatment program is needed. The prevalence of such preliminary testing in the field of counseling today indicates that the *objectivist* approach is still very much the predominant framework of thinking.

In many of the recent *eclectic* approaches in both pastoral and secular counseling which seek to integrate the subjective with the objective approach, this fundamental orientation is clearly evident. It is present even in those who explicitly espouse the client-centered approach which did so much to raise the fact of subjectivity to the consciousness of the psychotherapeutic world. In a recent work to come out of that school, that of Gerald Pine and Angelo Boy (*Client-Centered Counseling: a Renewal.* Boston: Allyn and Bacon, 1982), we find the subjectivist approach given major importance but as the way in which the counselor can gain an accurate understanding of that inner world of meanings and values of the client which will enable him or her to be more effective in directing the latter stages of the process. It has become the way in which a relationship of trust is built between the client and counselor such that the counselor might more accurately judge how to meet the client's needs. The client will then more easily be able to accept and integrate the suggestions of the counselor as to how best to solve his or her problem.

This same perspective is clearly expressed also in the latest edition of Howard Clinebell's popular work on pastoral counseling in which he writes:

> The pastor acquires a tentative understanding of the person's "internal frame of reference" — how life looks from within his or her world. This diagnostic impression includes some understanding of how the person defines the problem, the ways where his or her relationships are failing to meet basic needs . . . (the cause). On the basis of this tentative diagnosis, the minister recommends an approach (answer) to obtaining help [my emphases] (Basic Types of Pastoral Care and Counseling. London: SCM Press, 1984, p. 74).

Later Clinebell explicitly says that:

> Most counseling, regardless of its orientation, involves a process of understanding and evaluating the person's problems, then, in the light of this, making decisions about how to intervene and what type of help to offer or recommend (ibid., p. 82).

A similar situation can be found in another of the more popular eclectic approaches, that of Gerard Egan in his book *The Skilled Helper.* This is a widely used text in training counselors. He explicitly labels his approach *problem-solving* and, considers it essential that the counselor help the client to define as clearly as possible, in terms of specific experiences, behaviors and reactions of what exactly the problem is. Thus he writes:

*In view of the model just presented, it can be said that a problem is clear if it is spelled out in terms of specific and relevant experiences, behaviors, and feelings that relate to specific situations. Problem situations are more likely to be managed if they are clearly defined. If they are spelled out very clearly and concretely, then hints of ways to manage the problem begin to emerge more readily (*The Skilled Helper. *Monterey: p. 70).*

Furthermore, he sets up *effective interpersonal relationships* as the clear goal to be achieved which closes off the process and enables one to clearly delineate the *problems*. The hidden supposition is that what constitutes *effective interpersonal relations* is clearly known and fixed, psychologically and behaviorally, so that it can function as a commonly agreed upon ideal goal. He also refers to the findings of developmental psychology as normative. In using a specific case to illustrate a point he writes:

Jerzy really has little working knowledge of the developmental demands of a twenty-year-old woman (ibid., p. 11).

The implication here is that there is an objective set of demands specific to all twenty-year-old women which psychology has discovered and which can then be used as a reference point to interpret the young woman's situation and what the husband needs to do.

Furthermore, although Egan does have strict guidelines on the use of advice giving, nevertheless, we can see how, like Boy and Pine, his perspective is weighted toward the objectivist framework, especially in his explanation on the importance of the therapeutic relationship. He holds to the mainly subjectivist ideal of client self-determination as the goal and emphasizing the respect that the counselor should have for the uniqueness of the client. Egan nevertheless sees the establishing of a good relationship as not, in fact, the central medium of therapy as it would be in the subjectivist position, but as a means for establishing *social influence* over the client, helping him to become more amenable to the counselor's suggestions and directions (or advice, though he does not use this word). In this he is in agreement with other writers, particularly Stanley Strong and A. P. Goldstein. Thus Egan writes:

Goldstein (1980) describes the social influence process in a way that is complementary to Strong's. First, he calls behaviors by which helpers establish an interpersonal power base with their clients relationship enhancers. *He suggests that there are various ways of doing this: by providing clients with the kind of structure that enables them to give themselves more easily to the helping process . . . by modeling the kinds of behavior expected of clients so that they can imitate them . . . by attending, expressing appropriate warmth, by communicating accurate empathy, by sharing their own experiences and the like. Second, these behaviors, if carried out skillfully, lead to mutual liking, respect and trust. Third, this kind of relationship helps clients*

become more willing to engage in dialogue with helpers, reveal them-
selves more deeply, and open themselves to the DIFFERENT KINDS
OF DIRECTION helpers may provide throughout the helping process
[my emphasis] (Egan, op. cit., p. 134).

Confusion and Contradiction in Eclectic Approaches

Egan's view of the value and importance of the relationship and of the necessity of adverting to the subjectivity of the client is, like many other forms of counselings set within a predominantly objectivist framework. This results at times in a certain amount of confusion and contradiction. For instance, he emphasizes the paramount importance of the counselors awareness of the *principles* of reinforcement which come out of the objectivist framework of behaviorism. Knowledge of these will help the counselor direct the dynamics of the situation in order to benefit the client. However, Egan also acknowledges the subjective uniqueness of the client which relativizes the use of reinforcement and takes it essentially out of the control of the counselor, when he says:

The reinforcement is not a reward unless it is experienced as such by
the person whose behavior is in question . . . (and) the strength of
a reward also depends on how it is experienced by the person re-
ceiving it (op. cit., p. 17).

This is something that the counselor cannot control in the moment-to-moment process of the interaction. While the unique subjectivity of the client is acknowledged, the implications of this for the counselor's use of the objective principles of reinforcement are not worked out.

This uneasy fusion of the subjective and the objective approaches, with the former being located and subordinated to the latter, is characteristic of many of the eclectic approaches in counseling today. It is this which, for all their attempts to integrate the subjective perspective into their work, locates both Clinebell's and Egan's work, along with many others like them, in the objectivist camp, dominated by the mathematical, technological paradigm. If we were to label this approach, we might fruitfully call it neo-objectivism.

Summary

Compared to Patterson's assessment, it seems that the objectivist approach is still probably the more widely espoused in the counseling world: Counseling is still seen as advice giving on the part of the counselor based upon his knowledge of the normative principles of human functioning and his expertise in influencing the client to adopt what are considered by the counselor to be more positive perspectives and behaviors. It is interesting to note that in his latest work he has himself come to this conclusion. He now believes that: ''It appears that there is a trend (backwards) toward the more directive, controlling, authoritarian, or 'therapist-knows-best' approaches of the past'' (*Theories of Counseling and Psychotherapy*, New York: Harper & Row, 1986, p. 539). Whether this is a movement backwards or simply evidence that the subjectivist position was never fully assimilated is a moot point. I tend to this latter conclusion. However, it is evident that the subjectivist perspective has had substantial influence in modifying objectivist's more overt manipulative or directive tendencies and in holding back the counselor from simply subordinating the client to his or her own knowledge, values, or determinations. It has resulted, first, in the proposal in counseling that at the beginning of the relationship something of the values of the counselor and expectations on the client be made explicit and worked out. Second, it has highlighted the importance of the unique patterning of meanings and values of the individual client and the necessity of a personal relationship for their disclosure. And, third, it has introduced a note of caution into the giving of advice or guidance, moving it from a position of being a first-line approach to the later period of counseling when the core issues have emerged and become clarified.

However, this influence is more practical, and the resulting forms of counseling which seek to integrate it are, as we have seen in the case of Egan, somewhat hybrid in form. To reach a synthesis in which the real value of each approach is given its proper weight, one cannot stay simply on the level of practical usage. Although that may be instructive, especially in raising to consciousness the need to integrate the two perspectives, one needs to seek a new theoretical understanding of the relationship between the two sides. This essentially involves an exploration of the relationship between subjectivity and objectivity, or, as we have already put it, the relationship between objective common nature, and subjective unique personhood. Only then will we be in a position to judge the value and decide the proper use of advice giving in the helping process, or to reintroduce the terms already suggested between counseling, properly so called, and guidance.

2 Subjectivity and Objectivity in Psychology
Introduction: The Cultural Environment

Since the objectivist framework is the more dominant of the two forms, both historically and practically, we will look at this first. Its all-pervading influence on us today, as we have said, is clear in the way that we automatically respond to anyone who comes to us in difficulties. We wonder *what the real problem is* and worry, maybe, that we might not have the answer, or will fall short in our ability to give the client appropriate advice. In thinking about human difficulties in this way, we are implicitly making the assumption that we ought to be able as counselors to form a clear and definitive explanation of this person's situation and functioning so that we can decide the true nature of his difficulties and what the "solution" to them might be.

This is understandable since the cultural situation within which we function as counselors is largely dominated by the objectivist approach with its promise that through the scientific process human reality as a whole will one day be *figured out,* i.e., conceptually systematized so that definitively final answers can be obtained as to how the forces operating within it can be predicted and controlled. Rychlak describes the situation in these words:

> *Knowledge has been equated with scientific knowledge so that everyone believes that what is 'really factual' will be circumscribed by science someday* (The Psychology of Rigorous Humanism. *New York: Wiley, 1977, p. 82).*

This perspective tends to create an expectation of psychologists-as-scientists that they be able to do in the realm of human psychological functioning what their counterparts do in the more physical areas: i.e., create a body of knowledge that is both internally coherent, normative with regard to the meaning of experience, and utilitarian in its techniques and programs. Counselors are expected to know what that knowledge is and be able to pass it on to their clients.

And there are many psychologists who are prepared publicly on television and in the advice columns of newspapers to validate and satisfy this expectation by dogmatically offering advice over a wide range of *problems,* explaining the dynamics of particular situations and telling people what they ought to do to achieve the *best* results without having any real knowledge of the persons concerned. Their mode of operation is to catagorize *the problem,* i.e., place it in some common framework of meaning, e.g., mother-and-daughter problems, problems with anger, etc., and then, out of their theoretical knowledge of the problem area, describe the correct procedure to solve it. Many of the self-help books that crowd the shelves of bookstores are written on this premise. These books take a *problem* in the abstract and give clear guidelines as to how anyone with this particular problem can effectively and quickly eliminate it and so achieve fulfillment.

This mode of operation on the part of the *experts* has undoubtedly reinforced the general idea that advice giving is not only the primary but also the most effective way to help others and has been a major factor in that overuse of it that Ivey and Simak-Downey referred to above. It is understandable, therefore, that people who wish to be of help to others, seeing this model, would automatically assume that helping others essentially depends on the person's ability to *understand* the contours of the person's situation and, out of their experience of similar situations, or their study of the commonality that that situation has with others learned through their education, to then give advice.

In itself, of course, this is also quite an attractive proposition; it brings with it an image of mastery and power, and the promise of efficiency and effectiveness in our ability to help others, all of which promises a real sense of satisfaction and value. As Combs *et al.* explain:

> *It endows the helper with a special aura of respect and admiration from others and personal feelings of power over people and events (op. cit., p. 105).*

Recent writers have in fact openly proposed that this sense of power and mastery is intrinsic to the counseling relationship. Tennyson and Strom, for instance, have written:

> *First, and of fundamental importance, 'the counseling relationship' is grounded in the dominant power position of the counselor, who has the potential for exerting influence over others ("Beyond Professional Standards: Developing Responsibleness."* Journal of Counseling and Development, *64(5), January 1986:p. 298).*

Limitations on *Objective* Psychological Knowledge
De facto Limitations

Today, many scholars in the field of psychology would maintain strongly that this expectation exaggerates both the possibility and the extent of objective knowledge about human dynamics. With the espousing of this view, the field of psychology is brought into disrepute. This danger is nowhere clearer than in the public arena of the courtroom when psychiatrists and psychologists are brought in by both sides as *expert* witnesses to either explain why certain behavior occurred, or to render a definitive judgement upon the mental condition of the defendant and predict his future behavior. The disagreements which regularly occur are embarrassing, but to many in the field hardly surprising. *De facto* psychology is not a homogeneous body of established facts about human functioning which allow one to deduce the dynamics of specific situations by reference to its principles, but a disparate set of theoretical formulations and controverted explanations of causal connections which are, at worst, contradictory and, at best, only speculative possibilities.

This is particularly true in the field of psychotherapy. Stanislav Grof, I believe, is right in his assessment that

> *Even a cursory look at Western psychology reveals fundamental disagreements and controversies of enormous proportions concerning the dynamics of the human mind, the nature of emotional disorders*

and techniques of psychotherapy. This is true not only for schools that are products of a priori incompatible philosophical approaches, such as behaviorism and psychoanalysis, but also for those orientations with founders, who originally started from the same or similar premises (Beyond the Brain. Albany, N.Y.: State University of New York Press, 1985, p. 138).

Alvin Mahrer in his book The Goals of Psychotherapy has sought to examine and correlate the various families of psychotherapy in terms of their theoretical presuppositions and the goals they seek to achieve based on these presuppositions. His conclusion is a sobering one to those who look upon psychology as a homogeneous body of objective conclusions, validated by detailed and corroborated research. He writes:

1. Some goals of psychotherapy are shared by each family, even though they are described with different words, their meaning and significance may vary somewhat from family to family, and there are gross differences in the underlying rationale. For example, each family highlights such goals as the reduction of symptomatology, reduction of defenses, and reduction of anxiety. 2. The preponderance of psychotherapeutic goals is not shared by the three families. These goals may be relevant and meaningful for one psychotherapeutic family, while having less relevance or meaning within another. 3. Each psychotherapeutic family or personality model appears to be conceptually associated with a relatively unique set of psychotherapeutic goals. Thus, a meaningful association occurs between a given personality model and a particular set of goals (op. cit., p. 287).

The same situation, then, is likely to be interpreted differently by proponents of different schools, and, hence, what they understand to be the best way forward will likewise vary. Each school will have its own interpretation of the real meaning of what is going on and what is significant in terms of its dynamics. The advice as to what to do will likewise inevitably vary.

The very proliferation of psychological models and the goals deduced as desirable from them might of itself be sufficient to warn us against setting up any particular one as objective – in the sense of normative – so that someone who specializes in it is in a privileged position to advise and direct another in any dogmatic way as to what is really happening in any situation and how to manipulate the forces involved to achieve the optimum results. Jerome Frank has clearly acknowledged that, objectively, we still have very little clear scientific evidence linking specific therapeutic interventions to particular desirable results. He writes:

After decades of research, the amount of well-established, clinically relevant knowledge about psycho-therapeutic outcome still remains disappointingly meager. Although some relationships between determinants and outcomes have attained statistical significance, few are powerful enough to be clinically relevant, and most of those that have achieved this status are intuitively obvious (Converging Themes in Psychotherapy. Goldfried, New York: Springer, 1982, p. 281).

Response to *de facto* Limitations

However, instead of this fact leading psychology to entertain the possibility that it might in principle be impossible to establish a definitive body of knowledge about human functioning, all that seems to happen is that there is a continuous movement from one 'definitive' system to another. The faith in the possibility of formulating such a system remains, with each new discovery being presented as the missing piece, the ultimate explanatory concept, which solves the puzzle. Joseph Needleman has referred to the results of this phenomenon in these words:

> It is not only followers of the new religions who may fall victim to this tendency. . . . This tendency in ourselves also accounts for much of the fragmentation of modern psychology, just as it accounts for fragmentation in the natural sciences (Consciousness and Tradition. New York: Crossroad, 1982, p. 77).

We now have many different schools each claiming to have the definitive system. However, with each having its own body of orthodoxy and devoted adherents, based on a belief in their perspective as being the ultimate answer, they sometimes seem to have more of the character of religious systems rather than scientific schools. As with religions, there seems to be little attempt to participate in constructive dialogue with regard to the positions of other schools. David Martin has recently referred to this explicitly in these terms. He writes:

> Historically, schools of personality theory have been very like religions, with a guru who has disciples and followers who attack the followers of other gurus as clearly wrong and probably even infantile. The schools are even named after the guru, so that you know what I mean when I say something like "I know a Skinnerian who calls Freudians followers of Sigmund Freud" (Counseling and Therapy Skills. Belmont: Brooks/Cole, 1983, p. 85).

Just how long this process will continue before people become cynical about all psychology, it is impossible to tell, but the recent cutbacks in federal funding for mental health services may be an indication that under the surface, this cynicism may already be operating. There is increasing demand to show that the psychotherapeutic endeavor is able to produce identifiable success, such that it can warrant the public expenditure of providing this services. This is something that psychotherapy is finding increasingly difficult to do.

However, rather than leading us to view psychology as totally useless, the lesson that ought to suggest itself to us is that maybe we have given psychology a status that it cannot of its nature live up to and that we need to look at its value from another point of view. There may, in fact, be intrinsic limitations to our ability to form a purely objective conceptualization of the dynamics of human behavior which will be applicable to all human beings simply as human beings, but that nevertheless the very endeavor itself may be of enormous importance in furthering the growth and development of humankind. Its results may not be predictable, but nonetheless it may be an important and worthwhile service to make available to people.

Recognition of Intrinsic Limitations

The suggestion that it might not be possible to achieve any definitive objective picture of human functioning that gives us total control and predictability is being more clearly articulated among behavioral scientists today. These thinkers are willing to face the possibility that not only is it simply a fact that psychology does not offer a comprehensive, objective body of facts about human functioning which are generally applicable, but that in principle it might be unable to do so. The fundamental reason being given for this is that in psychology, even more so than in other sciences, the fundamental subjectivity of human reality is central both to its research and to its subject matter and that this imposes intrinsic limitations on our ability to formulate totally objective *explanations* which are comprehensive in their application. Sidney Callaghan pinpoints this when he says:

> The use of psychological findings is further complicated by the ambiguous standing of psychology as a science. . . . The subjective bias of subjective observers studying subjective actors is impossible to control, and consequently, the necessary public consensus which is the mainstay of scientific credibility cannot be obtained. Moreover, there is now no single established theoretical framework or dominant model in the multi-splintered field of psychology ("Personal Growth and Sexuality," Chicago Studies, Spring 1981: pp. 9-20).

This suggests that the fundamental weakness of the objectivist approach is that, whether used in a reflective, scientific way or in the unreflective, commonsense way of the man on the street, it is not objective enough, that is does not, in fact, take seriously enough the objective fact that subjectivity is intrinsically involved in any formulation of the way things *really are*. Not only do we have to take into consideration the fact that we are dealing with self-creative, self-determining subjects who live in a world which to some extent is unique to themselves, but also the fact that we are doing so from a subjective point of view and that, given the limitations involved in that, there can be nothing absolute about our findings.

Far from acknowledging this, however, psychology, along with other sciences, in its search for objectivity has sought as much as possible to eliminate that subjectivity from both its methods and in its subject matter, so as to arrive at laws of behavior which are true irrespective of the subjects observing them or of those operating within them. Richard Farson has charged that this has resulted in a false objectivity with regard to the results and a truncated view of the subject matter itself, the individual human person. He comments:

> We behavioral scientists hold to a scientism, a mis-understanding of what it means to be objective, that has led us to suppose that in order to be scientific we must view people as a set of systems, as a complicated machine and, hence, as an inert product of forces operating on him, rather than as a feeling, thinking, experiencing being. In the service of this view we have tried to operationalize and objectify and reduce the data of human experience, and so render them amenable to scientific scrutiny. But in doing so we have left behind the meaning and the man (Science and Human Affairs, p. 2).

The Challenge to Objectivism from Modern Physics

In this charge the *subjective* approach has the current backing of even the *hard* sciences themselves which have until recently laid the greatest claim to pure *objectivity* and have served as the model for scientific psychology. First, in physics, especially, the hardest of the hard sciences, it is being recognized that it is in fact impossible to achieve the sort of absolute objectivity that was promised by the classical framework. Heisenberg, through his discovery of the uncertainty principle in physics, has shown conclusively that there are intrinsic limits on our ability to *observe* what goes on at the level of subatomic physics, because through the very experiments we set up to observe we become part of the system and alter it. John Gribben comments:

> Today the key features of the Copenhagen interpretation can be more easily explained, and understood in terms of what happens when a scientist makes an experimental observation. First, we have to accept that the very act of observing a thing changes it, and that we, the observers, are in a very real sense part of the experiment — there is not clockwork that ticks away regardless of whether we look at it or not. Secondly, all we know about are the results of experiments (In Search of Schrodinger's Cat: Quantum Physics and Reality. New York: Bantam Books, 1984, pp. 160–161).

The Implications of a Subjective Point of View

In the first place, in the science of atomic physics, *known reality* is the *given reality* only as disclosed to us through our active, questioning relationship to it. We can never actually get to it as it is in itself, prior to the way in which we actively question it through our experiments. The constructs of Newtonian physics which led to the belief that we could formulate a total picture of reality may, in fact, be adequate descriptions of reality, but only at a certain level, and only as seen from a particular point of view. This does not mean that they are not true, only that their truth is limited. Just as there are many different ways of questioning reality, so there are many different but all partially true ways of describing it. Ilya Prigogine and Isabelle Stengers explain the results of the discoveries of Heisenberg and others in physics, thus:

> All description thus implies a choice of the measurement device, a choice of the question asked. In this sense, the answer, the result of the measurement, does not give us access to a given reality. We have to decide which measurement we are going to perform and which question our experiments will ask the system. There is an irreducible multiplicity of representations for a system, each connected with a determined set of operators. . . . This implies a departure from the classical notion of objectivity, since in the classical view only the objective description is the complete description of the system as it is, independent of the choice of how it is observed. . . . We have emphasized the importance of operators because they demonstrate that the reality studied by physics is also a mental construct; it is not merely given. . . . One of the reasons for the opposition between the two cultures may have been the belief that literature corresponds to a conceptualization of reality, to fiction, while science seems to express

36

objective reality. *Quantum mechanics teaches us that the situation is not so simple. On all levels reality implies an essential element of conceptualization* (Order Out of Chaos. *New York: Bantam Books. 1984).*

Subjective Influences on Scientific Objectivity

These discoveries on the level of subatomic physics are, from the point of view of science, highlighting for us in an especially vivid way a fundamental fact of epistemology that is applicable generally to the development of any knowledge, whether that be scientific or personal: namely that known reality is reality as exposed to our subjective questions. We have no way of getting to reality as it is independent of the questions we pose to it and that these methods of questioning are created tools, structures devised by the human subject in order to discover what he considers to be data relevant to his purposes. Heisenberg himself, is reported to have said concerning his own discovery:

> *What we observe is not nature itself, but nature as exposed to our methods of questioning (David Kolb,* Experiential Learning, *Englewood Cliffs, NJ: Prentice-Hall, 1984, p. 115).*

Malcolm Clark describes this fundamental fact of epistemology thus:

> *What facts we discover depends on the questions, purposes and interests with which we actively confront the world. . . . We look in vain for any building blocks which are given to all of us as the raw material of our experience (*The Need to Question. *Englewood Cliffs, N.J.: Prentice-Hall, 1973, p. 46).*

It was Kant who first highlighted in philosophy the notion that we can never attain to knowledge of the *thing-in-itself* but only as it is *for-me*. The hard sciences it would seem are just now beginning to catch up with Kant's central insight, and this they have done through taking the *in-itself* approach to its limits and discovering its inadequacy. According to Sidney Blatt and Howard Learner, it was in the nineteenth century that mathematics began to catch up with these insights, especially with the discovery of non-Euclidean and non-Cartesian geometries. Reflecting on the influence of these scientific and philosophical developments on the wider cultural and intellectual environment, Blatt and Learner write:

> *These discoveries led in part to the realization that the experience and conception of reality are influenced by the relative position and assumptions of the observer. As reflected in the formulations of Kant and Cassirer, there was increasing awareness that nature was not simply observed, but rather was a construction based upon the nature of a particular vantage point (*Clinical Psychology Handbook, *p. 87).*

The realization of this dynamic in scientific thinking is leading to a wholly different view of scientific theories. Hedges describes this view thus:

> *Current scientific thinking tends towards viewing theories as inventions or pictures to help organize our thinking and clarify vision. . . . Modern theories are understood as created points of view or conceptual lenses which momentarily brings into focus something one wants to look at (op. cit., p. 18).*

The Influence of Values on Objectivity

The *something one wants to look at* here indicates, furthermore, that in all constructs of reality, whether scientific reality or the reality of the ordinary individual, there is an intrinsic element of human intentionality, a desire to achieve a particularly valued result. Values are intrinsic to the search for reality; no view of what is really the case is independent of what I discern as significant for me. In the area of social sciences, Denis Goulet has written:

> *Ethical judgments regarding the good life, the good society, and the quality of relations among men always serve, directly or indirectly, as operational criteria for development planners and guidelines for researchers ("An Ethical Model for the Study of Values,"* Harvard Educational Review, *41(2), May 1971: p. 36).*

Research is not simply a dispassionate, intellectual exercise. It involves the whole person in his desire to achieve something of personal value. Abraham Maslow has highlighted in his work the fact that all intellectual activity is governed by need, ultimately the need to actualize our potentiality, to maintain and enhance our own being. This intentionality is prior to the scientific process itself; it is generated out of the human subjectivity of the scientist and governs the way in which the scientist relates to reality. The way in which the scientist, simply as a human being, formulates to himself the nature of that fulfillment will govern the particular way in which he relates to reality. This brings the role of subjective values right into the heart of all scientific endeavor. (By *scientific endeavor* here I wish now to include the much wider attempt to achieve an objective understanding of reality which is characteristic of human activity in all spheres, that of ordinary life as well as that of the specialized fields of study. In this sense we are all scientists in one way or another.)

This is something which science, in its attempt to be purely objective, had lost: the paramount importance of teleology in any understanding of human reality. All human behavior is intentional; it seeks a particular end and how that valued end is perceived dictates what sorts of questions we address to reality. It is this seeking for particular valued ends that governs the meaning of what we experience; it renders experience meaningful to a greater or lesser extent. It dictates the meaning of reality for us.

Although we have to accept that there is a level at which reality is intrinsically organized in a way that is prior to our encounter with it, such that it possesses a meaning-in-itself, it is disclosed to us only through the aims and intentions with which we approach it, its meaning-for-us. If we are able to get to a meaning-in-itself, it is only through its meaning-for-me. There is a prior process of selectivity based on the sense of what is significant to me which governs the scientific process. Adrian von Kamm describes the primary step in the process thus:

> *Man can only understand in a scientific way when he subjectively limits his original view. In order to be scientific he must adopt an attitude other than the open prescientific one. He has to change and reduce that which was originally given in his primary experience. What are considered to be objects in science are not objects which are given as such, but which are viewed in a specific frame because man*

orients himself subjectively in a certain way towards reality ("As-sumptions in Psychology," Insight, *3(3), Winter 1965: p. 43).*

Vitz rightly points out that this renders any simplistic idea of scientific objectivity obsolete:

Even to attend to a particular fact is already to give it a value with respect to those facts ignored. In psychology, in all social science, this problem becomes so pervasive that the notion of scientific objectivity must be seen as impossible when it comes to theory ("Empirical Sciences and Personhood: From an Old Consensus to a New Reality," Technological Powers and the Person. *St. Louis: The Pope John XXIII Center, 1983, p. 206).*

It is because of this intrinsic influence of values on objectivity that we can say to some extent at least, that we are responsible for what we discover and for the sort of world that we create, whether that be the private world of the individual or the public world of the community, since these value assumptions lie within ourselves and are to some extent at least available to consciousness. As Alan Waterman says:

We are organisms capable of intention, choice and purpose. . . . The range of choice in human functioning begins at the level of sensory experience. We do not automatically take our sensory inputs as reality but actively organize and construct from incoming data a probabilistic account of the world outside. While such choices are usually made below the level of awareness, we are capable of exercising volitional control in this sphere (The Psychology of Individualism. *New York: Praeger, 1984).*

The former *myth* of scientific knowledge, in which the conceptual pictures we formed of *reality* were accurate reflections of that reality which was there before and after man had looked at and discovered it, has now to be abandoned, as has the corresponding myth of the dispassionate observer scientists, simply reporting what it was he found. The picture that we are getting now is a very different one. The objectification of reality is now seen as the result of the activity of the human subject seeking to achieve something of significance for himself; it is a creative activity for which he bears a personal responsibility. It is no longer possible to simply hide behind the cloak of scientific objectivity, claiming simply to be reporters of what we find. We are to some extent morally accountable for the perspectives to which we give ourselves and allow ourselves to focus our attention on because these have a major influence on constructing the sort of *objective* world we live in. As Malcolm Clark puts it:

In adopting the viewpoint of the agent, we see how tenuous is the barrier between theoretical and moral. Movement in a given world can be described exhaustively in is *statements. But* is *joins* ought *when I preside self-critically at the very questioning which gives a world of a certain sort. I am responsible for my questions, for the way I formulate my alternatives, for the possibilities I disclose, for my habits of thought, for the discrimination in my perceptions, for the degree of self-presence I have achieved in my actions. I do indeed find myself in the world, but I find myself as an agent, responsible for what I make of it: it is my world* (Perplexity and Knowledge: An Inquiry into the Structures of Questioning. *The Hague: Martinus Nijoff, 1972, p. 37).*

This is becoming increasingly acknowledged by scientists themselves. Fritjof Capra, himself an atomic physicist, writes:

The patterns scientists observe in nature are intimately connected with the patterns of their minds — with their concepts, thoughts and values. Hence, the scientific results they obtain and the technological applications they investigate will be conditioned by their frame of mind. Although much of their detailed research will not depend explicitly on their value system, the larger framework within which this research is pursued will never be value-free. Scientists therefore are responsible for their research not only intellectually but also morally (The Tao of Physics. *2nd. ed. New York: Bantam Books, 1984, p. xvii).*

Historical and Cultural Limitations on Objectivity

With this emphasis on the centrality of the human subject in the generation of knowledge, we are also being brought up against the fact that the particular point of view and set of interests from which we view the data of reality is inevitably conditioned by the historical and cultural situation within which we are operating. As against the objectivist position which would seek to generate knowledge which is ahistorical, it is now being realized that this historical and cultural conditioning reaches to the very heart of man and is constitutive of his very essence in that he can never totally transcend it.

We can see this to be evident on the very foundational level of language. The individual, from the very earliest age, participates in the historical and cultural situatedness with all the limitations this entails through the assimilation of language. As we learn the language of our culture, therefore, we also inherit a particular world of meaning and value, and this intrinsically delimits and structures the way in which we view life and the sorts of questions we can then ask of reality. To a large extent we can never fully get beyond it. Ornstein highlights this when he notes that:

Our shared language and culture similarly limit our experience. Speakers of different languages may share a common structure of discourse and assumptions, but filter out much which is outside their own language, or worldview (op. cit., p. 17).

This inherited worldview, contained in the language we inherit, whether that be the language of ordinary discourse or the specialized languages of science, therefore, both discloses the meaning of the world of experience to us and yet at the same time limits it. It dictates what dimensions of reality are grasped by our conscious minds and their significance to us. Hence, it has been rightly said that:

The limits of a person's language are the limits of his world (Gerhard Egan. Encounter, Belmont: Brooks/Cole, 1970: p. 162).

Because of these historical and cultural limitations on the way in which we view reality, established at the very basic level of language, we all to some extent live in a world of our own. Bernard Lonergan talks about this under the notion of horizon. He explains it thus:

> There is a sense in which it must be said that each of us lives in a world of his own. That world usually is a bounded world, and its boundary is fixed by the range of our interests and our knowledge. There are things that exist, that are known to other men, but about them I know nothing at all. There are objects of interest that concern other men, but about them I could not care less. So the extent of our knowledge and the reach of our interests fix a horizon. Within that horizon we are confined. Such confinement may result from the historical tradition within which we are born, from the limitations of the social milieu in which we were brought up, from our individual psychological aptitudes, efforts and misadventures (The Subject. The Second Collection. *Milwaukee, WI: Marquette Press, 1968, p. 69).

Our ability then to get outside our historically conditioned horizons, both social and personal, is limited. We see reality only from within the meaning structures and values which we have inherited from our historically and culturally conditioned situatedness. This will radically condition the research that the scientist engages in and the sorts of results that he finds. In psychology, in the core area of normality, Offer and Sabshin have acknowledged the influence of these historically and culturally conditioned meanings and values on *objective* research into what is ideal in human growth and development. They write:

> It is apparent that any definition of normality will be affected by values influenced by philosophic, aesthetic and cultural theories. A scientist's original choice of one of the four perspectives of normality may be motivated by his or her past conditioning. Correspondingly, behavioral scientists' criteria of normality, which they proceed to establish experimentally or clinically, may not differ greatly from the criteria they have absorbed from the philosophic, religious or aesthetic values of their culture (op. cit., p. 389).

Because we are all born into a particular world, a world already constructed by the questions and answers of previous generations and embodied in its cultural, religious, and scientific myths, the way in which we address reality, the way in which we look at it, and the sort of meaning that it has for us and, hence, the questions that we ask of it, will vary with the culture and times into which we are born.

We can relate to reality, then, only from the standpoint of our historically determined and culturally inherited meaning and value systems. Although we may seek to go beyond them, they will still dictate the sort of questions we address to reality and hence what sort of picture of the world we build up. But more than this, they will also dictate what sorts of potentialities are evoked, and hence what sort of world we actually create.

Objectivity as Creativity

The second major perspective that is being offered to us by the hard sciences today, especially by the quantum theory in physics, is that our investigation of reality, while it is a search for what is, is also a creative structuring of what is. Quantum mechanics suggests to us that, at the level of the subatomic, it seems necessary to go even further than saying that objects appear to us in a certain way because of the way in which we are looking at them, and say in fact that they appear only because we look for them in a particular way. Gribben, agreeing with Eddington, comments:

> He stressed that what we perceive, what we learn from experiments, is highly colored by our expectations, and he provides an example, disturbing in its simplicity, to pull the rug from under those perceptions. Suppose, he says, that an artist tells you that the shape of the human head is hidden in a block of marble. Absurd, you say. But then the artist, chipping away at the marble with nothing more subtle than a hammer and chisel, reveals the hidden form. Is this the way that Rutherford discovered the nucleus? . . . All we see are the results of experiments which we interpret in terms of the nucleus (op. cit., p. 163).

The discoveries in quantum physics seem to indicate that to question an event in the atomic or subatomic world is to alter it, so that what is revealed is not the event in itself, as it is independently of me or as it is before I chose to observe it, but only as affected by the questions I address to it in my experiments. For instance the same phenomenon will appear as either a particle or a wave depending on the type of question addressed to it.

The phenomena appear in the way they do because we interact with the system in a particular way, and this is so because of the nature of tools that we have to use in order to question the system. To what extent this is true at all levels of reality is a difficult question. Insofar as any organism has an intrinsic unity within itself, it resists simply being determined from the outside, and it would in principle seem to be possible to remove ourselves from actively influencing that intrinsic unity so that its functioning can be observed in a way which does not significantly alter it. But nevertheless in highlighting the fact that individual entities are only such insofar as they are part of a field of interlocking energies, and indeed are only such because they participate in that field. It would seem to be legitimate to say that insofar as we are actually part of the system we are investigating we do have an influence on the way it appears empirically.

Creativity in Psychological and Social Research

We are becoming increasingly aware of this in the area of social and psychological research. To quote Goulet again:

> The most damaging bias held by empirical researchers is the belief that all social realities are amenable to objective study. But Clyde Kluckhohn and others report, significantly, "that when one studies values directly, the values are changed by the processes of study itself. . . . Thus the mere focusing of attention upon value problems changes the problems. In so far as this hypothesis is correct, the values

we discover are in part a function of the research approach." My
intention goes further: that problems are changed even when values
are studied indirectly. The mere presence of researchers on values
among people alters their level of consciousness regarding those
values. Wittingly or unwittingly, researchers are vectors of certain im-
ages of the good life and the good society; their passage does not
leave the values of a populace untouched (op. cit., p. 39).

In his discussion of what are known as *experimenter effects,* Ryschlak reports on the research of Rosenthal concerning the influence of the researcher
on the results of experiments. Ryschlak writes:

In an extensive survey of the extant research literature as well as in
his own researchers, Rosenthal was able to show convincingly that
the empirical findings of psychological experiments on humans are
influenced by such things as the experimenter's sex, race, manner of
relating to a subject (whether warm or cold), expectancy regarding
the likely outcome of a study, personal attraction to the subject, and
so on. Even when the experimenters were using rats as subjects, if
they believed the rats to be bright they obtained slightly better results
*than if they believed them to be dull (*Discovering Free Will and Personal Responsibility. *New York: Oxford University Press, 1979,*
pp. 104-105).

Their beliefs about their subjects evoked those potentialities. The result we
get then are results which are evoked by the experimental system itself. They
may be valid for that experimental system, but to what extent the findings can
be extrapolated to life outside the experimental situation is doubtful. This again
does not mean that the experiment has not yielded valid results, only that they
are valid only within the experimental situation itself.

In a somewhat different way, descriptive studies of human functioning which
do not require experimentation as such, inasmuch as their findings become culturally accepted, act upon the field in such a way as to actually produce that
which they purport simply to have found. They influence the system at the level
at which they actively participate in it, in this case at the level of education. Offer
and Sabshin give an example of this:

Erickson and other psychosocial theoreticians appreciate the cultur-
ally constructed and shared conceptual categories by which we jointly
organize and construct our experiences. Thus he and other investi-
gators report that some young people familiar with his ideas expect
to have an identity crisis. Cultural constructs seem to affect individ-
uals' expectations about their inner experience since, in a sense, giving
a culturally provided name to an experience makes it real to the in-
dividual (op. cit., p. 405).

This does not mean that they created the identity crisis as such or that they
did not discover something that could be called an identity crisis, but, in the first
place having delineated this set of experiences as *a crisis,* they have already structured the experience in a particular way according to their prescientific theoretical framework and given it a particular normative connotation. In articulating the
theory and propagating it as such, it then reacts upon the data, structuring peo-

ple's understanding of the situation in terms of crisis and hence creating expectations that it will occur. It now plays a part in actually evoking it: the explanation has itself created a new structure, such that to return to the empirical situation is to return to one which is different because the investigator has questioned it in a certain way. For instance, the more current expectation now coming out of the work of other theorists in the development school is the expectation of a mid-life crisis. Researchers having discovered something they have called a mid-life crisis, and, in making it a normative part of human development, can now expect to find increasing verification of their original belief as people come to expect to have this crisis at a certain period of their lives. They have also created a new empirical situation in that they will also find people who suffer from anxiety if at the appropriate time they do not have it, worrying that they may have repressed something important that leaves them deficient in some way, thus evoking a mid-life crisis of a different sort. The field of study is empirically altered by the articulation of the original findings.

If this is true, then it has implications for the current attempt to delineate and catagorize certain modes of behaviors as the result of *mental illness*. Illness is a particular social construct deriving from a particular view of biological functioning in which the individual entity can be affected impersonally by factors beyond his or her control. To apply the concept to mental functioning introduces an element which removes its cure from the person who is experiencing it, thus in fact producing a sense of being afflicted by impersonal forces beyond the individual's control. It thereby produces what in fact purports only to have been found empirically.

This concept also has important implications for the psychology of human relationships. Because of its objectivist basis, much of its effort has been directed toward the discovery of how to control, predict, and manipulate human behavior in order to achieve a better situation. If we now live in a world in which, as some psychological researchers believe (see Richard Restak, *The Self-seekers*. New York: Doubleday, 1982), *manipulation* is the dominant mode of relating to one another, then it is very likely that it is because, out of our scientific milieu, we have been so intensely concerned to look at the data solely in those terms. In the process of looking at human reality in this way, we have evoked and concretized these potentialities. Returning to these data, we now find that human relationships are primarily processes of mutual manipulation. Empirically, then, we might be tempted to deduce that human relationships need to be defined in terms of mutual manipulative patterns. But, in fact, we will only be discovering what we have already been instrumental in creating.

Implications for Psychotherapy

Following from this, in therapeutic psychology specifically, inasmuch as the therapeutic structure is an integrated system of its own, we come to the realization that the way the client is empirically in the relationship is partly a function of the person of the therapist. If, in the therapeutic relationship, we make central a sort of manipulative relationship based on a view of the process as being one in which an expert out of his or her superior knowledge is responsible for controlling and directing one who is ignorant and helpless to change and be responsible for their own lives, we are likely to produce people who are dependent and easily manipulated. The way in which we relate to the client, then will dictate what the client will become. If the central goal of counseling is the development of people who are essentially self-conscious and self-determining, then it would seem from what has been said that we need to relate to them in a way which actually evokes that potentiality.

Conclusion

In terms of our primary topic, then, what can we conclude from this discussion? There would seem to be three main points: in the first place, science itself is coming to recognize that the human subject is actively involved in the creation of whatever "facts" he discovers in the objective world, whether that be on an informal day-to-day basis or on the formal scientific level. He cannot simply stand outside of reality and contemplate it. Reality is not so much a puzzle to be solved but a mystery to be lived. Since it cannot ultimately be figured out, objectivity in science is not primarily an achievement but an ongoing process which can never be simply taken for granted. It is an active process rather than a passive reception.

Second, whether we be scientists wrestling with the formulation of the nature of the whole of reality, or simply ordinary persons seeking to make sense out of our daily experience, we are intrinsically limited in our ability to get a totally objective view of reality, either as it is or as it might be. We cannot rest simply in the belief that we have gained an objective picture of the way things are irrespective of who we are as persons. Whatever formulations we arrive at are intrinsically limited by the fact that they are the creations of subjects who relate to reality from a particular historically and culturally conditioned point of view of what is considered ultimately meaningful and significant. Our value system is a major factor in our ability to see our worlds objectively.

Third, because this viewpoint is to some extent under our control and plays a major role in what is evoked — in what becomes "real" — we ourselves bear a degree of responsibility for the sorts of data that are "discovered;" we are accountable to some degree, then, for the sorts of potentialities that are evoked through our active questioning of "reality," and hence the sort of objective world that results from our investigations.

At the very least this suggests that if, as scientists, we now have to be cautious about the status of our "objective" explanations of the world, as counselors we should be wary of the tendency to believe that we can gain an objective picture of the client's world such that we can thoroughly explain what is going on in it and how to change it for the better. It would seem that the movement back to the "therapist-knows-best" types of counseling which Patterson refers to is out of line with the developing perspectives in science generally, especially in those which are considered to be the paradigms of all sciences — the "physical" sciences. This does not of itself obviate the value of "objective" explanations and suggestions for action, but puts them in a different light. We need to see and relate to them differently.

Furthermore, we need to be much more aware and respectful of how the client himself has contributed to the creation of the world in which he lives and relate to him in a way that enables him to become more objective in his view of its meaning and what is possible within it. We need, then, to look at how we can help him involve himself in the process of achieving greater objectivity. We have to concern ourselves with how we can help people progressively come to a deeper self-awareness and gain the capacity to reorganize their own value investments such that they become more realistic in the way they relate to their worlds.

Finally, we need to be much more sensitive to the limitations on the person to be truly "objective" about themselves and their situation and their ability to reorganize their inner forces and their value-investments. Their past experiences, their current cultural and social situation, their intrinsic capacities are all limiting factors on their ability to see themselves and their world in an objective light and realize a better way of living within it.

We can see just what is involved in this endeavor if we again look at how scientists themselves become more objective in their work. This will enable us to assess the status and value of "objective" psychology in helping the individual achieve it in their lives and, beyond this, how our own "objective" understandings of the meaning of situations and advice as to what to do about them might be made available to clients in a way that actually helps rather than hinders them in their growth and development.

3 Philosophical Paradigms and Scientific Objectivity

Philosophical Assumptions and Objectivity in Science

It seems evident then that, in the search for a comprehensive explanation of human reality, even on the physical level, the scientist as scientist needs to be willing to take into account the complex of subjective meanings and values out of which he is operating. As John V. Knapp says:

> *The process of rationality involves unconscious and conscious decisions, value choices, and personal biases towards evidential considerations every step of the way. There can be no science without the scientist; human activity constitutes most of what can be called science, and like any other human activity, science is subject to emotion, inconsistency and will. To the extent that science tries to proceed without accounting for the human factor, it will flounder at precisely those points where human factors need the greatest attention* (Personality and Proof: The Mind of Science, *Revision 2, p. 8).*

And since science is essentially a social activity, there is in the first place a willingness to articulate and critique the philosophical presuppositions, inherited from his social environment, which inevitably influence the way in which the scientist views the data of his experiencing. The point is not to try to get rid of those presuppositions but to make them available to critique in order to see how well they do actually help us to organize and make sense of the empirical data. The fact is that no empirical studies can function without an underlying philosophy or myth about ultimate or essential meaning and value which is able to organize and interprets the data. John V. Knapp, summarizing the work of Ian Mitroff who has written extensively on the subjective dimensions of science, would concur with this. He writes:

> *Mitroff argues that scientists like other human beings cannot help but "postulate their own world views on the universe they behold in front of them." The selection of any particular experimental design is not automatic but is a function of one's world view as well as a response to particular technical requirements (Ibid., p. 8).*

These worldviews will dictate the sorts of theories that are formed. The result is, as Knapp, commenting on Freyerabend's work, goes on to say:

> *He notes that theory and observation, hence method and evidence are not separable. Thus all observation data is theory-laden (Ibid., p. 7).*

This is especially true of psychology as a science, as Joseph Nuttin observes:

> *The philosophic problem of man is inevitably involved in any general theory of human dynamism, because our theories about the moving forces in man depend upon our ideas as to what he is* (Personality and Psychoanalysis. *New York: Mentor-Omega Books, 1962, p. 264).*

There can, then, be no empirical study of man that can claim to be simply *factual:* the meaning and significance of what is determined to be *fact* about human nature is a product of our philosophical view of who man is. Every psychology contains some preliminary vision as to what human nature is and what it can become. In their studies of theories of normality, Offer and Sabshin point out an instance of this in a recent widely acclaimed work. They write:

> Levinson's work is often regarded as an example of some of the best clinical research on normal development. . . . Their view of what constitutes ideal development is so well defined that one wonders to what extent they imposed their vision of ideal man onto the lives of their subjects. Their presentation of theory, secondarily supported by case histories, suggests that the biographies have been used to illustrate a vision of ideal development (op. cit., p. 402).

Although, in terms of the process we have outlined, it might be possible to fault Levinson for not articulating what that ideal is and for not showing how it affects his choice of the data, one cannot find fault with him for having such a vision. This is both inevitable and necessary if we are to make sense of the data of our experience. But it can be an inhibiting and distorting factor if we are not aware of what those presuppositions are.

Raising to consciousness, then, the fundamental philosophical assumptions and values out of which we are operating is an essential element in the search for objectivity. We can transcend being locked into our subjectivity and actualize our intentionality toward objectivity only if we are able to raise to consciousness the meaning and value structures which we are projecting onto the data of our experiencing to see whether it accounts adequately for all the phenomena. This involves, then, a radical willingness on the part of the scientist to lay himself personally "on the line," so to speak, and render as good an account as he can of the basic framework out of which he is operating, especially as to how he views what is ideal.

Philosophical Background to Present Age

What is happening at the present moment in the scientific field illustrates this process. We are discovering the limits of the objectivist framework to account for the data of our experiencing and are being driven by that discrepancy to look at the philosophical assumptions out of which we have been operating. Under the pressure of experience, we are being forced to raise to consciousness the philosophical paradigm which we have been projecting upon reality and critique its ability to account for the data now being encountered. In the process of doing this a new paradigm is emerging which attempts to incorporate the subjective dimension into the search for objective understanding of the universe. It will be useful for us to look at this both in order to better understand the frame of reference out of which we may still be operating, and also to see what implications the new paradigm suggests for our understanding of the human reality with which we are dealing as counselors.

The term *paradigm* itself comes from the work of the philosopher of science, Thomas Kuhn. Grof describes its meaning thus:

> In the broadest sense, a paradigm can be defined as a constellation of beliefs, values and techniques shared by the members of a given scientific community (op. cit., p. 3).

48

The Cartesian-Newtonian Paradigm

The modern era until the present time has been dominated by the paradigm or world hypothesis inaugurated by Descartes. It was out of his philosophy, which proposed that human nature was constituted by two distinct dimensions — his mind and his body, each functioning on two independent planes, that the modern split between subjectivity and objectivity developed, resulting in the predominance of scientific objectivism in our approach to understanding reality. William Barratt comments:

> The fundamental feature of Descartes' thought is a dualism between the ego and the external world of nature. The ego is the subject, essentially a thinking substance; nature is the world of objects, extended substances. Modern philosophy thus begins with a radical subjectivism, the subject facing the object in a kind of hidden antagonism. . . . Nature thus appears as a realm to be conquered, and man the creature who is to be conqueror of it (The Irrational Man. Garden City, NY: Doubleday, 1962, p. 202).

This nature, the "objective," physical world, was a realm of discrete entities, or basic building blocks, whose interaction was governed by invariable processes which could be correlated into laws, the most fundamental and comprehensive of which were the laws of mathematics. These basic components were capable of being delineated conceptually and the relationships between them formulated precisely. He believed, for instance, that we should be able to formulate a language in which one word stood for one thing and that alone. He himself never attempted to do this, but some of his more enthusiastic students did. We gained knowledge of the external world, then, through analysis of these realities into their basic components and the differentiation of the "lawful" causal relationships between them. Carried through rigorously, the result was to be the creation of a systematic and comprehensive picture of the whole of reality through the formulation of clear, distinct, and internally consistent concepts in the mind after the model of mathematics. Malcom Clark comments:

> This assumption that ideas are atomic is to be found also in Descartes. Just as we analyze all numbers into prime numbers, so he held that we should be able to break down our common confused meaning into simple and ultimate ideas. . . . The idea of constructing a language which would avoid all the ambiguities of our ordinary words has persisted among philosophers, especially those with strong mathematical interests. (The Need to Question. Englewood Cliffs, NJ: Prentice-Hall, pp. 158, 160).

Out of this has come our emphasis on analyzing and categorizing reality and creating clear and coherent conceptual frameworks in the belief that these could clearly reflect and encompass the world "out there."

This Cartesian understanding of the physical world as a realm of fixed entities, essentially passive in themselves, whose activities were governed by mechanical forces that could be understood through the formulation of laws based on strict cause and effect, underpins the world hypothesis that came to dominate modern scientific thinking. The paradigmatic image is that of a clock with all its interlocking parts functioning in harmony. Its value as a fundamental and comprehensive perspective was reinforced as it began to yield spectacular results in our ability to control and predict the workings of various phenomena in the natural world. Newton's formulation of the laws of gravity which tied together the movements and behavior of solid bodies both in the heavens and on the earth ensured its success as the only true way to understand the physical world, and the Cartesian hypothesis gradually passed into common consciousness as a take-for-granted model of reality. Just how widespread and all-pervading its influence has been on the whole of modern scientific thinking has recently been detailed by Fritjof Capra in his book *The Turning Point* (New York: Bantam Books, 1983) in which he surveys all the major areas of scientific thought in order to show its influence and effects.

Although for Descartes himself, the Cartesian hypothesis was essentially limited to the physical world, through the work of such influential philosophers as Hobbes and Locke, it gradually became extended to encompass man as a whole, in his spiritual as well as in his physical dimensions. Barratt explains it thus:

Though man and nature are irremediably split off from each other, secretly what takes place is that the being of man is always understood in analogy to physical substances. While modern thought has split man off from nature, it has tried nevertheless to understand man in terms of physical substances (op. cit., p. 217).

The modern scientific study of man developed out of the assumption that human functioning could be analyzed into its component parts and understood as a mechanical system in which there was a strict relationship between cause and effect. Through the discovery of the strict connections between causes and their effects a complete picture of human reality could be built up and encapsulated in internally logical conceptual systems. Once formulated, it was believed, these ''scientific'' systems would be able to explain the functioning of every individual: human reality would have been totally ''figured out'' and brought under scientific control; breakdowns in the system could consequently be clearly analyzed and corrected. It is out of this that we evolved the belief that reality could be interpreted in terms of problems and answers; that we could analyze situations into their component parts and through an understanding of the mechanisms operating there intervene effectively to put them right.

Cartesian-Newtonian Paradigm in Psychology

It was this extension of the model to human reality that underpinned the growth of psychology as a science, both experimental and clinical. On the basis of this, the attempt was made to explain higher mental functioning on the basis of the interplay of underlying mechanisms either physiological, biological, or sociological which were believed to be more basic. The higher levels of human reality were assumed to be totally explainable in terms of the interaction of forces at the lower level since these were the building blocks out of which the higher functions were built.

We can see these elements in the following quotations from a work by Harold H. Kelley and John Thibout on interpersonal relationships which, on the face of it, would seem to be an area least amenable to the Cartesian–Newtonian paradigm. They write of their project:

It is our working assumption, then, that the total set of outcome matrices . . . account for all of social behavior. They account for everything that is or can be learned about social interdependence. Thus in their total effect they are totally responsible for both the successes and the failures of social interaction. . . . In short, when considered as the total set, outcome matrices provide a complete account of social behavior.

*This book is an analysis of outcome matrices (interdependence matrices). It considers their possible antecedents, the problems they pose in relation to their properties, how they can be thought about and provide bases for decisions, and what they make possible to learn about social life (*Interpersonal Relations: A Theory of Interdependence. *New York: John Wiley and Sons, 1978, p. 5).*

And they go on to say that:

It is possible to identify the major types of matrix patterns systematically. It is further possible to analyze the effect on the various patterns of (a) set of simple mathematical operations and (b) a set of simple sequences of the behavioral choices (ibid., p. 23).

Referring to an earlier form of their work, they see the value of their project in this way:

In its objective form the matrix was intended to have two other closely related uses. It may serve as a bench mark against which to evaluate the degree to which, at any stage in its development, the dyad is realizing the outcomes potentially available, and it may be used prescriptively to make recommendations about the joint behavior that ought to be performed in the interests of the relationship (ibid., pp. 13-14).

While not wanting to imply that their work has not produced anything of value for our understanding of the dynamics of interpersonal relationships, their use of such words as "total," "all," "everything," "complete," and their desire to attain a sort of mathematical exactitude and predictability, all illustrate clearly the presence of the Cartesian–Newtonian paradigm in the field of social psychology.

The Limitations of the Cartesian-Newtonian Paradigm

While undoubtedly this perspective has had enormously positive results in the extension of human knowledge, and has brought to conscious articulation dimensions of experience that had hitherto been obscure and untapped, what is becoming clear now, through the discoveries of science itself, is that the Cartesian–Newtonian paradigm has severe limitations for our understanding even of physical and biological phenomena. There are many areas and facets of our experiencing which it cannot explain or account for, especially the processes of transformation and growth. It is unable to account for the "intentionality" that is found in even the sub-atomic world, the dynamic movement to adapt to and integrate its environment into new and different complex unities. On the human level, it is unable to account for the role that subjectivity plays in the generation of knowledge and to the activity of science itself as an intrinsically subjective process with all its historically and culturally conditioned meanings and values.

Roger Poole would seem to be correct about the historical origins of this inadequacy when he says of Descartes that. . .

> . . . *[he] remained blind to one half of the problems he himself raised with his Cogito. He refused to discuss himself as embodied subject, his affective relation to the world, the questions of perspectives and the all important matter of how the world is built up inter-subjectively. All this he refuses to touch, shying away from experience of his own subjectivity and building barriers between it and himself by his dualistic primitivism* (Towards Deep Subjectivity. *London: Penguin Books, 1972, p. 85).*

This shying away from the implications of subjectivity passed into the general framework of thinking and resulted in a general devaluing of subjectivity in the quest for scientific knowledge. Whether, in the case of Descartes, it was a somewhat deliberate blindness, as Poole implies, or simply a result of the historical horizon within which he was operating is something that historians of philosophy alone can say. Suffice it to say, that in not adverting to the subjective dimension, Descartes did set in motion the perspective that has come to so totally dominate our thinking up until the present time: that the whole of reality, including man in his unique subjectivity, could be understood as a mechanical system of interlocking basic elements which could be accurately figured out in terms of cause and effect, discerned through a dispassionate observation which operated irrespective of the unique subjectivity of the scientist and capable of being ratified by the experimental method.

The Psychological and Moral Effects of This Paradigm

This sort of approach has also encouraged us to think that, in deciding what to do in our concrete particularized circumstances, we are on safest ground if we work downward from "scientific" theory to practice. It has elevated the abstractive dimension to such a privileged position that it has resulted in removing us from an openness to our experience as both a source of learning and as an important way of validating the concepts that we do generate about it. It has fed a certain mistrust of our own ability to make sense of our experiencing and ability to make adequate decisions on the basis of it. We have thus become remote from the ability to think about the meaning of our experiencing for ourselves and take responsibility for the decisions that we make on the basis of it.

It has also weakened our sense of personal responsibility for our actions by, in effect, creating two classes of people, those who know and those who do not know, with the latter being very dependent upon the former. If Kelley and Thibout are correct, for instance, in their assessment of their work, in order to live our lives "correctly," we would have to either become "expert" in their theory and its applications, or seek out their expertise and put ourselves entirely in their hands in order to discern how best to conduct our relationships. In either case, we are implicitly denying our own ability to discern the meaning and positive possibilities of our experiencing for ourselves and take personal ownership of the decisions we make about how to live in the particularity of our immediate situations.

Especially in the area of human intra- and interpersonal experiencing, then, we are left with a legacy of over-confidence in the abstract conceptual knowledge of science, such that we tend to equate its abstractions with reality and try to subsume the everflowing uniqueness of our experiencing in all its complexity into these abstractions. And since that body of knowledge is believed to be able to give us the hidden causes of things, we look to it for information as to what we need to do in the particularized and ever-changing flow of experiencing in order to achieve fulfillment. We have, as a consequence, come to rely upon working downward from formalized theory to practice in living and to rely on technique as being the predominant way of conducting our relationships. It has weakened the individual's ability to engage with confidence in the process of achieving objectivity in the conduct of their personal lives and formented an increasing dependency on the part of people generally on the knowledge and expertise of those who specialize in the human sciences. This has left people somewhat adrift in their ability to relate to and operate satisfactorily within the uniqueness and variability of their immediate experiencing. Especially in the realm of human relationships, instead of the confidence that we can understand and make adequate decisions for ourselves as to the best way to live and act, we tend constantly to be looking to the experts in psychology for the knowledge and skills as to what to do and how to do it. The result is a sort of mechanical, stereotypical responding, a concern to operate "correctly" according to certain theoretical postulates accepted as accurate formulations of the way things are and ought to be.

Emergence of a New Paradigm

The Centrality of the Subject

However, because of the recent discoveries of atomic physics, the realization of the intrinsically subjective nature of all knowledge and the implications of this for our understanding of reality which are now surfacing, a new world hypothesis or paradigm of reality is being forged. Philosophically, the ground had already been prepared for the emergence of this new paradigm. It had been in formation ever since the reaction of Kierkegaard to the philosophical systems of Hegal. It has been fed by the streams of Kant and latterly of Husserl and Heidegger, finding its modern expression especially in the existentialist movements. Joseph Lebacqx has described this emerging philosophical revolution thus:

> It is often said that much of today's philosophy is a philosophy of subjectivity. The view is that the philosophies of the past, concerned as they were to produce a systematic account of the whole of the universe, had too often reduced man to the status of being a simple piece inside a huge organized cosmos, where everything seemed so predetermined, so completely "already there" beforehand that there was no place for real history, or the historical process. In reacting against this distorted view of human reality modern philosophy. . . , emphasizes the central and privileged status of man. Far from being swallowed up by an anonymous and rigorously determined process man as endowed with freedom has himself to decide what to make of his life in the world. He has, in a true sense, to make himself, not according to a pre-established pattern, but according as he decides ("Subjective and Objective," Heythrop Journal, vol. VIII, April 1967: p. 191).

Man as an individual, self-conscious subject, irreducible to any underlying phenomena, and possessing a certain creative freedom as to what he can become, is now at the heart of the emerging worldview. Having received radical reinforcement from the findings of the hard sciences themselves which has highlighted the subjective dimensions present in all "objective" scientific formulations of reality, this new paradigm is highlighting the distinctive properties of self-consciousness and is giving it new weight in scientific theorizing. Fritjof Capra describes how this is affecting scientific research in these words:

> The ability to recognize order seems to be an essential aspect of the rational mind; every perception of pattern is, in a sense, a perception of order. The clarification of the concept of order in a field of research where patterns of matter and patterns of mind are increasingly being recognized as reflections of one another promises to open fascinating frontiers of knowledge (The Turning Point. New York: Bantam Books, 1983, p. 5).

Features of the New Paradigm

The name currently given to at least one form of this new paradigm is general systems theory, and as explained by Fritjof Capra, it has several dimensions that are important for our purposes. In the first place, what is being proposed in this new scientific outlook is that the whole cannot be reduced to its parts. Especially with regards to living systems, such as the human being, what is higher in its level of structure and dynamism cannot be explained simply through an analysis of its parts or its underlying structural components: the higher levels possess potentialities not contained in the sum of its components. As a result, for instance, "self-consciousness" is no longer seen simply as an inconsequential epiphenomenon of the interplay of physical forces, but as a unique and realized potentiality of the biological organism as an integrated, dynamic whole.

In the second place, consciousness as such is seen to be an intrinsic element of all reality even at the lowest level of the subatomic world, a consequence of the dialectic tension between the intrinsic structure of an entity, its dynamism toward growth and development, and the environment in which this growth has to take place. Self-consciousness from this perspective is the endpoint or fulfillment of the intrinsic dynamic in the universe to ever-increasing levels of complexity and simplicity. The universe then has reached its apogee in human self-consciousness which in its ability to reflect upon itself has realized a new level of unity with the world: the world of nature is now conscious of itself in a new way — as a system it is present to itself and knows itself as a system.

It does not seem to be too much to suggest that with the emergence of human self-consciousness, the fabric of reality itself has been changed. It would seem that the evolutionary dynamisms which produced self-consciousness are no longer in operation. In reflecting upon nature, therefore, and discerning its objective meaning, the primary source for human consciousness is its knowledge of itself. The new paradigm, then, instead of mechanizing the personal would seem to be calling for a personalizing of the mechanical.

In the third place, activity is being seen as intrinsic to reality, that all entities of their very nature are dynamically active forces of energy rather than passive solids. Entities in nature are not motivated to act primarily by forces outside of themselves but of their very nature are actively seeking a certain condition of being. Capra writes:

> The dynamic aspect of matter arises in quantum theory as a consequence of the wave nature of sub-atomic particles, and is even more central in relativity theory, which has shown us that the being of matter cannot be separated from its activity. The properties of its basic patterns, the sub-atomic particles, can be understood only in a dynamic context, in terms of movement, interaction, and trans-formation (The Turning Point, p. 87).

Nature then is actively seeking self-actualization and its structure is formed in interaction with its particular environment in order to make that possible. George Lock Land, quoting Robert D. Coghill, writes:

> The organism acts on the environment before it reacts to the environment. The drive of both physiological and the psychological processes of living is to assimilate external materials and to reformulate them into extensions of themselves (Grow or Die. New York: Random House, 1973, p. 8).

Where it is not possible simply to assimilate the environment to itself, matter seems further to be open and willing to seek self-modification or transformation in order to achieve on-going growth.

In the fourth place, the universe as a whole is seen as an indivisible unity, a system, containing in itself different levels of interlocking systems, the highest being that of the human person, the lowest that of the subatomic world. The activity of these living systems cannot be understood as totally governed by mechanical laws of cause and effect which can be rigorously analyzed, though something of this is present, but as also governed by the intrinsic structure of the reality as a whole and the dynamic purposefulness of that structure as it seeks to grow and develop and realize its potentialities within the context of its particular environment. The activity of the lower parts, then, is also governed by their place in the overall structure of the system in its dynamic movement toward higher levels of integration.

While it is primarily just speculation that the intrinsic structure of nature was changed by the emergence of self-consciousness, we are on surer ground when it comes to the influence of personal self-consciousness on the intrinsic structure of the brain. Roger Sperry for instance, in commenting on the way this revolution has touched brain research, maintains that the personal constructs of the individual as to both meaning and value has a major influence on the actual formation and structure of the physical reality of the person, including the brain. Hence, he says:

> The key realization was that the higher levels in brain activity control the lower. The higher cerebral properties of mind and consciousness are in command. They envelop, carry and overwhelm the physiochemical details. They call the plays, exerting downward control over the march of the nerve-impulse traffic. Our new model, mentalism,

puts the mind and mental properties to work and gives them a reason for being and for having evolved in a physical system (Interview, Omni, August 1983).

He draws the conclusion that:

. . . according to our new views of consciousness, ethical and moral values become a very legitimate part of brain science. They are no longer conceived to be reducible to brain physiology. Instead, we now see that subjective values exert powerful causal influence in brain function and behavior (ibid.).

Implications for Pathology

In contrast to the view maintained by the Cartesian-Newtonian model that biochemical imbalances in the brain cause mental, perceptual, and behavioral disturbance, this perspective would suggest that the opposite process is likewise a real possibility: that perceptions and values can create brain disturbances with their biochemical correlates. The meaning structures and value investments we make on the conscious level actually affect the structures and dynamisms operative on all the substructures that constitute the interlocking series of systems of the human person. Intrinsic to an understanding of the subsystems in any particular person is an understanding of the structure of the world in which he lives, and this is primarily a function of his interpretation of the meaning of his experiencing.

This in itself does not rule out the influence of biological structures on conscious processes. If conscious mental processes can alter the bioneurology of the brain and of the body as a whole, then a sort of automatic response to the data of experiencing can be fixed in a way that functions below that of consciousness. The body is programmed as it were to discern those meanings in its experiencing. Once fixed as patterns of interpretation, they may very well "cause" a conscious interpretation in line with them. There does seem to be some evidence, through the study of identical twins of pathologically disturbed parents, raised by separate adoptive parents, that these patterns can be passed on genetically such that they predispose the person to similar pathologies. In this sense, one can see the biochemical imbalances as one of the causes of the illness in certain people. Insofar as Cartesian-Newtonian science has enabled us to discern the cause and effect mechanisms of the biochemical structures, it has enabled us to intervene to some extent in their operation and correct them. Those in whom the illness was biochemically caused can then be said to be cured of the illness.

The Notions of Causality and the New Paradigm

However, the paradigm would suggest that in discovering these mechanisms, one has by no means explained the phenomena. Returning to an older scientific point of view, that of Aristotle, Rychlak has shown that, to explain a phenomenon, one has to look for at least four causal factors, what are traditionally known as material, formal, final, and efficient, or as he calls them: substance, the underlying essence of a thing at any particular time; pattern, the style of organization and internal consistency of an object; intentional or formal, the dynamic seeking, the "for the sake of which" the activity is in motion; and impetus, efficient or mechanical causality, the interactive effects that produce a succession of events over time. From this perspective Rychlak sees the new paradigm as, in some ways, a rediscovery of a tradition that had been submerged by the rise of modern science. He defines the reductionism that characterizes modern science as

> . . . *reducing pattern and intentional construct meanings to substance and impetus construct meanings* (Introduction to Personality and Psychotherapy. *Boston: Houghton Mifflin, 1973, p. 7).*

In psychology this entailed the reduction of the dynamic intentional activity of the person in all its uniqueness to the relational dynamics of our common nature. It sought to delineate and categorize the common features of human nature and sought the laws which govern their interaction while ignoring the part all those features played within the intentional world of the particular individual. The reductionism went further, however, in seeking to explain all the common elements of human nature on the basis of those elements that it shares with the rest of nature.

One of the reasons for this loss was the movement to wrest science from the clutches, so to speak, of philosophy and theology and give it its own autonomous rationale. The notion of intentionality in nature bespoke too closely the idea of the involvement of some ultimate personal agency which had formed everything with a particular intention in mind. It was considered impossible to understand anything except in reference to that particular divine intentionality. Science, on the contrary, sought an explanation of the way things were from within nature itself, by the analysis of its inner working and effective relationships with its environment and through this study gain control of nature in order to direct it to rational ends.

The Implications of the New Paradigm

What the new paradigm seems to be doing, however, is to be rediscovering, in a fresh and more discriminating way, the nature and importance of the pattern and intentional nature of reality. To understand the nature of any phenomenon one has got to take into account the pattern of the whole and its dynamic striving for growth.

Particularly in the light of Sperry's comments, this has important repercussions for our understanding of what health and illness are: in discovering the mechanical components in an illness one has not as such discovered "the" cause of illness. In altering or "correcting" those biochemical imbalances one is correcting the symptoms, not the cause. From this perspective, health cannot be seen as it often is today simply in terms of a particular physiological or even psychological condition, i.e., the absence of identifiable disease emotionally or physically. Both these conditions can be achieved from and sustained by sources outside the person through chemical means of one sort or another. It is conceivable that with the development of the biological and medical sciences it would be possible to chemically maintain particular physical or even emotional conditions over long periods. However, the new paradigm would suggest that one cannot necessarily consider this health as long as the basic psychological, spiritual, and social patterns of a person's life which may have caused the imbalances in the first place remain. One can, then, have an absence of physiological or psychological distress while still being radically unwell.

Contrary to overwhelming popular belief, therefore, to have the symptoms removed is not necessarily to have been cured of one's sickness. An important component in illness is the overall condition of the person. Why will one person fall sick of a particular illness while others exposed to precisely the same situation will not? The answer seems to lie in the way a whole pattern of life affects the immune system, the body's ability to maintain itself in health. Stress seems to be an important factor here: in what ways is a person being stressed and how is the person coping with it? Intrinsic to this is the way the person internally construes the meaning of his experiencing and the values that are involved. Lack of a core integration at this level produces a core lack of integration on all levels of the organism, weakening its ability to maintain its integrity as an organism. Speculating on the origins of the disease of modern times, cancer, Capra writes:

> A state of imbalance is generated by prolonged stress which is channeled through a particular personality configuration to give rise to specific disorders. In cancer the crucial stresses appear to be those that threaten some role or relationship that is central to the person's identity, or set up a situation from which there is apparently no escape. Several studies suggest that these critical stresses typically occur six to eighteen months before the diagnosis of cancer. They are likely to generate feelings of despair, helplessness, and hopelessness. Because of these feelings, serious illness, and even death, may become consciously or unconsciously acceptable as a potential solution (The Turning Point, p. 354).

This is not to say that the removal of the symptoms cannot be an important part of the curing process. Inasmuch as they do give relief from certain debilitating situations, and interrupt the automatic interpreting of life in a particularly pathological way, they can give a person the opportunity to see life differently and to restructure their outlook and behavior with the hope that internal conflicts can be resolved and a better condition can be attained. However, because of the prevailing Cartesian-Newtonian paradigm, this is not the way generally in which the situation is viewed today. The tendency is to view both mental and physical illness impersonally as a product of forces operating at a level lower than that of self-consciousness and self-determination and hence as something that one personally has no responsibility for or control over.

In that this perspective has removed large areas of human life from personal reflection and control, it may actually be encouraging the emergence of a frame of mind that is increasingly susceptible to stress because it views its well-being as something essentially dependent upon external, impersonal forces over which one has no control. With the reduction of the sense of responsibility for their own well-being, people are becoming increasingly susceptible to those forces. One might speculate that with increasing ability on the part of the medical and psychiatric world to intervene and create a condition of well-being biochemically, the incidence of disease could increase. Recognition of this possibility would not suggest a reduction of the efforts to achieve the possibility of effective intervention, but rather that it should be combined with a counterbalancing educational process that would highlight the linkage between one's meaning structures and value system and the susceptibility to mental and physiological diseases.

To view events, then, from the perspective of the new paradigm would also alter the view of the nature of illness or physiological and psychological distress, or at least enlarge our ability to discriminate the meaning of various illnesses more finely. While leaving intact the real possibility that there are illnesses which are the results of impersonal forces either in one's internal or external environment, it would also enable us to see, on one side, that some illnesses are positive, if painful, indications of the need to change one's internal and external life patterns, and to revamp one's meaning structures and value systems. On the other side, some illnesses may be seen as indications of growth itself as one set of perspectives and investments is disintegrating in order to allow the emergence of higher levels of growth and hence as something one needs to understand and live through rather than simply get rid of.

The Notion of Law in the New Paradigm

Finally, this new paradigm seeks to articulate and develop general laws which govern all levels of reality as interactive energy systems. In this new way of understanding reality, the search is still for the discovery of principles which are applicable universally, but they are different sorts of laws from the simple cause and effect laws of the previous paradigm. They look for the process patterns which are present in the systems as a whole. The search now is for laws which are intrinsically involved in any system simply because it is. What results are isomorphic laws, principles of operation which are the same at any level yet distinct according to each level. They are essentially what used to be called in metaphysics analogical principles. George Lock Land writes:

> Of late, the discipline of formalized analogy and the construction of analogical models have become techniques whereby new, logical, and profound relationships have been discovered in the physical and natural sciences. It was formalized analogy that revealed the nature of systems to cyberneticians, the structure of DNA to molecular geneticists, and produced a wide variety of discoveries . . . (op. cit., p. 6).

The important differences between these laws and the Cartesian–Newtonian laws is that, while they are generally applicable and hence govern all reality, they yet operate in distinctly different ways in the concrete reality of each system. They are, therefore, able in principle to allow for the distinctness of the levels of beings involved. They will not apply in precisely the same way at each level. They will apply at the level of human reality yet be different from the way they operate at lower levels and be essentially irreducible to them. While being able to reincorporate subjectivity and its very highest spiritual activities into the formulation of the meaning of the whole of reality, the temptation to a simple reductionism in which all reality can be explained in terms of the interaction of its lower elements is removed.

Furthermore, those who search for those comprehensive laws are well aware that they may never attain a totally comprehensive explanation. Fritjof Capra writes:

> The recognition that all concepts and theories we use to describe nature are limited has been one of the main lessons that physicists have had to learn in this century. It has given rise to the idea that the

science of the future may not produce any more broad unified the-
ories but may well consist of a network of inter-locking and mutually
consistent models, none of them being any more fundamental than
the others. Such an approach seems to be suited ideally to describe
the multi-leveled, interrelated fabric of reality. Ultimately, the various
models will go beyond disciplinary distinctions, using whatever lan-
guage will be appropriate to describe aspects and levels of reality
(The Metaphors of Consciousness. New York: Putnam, 1981, *p. xi).*

Overcoming Cartesianism in Psychology

On the basis of the new paradigm, then, man has to be understood in his
distinctive reality. If there are principles of operation which he shares in common
with other living systems, they operate differently here than they do at lower
levels, and our understanding of their operation at lower levels derives from our
understanding of their presence in man. Reflection then on the intrinsic nature
of human being as disclosed in human self-consciousness is essential to understanding the nature of being as such.

The Philosophical Critique

This is primarily a philosophical task rather than a psychological one. In
modern times it has been attempted primarily by the existential philosophers,
particularly Heidegger who is considered by many to be the most important philosophical thinker of our age. In Catholic thought, the school of transcendental
metaphysics has attempted to articulate the intrinsic dimensions of being *a priori*
disclosed in the dynamics of subjectivity. Lonergan and Clark, whose work we
have already referred to, are important figures in this school. However, Hedges
believes that the modern philosophic reflection on the basic Cartesian assumptions of modern psychology, especially as formulated by Gilbert Ryle, has been
a major influence on restoring the human mind to its unique position in modern
psychology. To what extent this is true is difficult to determine but it would seem
that Ryle has been able to highlight the major weakness of the Cartesian system
as a philosophical framework in a way that has caused many in the field of psychology to reevaluate its validity. And in the process, he has furthered the effort
to reinforce the preeminence and irreducibility of the subject. Hedges writes:

> *Ryle (1949) has shown the Cartesian myth to be an historical curiosity*
> *in the form of a categorical error. According to Ryle, Galileo's framing*
> *of the universe in a vocabulary of mechanics led quite unnecessarily*
> *to a "Ghost in the machine" conception of man. Propositions re-*
> *garding mental causes, states and processes were cast into an anal-*
> *ogous mechanistic and deterministic vocabulary. Ryle examines the*
> *historical, logical and grammatical considerations which erroneously*
> *led to considering mind and body as concepts within the same uni-*
> *verse of discourse. He demonstrates the unfortunate consequences*
> *which the perpetuation of the Cartesian manner of thinking has had*
> *on the subsequent development of clinical and theoretical proposi-*
> *tions in psychology (op. cit., p. 19).*

The categorical confusion which he highlighted is the tendency from the
objectivist framework to see mind and body as different objects and interpreting

the former on the basis of the latter. This in fact is to reverse the process. Mind is that by which we discern objects as objects; the objective world of objects as objects only appears in and through the activity of the mind. Mind, then, is a function of that intrinsic self-presence, the ability to know ourselves in our knowing, which enables us to differentiate objects as objects and, hence, body as body. Mind, although itself an abstraction, is the term we use to describe the subjective activity by which we are able to recognize ourselves and the world as other than ourselves and so objectivize it through our concepts. It is not itself an object and cannot be reduced to the mechanical determinisms we can discern at lower levels of reality.

We can see this categorical confusion in a very recent book on the brain by Richard Restak which was the basis of a very popular television series. He writes, in his discussion of the relationship between mind and brain as shown by the ability of the person to watch his own brain activities on a P.E.T. scan,

> Consider the paradox involved: the inquiring organ, the brain, is itself the object of its own inquiry. The brain is the only organ in the known universe that seeks to understand itself (The Brain. New York: Bantam Books, 1984).

The categorical confusion is evident here: the human person in his mental activity is equated with the physiological functioning of the brain. However, the notion of the brain is itself an abstraction, a conceptual categorization of a dimension of human reality, and what appears on the screen is a further abstraction based on the technological instruments involved. It is not, as such, a picture of the human mind that is watching it; it is an objectification of certain physiological dynamics delineated as the most significant and defining characteristics of what has been decided to be brain by the human mind. The concept *brain* does not as such simply equal some thing out there; it is the way in which the human mind differentiates some aspect of reality in order to discern its internal relationships and external effects. Where the brain actually begins and ends is a scientific convention for the purpose of research and dialogue. In that it is responsible for differentiating and discerning it as brain, mind, in itself, is transcendent to it.

The Transcendence of Spirit

Mind as such cannot be seen, only body can be seen. Mind is the light by which we as subjects see it. In watching certain mechanical operations of the brain on the screen, we are not, as such, watching the human mind. We know of mind only in the subjective operation of distinguishing, correlating, and grasping objects as objects, i.e., as other than ourselves as subjects. Mind as such then cannot be equated simply with brain activity as capable of being discerned by human technological ingenuity. Its emergence may in fact be a result of the development of brain organization, but that organization has produced a reality which, though dependent in many ways on that underlying structure, possesses a potentiality which is not reducible to the parts that underlie it, namely the capacity to reflect upon itself and know itself, and hence differentiate objects from itself. Rather than saying produced, some scientists, such as Bohm, now prefer to say that the process has "enfolded" what was previously "infolded" in matter, namely consciousness. Consciousness cannot then be explained by the operations of its constituent parts. It may also be that, in order to grasp this properly,

61

we have to revise our way of interpreting matter. Rather than talking of self-consciousness as nonmaterial, we need to interpret matter as non-self-consciousness, that is, it is some aspect of reality that limits self-consciousness. This would make more sense of the scientific data concerning the teleological tendencies in "matter." Nature can then be seen as a dynamic movement to realize its own intrinsic potentiality for self-consciousness. This way of looking at it would also make sense of a cryptic remark attributed to Sir James Jeans to the effect that "the universe is beginning to resemble more and more a gigantic thought rather than a machine."

The concept mind, however, although itself also an abstraction, is one which delineates not an object but a process, a process which emerges out of and is intrinsically constitutive of a deeper reality which lies at the core of human being rendering it transcendent to any objectification. John G. Finch uses the word *spirit* to cover this core element which is irreducible to any objectification. He describes it thus:

> *Thus, from a psychological point of view, it would appear that spirit can be defined as that quality unique to man which is able to objectivize but incapable of objectivization, has the characteristic of self-transcendence, and gives man a quality of freedom and responsibility which ascribes to man powers of creatorship ("Spirit and Psyche," A* Christian Existential Psychology: The Contribution of John G. Finch. H. Newton Maloney, ed. Washington, DC: University of America Press, 1980).

Spirit, then, is that foundational presence to self as an integral subject seeking to discover the intelligibility and significance of the data of its experiencing in order to realize itself. In its unity with itself, in which it both knows and affirms itself as significant, it both affirms the unity and significance of reality as a whole and is able to differentiate what is not-self, that which yet awaits discovery of its intelligibility and value.

The dynamism toward objectivity then, is essentially the spiritual activity of the human subject, in and through its mental operations, gradually differentiating the "not-I" from itself, discerning and articulating its contours and potentialities, or objectivizing it, in order to integrate it into human purposes, enabling it to become part of the "I" at a higher level of integration. It is a process of differentiation and reintegration.

The Dynamic Process of Objectivity

Crucial to the growth in objectivity is the ability and willingness to touch and recognize our ignorance about the meaning of the empirical data. Objectivity begins, we might say, with an attitude of "reverent puzzlement" in which we are faced with the possibility of having to revise and transform who we are in our knowledge of ourselves and our world. We are most in touch with reality, with that which is, when we are actively willing to reach out to the other as significant to us in its distinct reality and able to recognize and accept that what it is we are experiencing does not wholly fit our existing conceptual structures, what it is we already know.

The ability to be open to our ignorance, we might say, is the cutting edge of our ability to grow in objective knowledge. Far from being a passive reception of impressions from the outside, therefore, growth in objectivity demands a courageous commitment in faith. It is an active searching for and holding open to that which is opaque, which does not fit what we already know; it is a willingness to move out of where we are into the unknown, to be on the edge of what we already are and moving into becoming something different, without any concrete guarantee that it will be more comfortable, secure, or satisfying. As Abraham Maslow put it, we are in a fundamental tension between the desire to know and the fear of knowing (see *Towards a Psychology of Being*. New York: Van Nostrand, 1968, p. 60).

It is also a commitment to love, to be willing to differentiate the other from ourselves in its own reality and to be willing to recognize and affirm it as such. There is therefore a corresponding tension between the need to act and the fear of acting, between the need to be responsible and the fear of responsibility. As Maslow has pointed out there is an intrinsic link between these two. New knowledge requires new and different actions and demands a change in us. This can be difficult and frightening; it demands that we leave who we are and become something different, to leave the security of the familiar and enter into unknown territory without any certitude that it will be a better place. This is especially true when we are dealing with self-definition, with our objective understanding of who we are and what we can and should become. Fear of becoming different, of having to change, and take responsibility for that change, can pressure us to avoid knowing ourselves.

Freud was the first of modern psychological thinkers to point to a force in the human person which seemed to resist any new self-knowledge that would require becoming different. He called it the *death-instinct:* an inertial impulse to stay the same out of a sense that death is the natural end of the organism, a state of stasis and nonchange. There is a primitive wisdom within the person that says it is pointless to give up the security of what one is to change and become different. This instinct is also called the *nirvana principle* which in some ways would seem to be a more appropriate name for it in that it looks to a condition of rest and peace. This is a projected understanding of the state of death which might in fact be drawn out of the early experience of the womb: death is seen then as a return to the peace, quiet, and passivity of the womb.

The Intrinsic Dynamics of the Process

Whatever the validity of these understandings, they do point to the fact that the search for deeper objective knowledge with its concomitant need to become and behave differently is not something that "comes naturally," though within the human organism there is a pressure so to speak that demands it. It is something that requires choice and commitment; it is essentially a moral task in which there needs to be a core commitment to certain central process values. It has been one of Lonergan's important contributions to elucidate what these imperatives are. John Haught diagrams these in this way:

(1) Be attentive	(be open)⟶	experience
(2) Be intelligent	⟶	understanding
(3) Be reflective	(be critical)⟶	judgment
(4) Be responsible	⟶	decision

Although this seems simple and obvious enough, it does indicate that we are involved always in a circular process which demands a personal commitment. It is the movement from openness to our primitive experiencing, the locus of our ignorance, through the steps of articulation (understanding) and dialogue, both intrapersonal and interpersonal (reflection), to evaluation and a decision to act (personal commitment) and then a return again to primitive experiencing. John Haught comments:

> The above scheme would perhaps be inconsequential, and our disclosure of its native invariance in man's consciousness would be without import were it not for the obvious and perplexing fact that we humans are continually violating its norms. We are not always sufficiently attentive, intelligent and critical, let alone responsible. The evasion of understanding, the "flight from insight," is a pervasive temptation. Thus our bringing the above structure into reflection is intended to make us more aware of what is involved both in the quest for the real and the flight from it" (Religion and Self-acceptance. New York: Paulist Press, 1976, pp. 19–20).

A similar pattern of growth in objective knowledge, but from a psychological perspective, has been recently detailed in the work of David Kolb. He considers that there are four basic learning modes: concrete experiencing, in which one is immersed in the fluctuating data of the immediate moment, sensitively accommodating and responding to its ever-emergent newness; reflective observation, in which one reflects imaginatively on its patterns of meaning both in itself and personally; abstract conceptualization, in which one attempts through analysis and abstraction to see commonalities in the data in order to build up theories and explanations and so grasp the data in as comprehensive a framework as possible; and active experimentation in which one then moves back out into reality to try out different ways of relating suggested by the theories. In this process, the data of one's experiencing is altered and the process continues.

While Kolb sees each of these modes as, through specialization, independently valid ways of achieving knowledge, he also sees a prior intrinsic unity among them such that growth in learning is a gradual integration of these four modes of learning. We can relate them to Lonergan's framework thus:

(1) Be attentive (be open) →	experience	Concrete experiencing
(2) Be intelligent →	understanding	Reflective observation
(3) Be reflective (be critical)→	judgment	Abstract conceptualization
(4) Be responsible →	decision	Active experimentation

The ability to live these four imperatives would seem to be a basic description of the movement toward objectivity in any area of human knowing, whether that be the realm of scientific investigation or of personal social living, although, in the former, abstract conceptualization and active experimentation will dominate while, in the latter, the concrete experiencing and reflective observation modes will be foremost. The task of scientific integrity will depend on the development of the two less dominant modes of concrete experiencing and reflective observation and that of personality the other two. We have seen something of this happening in the search for a synthesis between the various approaches to counseling and psychotherapy. As we said there, the research is focusing on what is actually happening in the therapy session, on the actual experiencing rather than looking for reconciliation at the level of theory. It is utilizing the reflective observation mode of learning. It shows that in practice, therapists themselves in their actual activity may very well act in ways which are not justified by their overt theory. They instinctively act out of the demands of the moment rather than being locked into simply the demands of abstract theory.

Therapy, Objectivity, and Psychological Health

It would seem that on the basis of this process we can formulate a core understanding of the meaning of mental and emotional health which is the goal of the process of counseling and psychotherapy. To be healthy from this point of view is the capacity to be objective, to be fully present and open to all of one's experiencing, capable of articulating what it is one is experiencing, a willingness to understand it and evaluate it through interpersonal dialogue, and a willingness and courage to act responsibly on the decisions made without any explicit guarantee of success.

The ability to do this is something that is formed in and through interaction with the environment one grows up in and the extent to which it has enabled the development of that inner sense of one's own identity which enables us to gradually come to terms with the intrinsic limitations imposed on us by the world and so be able to distinguish it from oneself and one's personal desires. It is the movement out of what has been termed primitive narcissism to mature narcissism which is the concern of the Object Relations School of Psychoanalysis.

Jeffrey Urist summarizes the perspectives of this school by stating that objectivity develops in this way:

> Most of them recognize an "objectless" or autistic period at the beginning of life, which gives way to the development of object relations. In the opinion of most theorists, object relations begin with an early "symbiotic" or "primary narcissistic phase," involving a lack of differentiation between images of self and images of not-self. They then posit a second stage of "separation-individuation," "secondary narcisism," or "need satisfaction," where there is clearly a psychological distinction between self and other but where the young child's interest in others is essentially narcissistic. Here, others are experienced predominantly in terms of the needs of the self, in the sense that others are defined as though they were extensions of the self. In the third stage, definitions of self and other achieve a sense of wholeness and continuity; others are interesting in their own right, no longer exclusively as potential providers of pleasure or frustration. Terms such as object love, object constancy, ego identity and self-constancy have been used to delimit and describe this third stage. (Encyclopedia of Clinical Assessment. *San Francisco: Jossey-Bass, 1981, p. 825).*

The capacity to be able to discriminate the unique particularities of our experiencing, especially our experiencing of other people, and so be able to continuously revise our meaning structures and values would seem to be radically dependent upon the development of a distinct sense of self so that one is secure in the understanding that one's personal reality and value will not be destroyed in the process.

From this point of view we can say that the goal of counseling is the development of a person who is able to become more objective about himself and his situation. He will be able to stand off from the data of his experience, see it from a various point of view, revise his current understanding, and reevaluate his goals, and then generate alternative ways of behaving. He will responsibly commit himself to what he has decided is best, fully aware that his ongoing experience may very well demand further revision in his understanding of himself and his situation and reevaluation of his behaviors. Objectivity, then, also demands that a person be confident enough in his own inner stability and competancy not to be afraid of the risks involved in making those choices and in being responsible for the consequences.

The counselor aids in this by creating an environment in which one need not be ashamed or afraid to touch one's actual experiencing, especially in its affective and emotional overtones, no matter how bizarre they might be, by being able to aid in the articulation of that experiencing, by being willing to challenge the person to evaluation and encourage the person to take the risk of acting responsibly.

He or she is unlikely to be able to do this if they themselves are not open to the concrete experiencing of the therapy session, reflectively and imaginatively formulating the patterns emerging within and through it irrespective of what their theory might dictate. To be simply attempting to diagnose what is happening in terms of some theoretical framework and seeking covertly to manipulate the client in accordance with some present goals suggested by it is not, in fact, to be acting objectively, but rather subjectively. One is forcing the client to conform to oneself rather than the other way around. The tendency is then simply to use the client as a way of validating one's own theories and of satisfying one's own need for cognitive security and personal effectiveness. It is inevitable that in this framework of operation there will be a real pull towards having the client adapt the counselor's theories, goals, and values.

There does seem to be evidence that in the objectivist approach we have described, the client gradually grows to accept the counselor's explanations, goals, and values and that this is then interpreted as evidence of real growth on the part of the client. Everett L. Worthington reports:

> There is some evidence that when counseling is effective, clients change their values. During effective counseling, the client's values move in the direction of his or her counselor's values ("Religious Counseling," Journal of Counseling and Development, (7), March 1986: 425).

Interestingly, Freud himself seems to have been aware of this danger in the use of psychoanalysis. Joseph Nuttin writes:

> Let us conclude this introduction by quoting Freud's advice to his followers: "The analyst respects his patient's personality; he does not

try to mould it according to his own personal ideas; he is satisfied when instead of giving advice he can obtain his results by arousing the patient's own initiative."

This remark of Freud's, which we would like to emphasize, appears highly significant in connection with contemporary developments in psychotherapy . . . The first point Freud makes, his advice to the analyst to respect the nature of the patient and to avoid forming it according to his own ideals, is a principle too often forgotten by analyists, and it is the failure to observe this dictum which justifies what is perhaps the most important complaint that can be made against psychoanalytic treatment as applied by certain psychoanalysts to patients with a religious background (Psychoanalysis and Personality. New York: Mentor-Omega, 1962, pp. 52–3).

Worthington has outlined how this process takes place:

Worthington and Scott (1983) hypothesized that counselors influence clients' beliefs by the goals they lead clients to select in counseling. They surveyed 81 counselors and counseling students in explicitly Christian settings . . . or in secular settings. Professionals in different settings defined the problems differently and set different goals for the client, depending on the client's stated perceptions. . . . Of course goals are not selected unilaterally by the counselor but are negotiated between client and counselor; however, these data indicate that counselors might guide clients subtly towards or away from religious considerations through their problem definition and selection of goals for counseling (op. cit., p. 425).

Conclusion

It is necessary, then, in order to become truly "objective" and "scientific" in their work, for counselors to be willing to reflect philosophically on the fundamental belief system with regards to human nature out of which they are operating, and to be willing to assess its influence on the way in which they are relating to the client. In particular, they need to ask to what extent they may be imposing an interpretation of human being onto the client from which they may be in practice implicitly exempting themselves. Are they assuming a capacity for grasping objective truth about reality, a capacity which they are denying to the client? This seems to be inherent in the objectivist framework of thinking with its division into those who know and those who do not. Mary Van Leeuwen has referred to this as adherence to a double standard of humanness. She writes:

I will argue that most of the concern about both metaphysical and applied behaviorism arises when the impression is given that the behavioral psychologists are a different and somehow more privileged group of people than those whom they study, and when it is implied that they therefore have both the ability and the right to become a species of managerial elite within society (The Person in Psychology. Grand Rapids, MI: Eerdmans Publ. Co., 1985, p. 116–17).

This double standard arises out of a failure to reflect upon the implications of their own subjectivity. In failing to acknowledge the subjective basis of all objective knowledge, they are not able to be present to and acknowledge the same dynamics in their clients. They therefore fail to take them into account in their dealings with them and it is this which enables them to impose their own meanings and values on the client.

Without an awareness and acceptance of the intrinsic dynamics of their own subjectivity, counselors will not be open to the fundamentally empirical fact of the client's own subjective personhood which is essentially the creative capacity to interpret the meaning of his experiencing and act responsibly in the unique circumstances of his life. In missing an important empirical dimension of their clients' reality, they can be a real hindrance to their growth rather than a help. It clouds their ability to recognize that possibly, in working to influence the client to adopt their own meanings and values, they may in fact be vitiating the client's own ability to grow in the capacity to become more objective in his own psychic life and hence more mentally healthy and socially independent of the counselor.

If the counselor, then, wishes to be truly scientific and objective in his work with people, he is obligated to work to become aware of the dynamics of his own subjectivity in order to be able to differentiate that of his clients. It is a challenge to personal and spiritual growth. It demands commitment to a humility about one's own ''objective'' understanding of the meaning of reality which is solidly based on an awareness of the intrinsic limitations on ''objective'' truth, imposed by one's own historical subjectivity. More than in any other field of scientific endeavor, the success of the enterprise is intrinsically related to the quality of the counselor's own life, morally and intellectually. It is not too much to say that the counselor will be helpful to the client in terms of mental and spiritual health only to the extent that he himself is mentally and spiritually healthy.

This is not to say counselors have to deny their own interpretations and values, which may in themselves be valid — but it calls for a willingness to become aware of what these interpretations and values are and how they may be influencing the relationship with the client. Counselors need to be able to hold their values in abeyance, so to speak, in order to enable them to be open to the different meanings and values out of which the client may be operating and to be capable of articulating values for the client so that the latter can himself gain a deeper self-knowledge and self-determination around these values and so become more objective himself. This raises the question of what role the counselor's own understanding of the client's reality, derived from his theoretical knowledge of human dynamics, might play in facilitating growthful change in the client. It is to this question that we now turn.

4 Objective Psychology and Psychotherapeutic Practice

The Goal of Human Becoming: Self-Actualization

Self-transcendence: The Growth in Consciousness

Just as in the progress of science in its formulation of ever more adequate understandings of reality on the general level, so analogically, personal self-development is essentially dependent on the ability to continually revise and reformulate the meaning and value structures out of which we are operating so as better to account for and integrate these data of our experiencing in an on-going way and so formulate more adequate ways to acting and relating. The life and behavior of the individual will change in a growthful way only to the extent that he or she is able to do this, i.e., until the individual is able to be conscious of the assumptions and values out of which he or she is operating, they will continue to be determined by these assumptions and values rather than being self-determined. The less consciousness there is of them the more the person will be dominated by them for good or ill.

The operative words here are growthful change. Change in behavior itself can be achieved in many ways and in much of its study psychology has attempted to discover ways to do this. Behavioral change is the rationale for objectivist psychology. It has looked for those determinants of human dynamics and the principles that govern them that would enable an outside agent to affect behavioral change in another. A recent book on interpersonal communication illustrates this:

> *It will give you the tools and techniques you need to gain power with people and win mastery over them through the art of conversation. You will be shown how to influence and control specific key individuals in your life by what you say, so you can achieve your goals and become highly successful (James Van Fleet.* Lifetime Conversation Guide. *Englewood Cliffs, NJ: Prentice-Hall, 1984, p. vii).*

Much of objectivist psychotherapy has had a similar objective: to discover how to manipulate the client to behave in a more effective and fruitful ways as that is determined by the therapist, and it can hardly be denied that it is possible to do this successfully. Its success rests upon the fact that the human person is vulnerable to being determined by that of which he is not conscious. If we are able to determine the unconscious motivations of the client, we are able to utilize them in order to get him to do what it is we want.

For these methods to work, however, the client has to be kept ignorant of the fact that he is being manipulated. If the client becomes conscious of what it is we are doing, of the technique that we are using, these methods lose their power. In the long term this is self-defeating. To publish a book such as the one quoted above not only teaches how to manipulate but also how to become aware of when one is being manipulated oneself. It will be effective, therefore, only to the extent that the other does not know how he or she is being manipulated. If it continues to have an effect on the behavior of the other even after they have become aware of what is going on, then, although on the surface, things seem to remain the same, on the level of human intentionality, the activity is now something different, it means something else. Either it becomes collusion in some sort of game playing, or in turn becomes a sort of manipulative compliance whereby the therapist is bought off and the person able to protect his or her personal status quo. This changed character of the activity cannot be known from the outside but only through the disclosure of the individual as to its subjective meaning, what the activity means from within the particular intentional world of the person.

The change in the other even when on the surface it might seem to be for the client's own good is not growthful change. Growthful change can take place only when a person is able to gain a deeper understanding of the meanings and values out of which counselors are operating and critique and change these in ways which clients themselves have determined them to be most helpful in attaining their long-term fulfillment. Growthful change then is change in the intentional world of the person in the direction of increased self-awareness and self-determination toward those self-accepted values which will be better able to bring integration into the particularities of his personal existence.

Goals, Values, and Human Development

Intrinsic to fruitful change is a change in the goals the person is invested in. For the client to be able to act differently in the circumstances of his actual situation depends upon an alteration in the personal world in which he or she actually lives: the actual way in which he or she uniquely construes the meaning and significance of his or her experiencing.

As we have seen, the meaning of our world is radically influenced by what we intend. Human beings are fundamentally teleological: we act for a purpose, fundamentally in order to achieve goals deemed most conducive to achieving the protection, maintenance and enhancement of our being. How we have actually formulated to ourselves what this entails will dictate the way in which we perceive and construe our world, the meaning of our experiencing. Furthermore, the extent to which we construe the importance of some particular goal will dictate the depth of self-investment we have in it. It is this degree of self-investment in goals which is at the core of our uniqueness. The particular way in which we formulate our actual goals, the complex patterns of meaning that our experiencing has for us, both in general and in the unique situation that we encounter, together with the degree of self-investment involved is what constitutes our unique operational selves.

People are motivated to come to counseling when in some way or other their unique operational selves, the structure that they have formed as the way to growth and development, are not adequate to the realization of their fulfillment. As a result of this discrepancy, they are suffering physical, emotional, mental confusion, and pain: They *don't know what to do for the best,* as many often put it. Counseling, then, is centrally concerned, not with the giving of information, no matter how accurate that might be in and of itself but with the discovery ON THE PART OF THE CLIENT of what, operationally, he or she is seeking to achieve, what specific goals and values are dictating the way he or she is construing the meaning of his or her experiencing so that, where necessary, they can alter the degree of investment in those goals and meanings and reinvest in more adequate ones. The aim of counseling then, is the reorganization of these values and goals, so that they are more adequate to realizing the client's fulfillment as a human being.

The Core of the Therapeutic Relationship: the Acting Person

The Core of Uniqueness

Discovery, then, of the meaning of any particular situation for a person is the discovery of what he or she is seeking to achieve in the situation and the degree of self-investment in those goals. It is this degree of self-investment as well as the particular combination of meanings that make up a person's operational self that renders the person unique, rather than the meanings or goals themselves which on the basis of a common humanity and cultural situation will be shared by many. As counselors, we can know about these various meanings and goals, but we cannot know from the outside the particular combinations of meaning and value together with the degree of self-investment that make up the unique operational self of the client. It is this which is the primary area of concern in counseling. If this is to change in a growthful way, the person must be conscious of himself as a unique person, of the uniqueness of the situations within which he or she has to live and work, and the values that he wishes to give himself to must be fully engaged. The core of therapeutic counseling then is the active relationship whereby the person's own capacities for self-consciousness and self-determination are enhanced.

The Development of Consciousness

The extent to which we are able to become aware of what our current meaning structures together with their concomitant values are will obviously vary from individual to individual and in all of us will always to some degree be limited. Hence, there will always be a great deal that can be discovered in terms of commonalities of meaning patterns and their behavioral correlates through the sort of empirical observation employed by psychology.

The capacity for full self-conscious formulation and evaluation is something that develops slowly through childhood and adolescence, coming to full maturation only with the onset of puberty. The person is more susceptible to external determination, then, prior to puberty. The meaning structures and behavioral forms that come to determine the individual are formed largely unconsciously through socialization and personal experience during childhood, especially in the period before the child has the vocabulary to articulate in any consciously discriminating way the personal meaning of that experiencing. To some extent, and to what extent we do not know in any individual case, these primitive meaning structures, precisely because they are formed below the level of consciousness, are likely to remain as determining factors throughout life. If they severely distort enough of the core of the person they are likely to form the basis of future pathology.

It is this dimension of the human being that psychoanalysis has explored so fruitfully. Behaviorism too has made great contributions here in its study of the social reinforcements that lead to the stability of even inadequate behavioral patterns. However, once puberty has been reached and the capacity for critical thought has developed, the person gains a real yet relative freedom from determination, even from those patterns formed during the crucial period of childhood and reinforced through the socialization process. At this point the person to some extent becomes capable, through self-reflection, of taking possession of the meanings and values out of which he or she operates and of either accepting or, if necessary, altering them. Leon J. Saul writes of this:

> And we know that in its psychological and historical aspects . . . the unconscious is essentially the persistence in the adult of the infantile emotional patterns. We know from psychoanalytic experience the impressive extent to which the unconscious can be reclaimed and unconsciously motivated symptoms can be ameliorated, but how much can be corrected and how much might have been prevented? Certainly we cannot imagine a human being without persisting infantile impulses. However, this means only that the infantile, more particularly the traumatic infantile, if not too warped and pathological, can be outgrown sufficiently and to such a degree that the mature attitudes predominate, and the remaining infantile impulses can be integrated with the mature drives and can be handled maturely (The Childhood Emotional Pattern and Maturity. New York: Van Nostrand Reinhold, 1979, p. 19).

The Use of Psychological Constructs in Therapy
Dangers in the Use of Psychological Constructs

Psychology can to some extent enable the individual to grow in self-awareness and take possession of him or herself and thereby become more self-determining. To that extent psychology can be helpful. However, it will only be helpful to the extent that the unique individual is able to find him or herself in its concepts and suggestions. When offering the practical knowledge of psychology, the counselor must be careful to see that the individual is free to discover him or herself in those psychological constructs insofar as they are able.

It would seem that this information would best be offered to individuals in an educational setting, clearly delineated as such. This gives the individual the freedom and space to take whatever does illuminate his own experiential world, discarding that which does not without fear of breaking the relationship with the one giving the information. If this essentially educational process does take place within the context of counseling and psychotherapy, then it ought to be clearly offered as such and if possible in its own time slot distinct from the counseling session proper.

Undoubtedly the offering of some explanatory conceptualization of some particular situation, experience, or condition may enable someone to more clearly objectivize who they are and what it is they are doing. Thus, the experience becomes a freeing one. In particular it can have a reassuring effect on the client in that he can come to see that he is not entirely isolated from others, that he participates in a common human condition. It can, on one level, help to reintegrate him with the rest of humanity.

However, that reintegration is incomplete in that it does not reach the person in his unique personhood. The integration of the person as a person into the human community requires a different level of relationship, one that will allow for and encourage the living into that uniqueness as it is continually being unfolded and recreated. This is not achieved simply by seeing how the person is like others but through being able to touch and relate in a positive way to that which renders him a unique person.

Given the fact that psychology as an explanation of human beings in their common nature is subject to all the historical limitations of any scientific endeavor, simply to subordinate the individual to the abstract schemes of any psychology elevates that psychology to a comprehensiveness and an absoluteness which, as we have seen, it cannot possess and in this it simply becomes fraudulent. It can, in fact, do violence to human nature and can itself become pathological, radically distorting the possibilities of human growth and development. Étienne Gilson vividly highlighted the dangers of the *definition* in all human knowledge when he wrote:

> *It would be a fruitful subject of reflection to consider the dreadful consequences of what might be called the* spirit of abstraction. *In speculative matters, it invites the substitution of the definition for the defined, which is a sure way to render definitions sterile. It also invites the illusion that one can increase knowledge by merely deducing consequences from already coined definitions, instead of frequently returning to the very things from which essenses and definitions were first abstracted. In the practical order, the spirit of abstraction probably is the greatest single source of political and social disorders, of intolerance and of fanaticism. Nothing is more uncompromising than an essense, its quiddity and its definition* (Elements of Christian Philosophy. *New York: Mentor-Omega Books, 1960, pp. 51–52).*

Something of this is beginning to be recognized today in psychology and serious questions are being raised. For instance, there are questions as to the possible pathological effects of psychological labeling in fixing a person into a particular category of functioning both in his own eyes and that of society thus rendering difficult if not impossible any growth and development toward health. David Kolb has referred to this tendency when, in his discussion of the categorization of people into psychological types, he says:

> *Psychological categorization of people such as those depicted by psychological types can too easily become stereotypes that tend to trivialize human complexity and thus end us denying human individuality rather than characterizing it. In addition type theories often have a static and fixed connotation to their descriptions of individuals, lending a fatalistic view of human change and development. The view often gets translated into a self-fulfilling prophecy, as with the common educational strategy of tracking students on the basis of individual differences and thereby perhaps reinforcing those differences* (Experiential Learning. *Englewood Cliffs, N.J.: Prentice-Hall, 1984).*

What is true of *type* theories is also true of psychiatric diagnostic labeling. As we have said, people generally do exhibit patterns of thinking and behaving which have sufficient commonalities to be put in one category or another, and knowledge of such categories is enormously helpful in understanding the present experiencing and future behavioral possibilities of such people. But categories, too, can become constricting of future change and development when seen as static, fixed states. Indeed the very use of categories can bring about such a fixed condition. They are at best useful abstractions to achieve a particular limited purpose, not total pictures of the unique, living personal reality.

Therapeutically there is a twofold danger in the use of theoretical constructs, whether psychopathological or more general. In the first place, the use of theoretical constructs can narrow down the counselor's ability to help in that it can restrict his vision to only certain areas of that experiencing, i.e., that which he is looking for, which fits his theoretical framework. Rollo May points to this danger when he says:

> Can we be sure, one such question goes, that we are seeing the patient as he really is, knowing him in his own reality; or are we seeing merely the projection of our own theories about him? Every psychotherapist, to be sure, has his knowledge of patterns and mechanisms of behavior and has at his finger tips the system of concepts developed by his particular school. Such a conceptual system is entirely necessary if we are to observe scientifically. But the crucial question is the bridge between the system and the patient . . . does not this patient, or any person for that matter, slip through our scientific fingers like seafoam, precisely to the extent that we rely on the logical consistency of our own system? (Existence. New York: Touchstone Books, 1958, p. 3).

Second, to seek to subordinate the client to *objective* schemata can not only limit the capacity of the counselor to help but it can also seriously hinder the ability of the client to discern the unique contours of his inner world and particular social situation with all its unique dynamics and, consequently vitiate the possibility of changing it in positive ways. At its worst this can seriously harm the individual, further alienating him or her from experiential life and hence the ability to bring that life under rational control. It may indeed be one of the main sources of what has been called iatronic illness, i.e., mental or emotional dysfunction brought about through the therapeutic relationship. At a less destructive level, it has been observed how clients tend to take on the vocabulary and theoretical constructs of the therapists. In this there seems to be a covert collusion between them that in fact results in both finding only what they have already decided must be there. Rollo May, referring to the various psychologists of the existentialist school, comments:

> They were aware, as Straus puts it, that the unconscious ideas of the patient are more often than not the conscious theories of the therapist (ibid.).

Dangers of Problem-Solving Modality

The same is true when we seek to categorize people's lives in terms of *problems*. We can do violence to another when we try to subsume them under our own understanding of the particular situations they are in which may be causing them difficulty, or when we assume that our understanding of the *real* situation is the *objectively* true one such that we feel able to tell others what they ought or ought not to do. Egan, whom we have previously categorized as being influenced by the objectivist framework in his use of the problem-solving categories, has in another context referred to some of the negative consequences of this Cartesian way of thinking of therapeutic work in these terms:

> *One of the* problems *is the word* problem *or at least the word* solution. *It is true that men refer to disturbances in interpersonal living as problems, and when they come to mental health professionals, they are looking for* solutions. *Behavioral scientists have, more or less, followed this problem-solution paradigm in their approach to psychopathology. But while this paradigm is obviously well-suited to mathematics, it is not clear that it is generally applicable to human relationships. Too many people think that they have the problem and that the professional has the solution. But impasses in interpersonal relationships are more properly transcended than solved; . . . The problem-solving paradigm is too neat and pat to fit . . . the complexities of disturbed communication* (Encounter. *pp. 201–2).*

Later on, he correctly observes that:

> *Life is not the compartmentalized or atomistic entity that the proponents of the* problem-solution paradigm *envision. Life is principally interpersonal living, but to cast interpersonal living in terms of problems and solutions tends to make objects out of people. . . . Perhaps the use of such terms as* problem *and* solution *appears unhealthy or inappropriate because such language is symptomatic of overly mechanistic attitudes towards oneself and one's relationship with others* (ibid., p. 354).

And Curran, who has been one of the most severe critics of the Cartesian paradigm, especially as it relates to the problem-answer modality, points up the essential distortion that it can bring to therapeutic work thus:

> *People often resent being* figured-out *in this way or subjected to such analysis because, in a way, it puts them at the mercy of the one solving the problem and gives that person control over them. Even though there may be a genuine attempt to be helpful to the other, it is often too depersonalized. In this sense, I may focus on your problem but totally bypass you as a person, missing entirely your unique and spontaneous real self. I have thus unconsciously moved into a relationship with your* problem. *As one can see, this is a highly depersonalized notion of understanding because it renders communication static. There is no dynamic interplay of two living people* (Understanding, p. 50).

The Value of Psychological Knowledge in Counseling

Since the problem-solving mode of viewing the counseling process rests upon the *objectivist* framework of looking at human life fitting the person into some *normative* view of reality and interpreting his situation from within it, it is radically inadequate. Egan, in his attempt to give proper weight to the subjective dimension, prefers to refer to the client's situation as problematical rather than a problem as such. This is a much more subjectivist understanding and leaves room for the fact that problems are only such from within the individual teleological framework of the persons involved and as such are far too uniquely multifaceted to be understood simply from within generalized categories.

In making a choice then between the subjective and objective approaches to counseling, priority has to be given to the subjective. However, as should be evident now, this is not to say that the objective knowledge of the counselor has no place to play in helping the client. It can do so in two ways. First, if, through his study and reflection, objective knowledge has enabled him to be sensitive to the dynamics operating in people and their situations and has enabled him to differentiate aspects of his own experiencing, it can aid him enormously in differentiating for the client the data of his experiencing. It alerts and enables him to articulate elements of that experiencing for which the client himself may not have words. This does necessitate a translation of those concepts into a language that the client can experientially understand, otherwise the client may end up using the counselor's vocabulary, but in a way that prevents real articulation of his unique experiencing.

In the second place, in that it is enabling us to gain both an understanding of the patterns of meaning and value that we actually live out of on an unconscious level, and also a deeper grasp of some of the dynamics that may govern human functioning, the objective approach has its own level of validity. It is an important aspect of our overall attempt as a race to come to understand ourselves and so grow and develop and realize our full potential. However, since its findings are generally relevant to the many, in that it deals with the commonalities shared by groups of people, the offering of those understandings to the individual more properly belongs to an educational setting rather than a counseling one. It is what we have termed guidance as distinct from counseling. However, inasmuch as these findings might be relevant to the particular individual and it is judged that they may in fact illuminate his or her situation, then education may very well be legitimate within the overall process of helping. However, this psychological knowledge is theoretical and it must always be subordinate to the unique, living reality of the client; it is only of help insofar as it does illuminate that reality for the client. In counseling, it is that unique living reality of the client which has to be made central, and the counseling skills are primarily related to helping the client raise to consciousness the assumptive world in which he or she lives, enabling the client to take more conscious control and direction of his or her life, augmenting personal freedom and the capacity to be responsible. David Kolb is entirely correct, I think, when he says:

> Immediately apprehended experience is the ultimate source of the validity of comprehensions in both fact and value. The factual basis of a comprehension is ultimately judged in terms of its connection with sense experience. Its value is similarly judged ultimately by its immediate affective utility (op. cit., p. 107).

Knowledge of those generalized categories can be enormously helpful in enabling the client to secure an *objective* perspective on himself and his operations and hence in recognizing himself, but these categories are only of value therapeutically insofar as they do so. As a living experiencing subject the client remains transcendent to them and is the final judge of their value to him. Before they can be of value to the client, he or she must be strong enough in their inner understanding of themselves and their situation to be able to rationally assess the explanations. They must be at a point in their growth where they are able to articulate and rationally assess for themselves the contours of their experiencing so that they are in a position to assess the value of the explanations and solutions suggested.

Where this point is held paramount in the counseling situation, then the dialogue between the client and therapist which utilizes the therapist's reflective, *scientific* understanding of human functioning becomes the dialogue between two subjects collaborating in the gradual objective elucidation of the unique subjective situation of the client. To be valuable, theoretical constructs should elucidate the unique experiencing of the client, otherwise they can be a hindrance. Reflecting upon the study of consciousness itself, Needleman touches on this point when he says:

> *From this latter perspective, the main requirement for understanding the nature of consciousness is the repeated effort to be aware of whatever is taking place in the whole of ourselves at any given moment. All definitions or systematic explanations, no matter how profound are secondary. Thus teachings about consciousness, both of the ancient masters and of modern psychologists, can only be a distraction if they are presented to us in a way that does not support the effort to be aware of the totality of ourselves at the present moment (op. cit., p. 78).*

Recognition of this as the crucial element in human growth and development should enable the counselor to disengage himself from any strong desire to advise the client as to the *real* meaning of his situation and what to do about it. The counselor himself must be freed from any overidentification with his intellectual constructs as to the meaning of what is going on with the client and what he should do within that and must be capable himself of learning from the uniqueness of his client.

5 The Dynamics of Counseling
Abstract Knowledge and Operational Effectiveness
Distinction between Abstract and Operational Knowledge

It would seem that the capacity to help another person in his or her struggle to grow and develop is not essentially dependent on the ability of the counselor to explain why the client is the way he or she is, though, used wisely and at the proper time, the offering of some possible explanation, drawn from objective psychological research, might be of enormous benefit in helping the client gain a more objective view of himself. But it would need to be offered with the explicit acknowledgement that it is only one of several *possible* explanations that may be helpful.

The possibility of this knowledge being helpful is enormously enhanced if the counselor is first of all willing and able to gain as deep an understanding as possible of the unique person and situation of the client. As we have said, many counselors would see their service as being precisely this. Their way of relating to the client is essentially one of gleaning a precise knowledge about the unique situation of the client so as to accurately locate the problem within their own personal or professional psychological research and come up with the most helpful answer. Their methods of research into the unique world of the client may be various, ranging from in-depth interviews to the use of standard projective tests such as the MMPI or the Rorschach.

We can term this the process of guidance. Based on what the client reveals about him or herself, the counselor can see the similarities between the client's situation with either those analyzed and studied in psychology and cataloged under the heading of PROBLEMS or with those that he himself has experienced. Out of that awareness, he forms some sense as to the general directions which personal experience or psychological research suggests as to the resolution of those problems and is able to pass on that knowledge to the person in a way that relates closely to the situation in question.

This approaches much more the ordinary situation in which advice giving usually takes place. Someone outlines something of his or her difficulties and the counselor, through listening, asking questions, etc., tries to get a clear picture of what the situation is; then out of that fund of knowledge and experience, whether everyday or clinical, he decides what the source of the difficulties is and what might be best done about these difficulties. The difference between the amateur and the professional here is the depth of their knowledge of what the science of psychology might have to say and the guidelines that are suggested by its research findings.

Although, where based primarily on what is gleaned from the client through the actual interview, an explanation as to the meaning and significance of what is going on might be much closer to the unique reality of the client, it will not, in and of itself necessarily be effectual in helping the client in the process of self-transcendence. It may, indeed, be accurate knowledge ABOUT the client's situation and how he should act in it, but it will not necessarily be helpful unless and until, as with the educational process, the client is able both to see its accuracy and be able to operate on it. In short the client must be able to own it as her own; this means that insights and explanations will remain simply abstract until the client is able to integrate that knowledge into her ACTUAL OPERATIONAL living.

In counseling what we are primarily concerned with is not to glean knowledge ABOUT the client but to help the client gain self-knowledge. It is the client's knowledge of himself that enables him to change himself in an increasingly mature way. This knowledge of himself is precisely that which pertains to him as a unique PERSON rather than that which pertains to him as one possessing a common NATURE with others. It is not, in the first place, the knowledge of himself as being like others that is important but the knowledge of himself in the unique configurations and possibilities that pertain to him as a person. The core of counseling is how to relate to the person of the client in such a way that he can come to this knowledge of himself.

The issue is not one of explanation in terms of efficient causality but of clarification of the formal causality that is of the essence of being human. The client needs to come to some understanding of the meaning-for-him of his experience and the values that dominate his search for fulfillment.

The Unity between Abstract Knowledge and Operational Competency: An Ideal

Simply explaining to people the dynamics operating in a particular situation, the goals that are most adequate to the realization of fulfillment and how best to go about realizing them is the most effective way of helping people. The belief that this approach is helpful comes out of an almost automatic assumption in our culture: If you know what to do, then you ought to be able to do it. This is undoubtedly an ideal and, as such, something we might hope for, but, in fact, both common sense and psychological data suggest that intellectual knowledge about a situation and what to do in it do not automatically mean that we will so operate in actual situations. St. Paul highlights the common experience of this gap in his famous outcry in the Epistle to the Romans:

I have the desire to do good but I cannot carry it out. For what I do is not the good I want to do; no, the evil that I do not want to do — this I keep on doing (7:18b-19, N.I.V.).

Freud with his discovery of unconscious motivations to action and how these can rule reason hammered home the fact that between intellectual knowledge and operational possibility there is often an enormous gap. Recognition of this gap is a commonplace in skill education. A person does not acquire a new skill simply by learning about it intellectually but mainly by repeated practice which gradually brings intellectual knowledge right into the actual particularities of experiencing. Only when a person correlates the two in the moment of operation can he or she be said to have learned the skill. This is called the moment of internalization or insight. There is an element of unpredictability in it in that we can never tell if or when it will occur.

Arthur Combs et al. sum up the essential difference between abstract knowledge and operational knowledge this way:

> There is a vast difference between knowing and behaving. Knowing comes from getting new information. Change in behavior comes from the discovery of personal meaning (Helping Relationships. Boston: Allyn and Bacon. 1978, p. 58).

Personal meaning here is the meaning that something actually has for me as a person with specific important goals, goals I am fully invested in. Information only becomes operational insofar as it becomes part of one's actual operational self-system, and insofar as the goals contained in it become one's own and, hence, the meanings and values really are one's own values. To become operational, knowledge must be *in-formed*, as Curran puts it, by the individual's own reason and desires; he or she must understand its meaning and own its value in the unique particularity of the situation.

The Principles Governing Action

The important difference between knowing about a situation intellectually and the sort of knowledge that guides and directs actual operations lies in the degree of abtractness involved. In intellectual knowledge we distance ourselves from our experiencing in all its particularly and complex unity in order to catagorize it and see its commonalities and its possible relationships to other theoretical meanings that we hold about ourselves and our world. But action, on the other hand, always takes place in the immediate particularities of a situation and will always be based upon the immediate formulation of its meaning to us at that moment. With hindsight or from a distance, we may be able to formulate different understandings of the situations we are in, but at the moment of experiencing we will act out of those which immediately impress themselves upon us: the personal meaning that it has for me at that moment.

These personal meanings, as we have seen, may not be conscious formulations but patterns of interpretation and evaluation which we have built up from childhood and of which we are no longer overtly conscious. Curran explains it thus:

> As we have seen, these values may sometimes be hidden in one's psychological matrix and carried over from early childhood or they may be in the culture itself. Until now, such values have only been implicitly accepted by the person. But they could be governing his life even though he never consciously recognized or evaluated them (Counseling and Psychotherapy: The Pursuit of Values, East Dubuque, IL: Counseling Learning Institute, 1976, p. 156).

Gendlin would say that these personal meanings and values are written into the body, so that they are organismic assessments and reactions rather than simply intellectual ones (Gendlin, "Experiential Psychotherapy" in *Current Psychotherapies*, Corsini, ed., p. 353). And they become written into our organisms mainly through our childhood experiencing. Lock Land has referred to this in these terms:

> We repeat again and again for our children those behaviors, habits, and values that ensure their doing those things most acceptable in

their cultural environment. In this process of repetitive acquisition this information forms those behaviors that are so spontaneous and un-thought as to be classified as emotional, *producing what we often call* thoughtless *acts. In such cases, logic or reasoning — active thinking — is unnecessary because the system is responding automat-ically. A threat to life, an act against conscience, or an instant liking or anger can be a response to environmental situations that are so fitting or unfitting to this redundancy that spontaneous recognition of foreignness or likeness occurs (op. cit., p. 106).*

These personal meanings, however, are not just those drilled into us by parents or our environment, but those generated out of our own experiencing too.

This is a mysterious phenomenon, one that needs more research. It means that many of the meanings and values out of which we live are not verbalized to ourselves; our awareness of the meaning of events and our ability to respond to them is, for want of a better term, nonlinguistic and unreflective. In this sense we can say that they are *unconscious* or automatic. The act of driving a car, for instance, is something we can say we do *instinctively*. Though it is a thoroughly human activity, it shares something of the same character as the behavior of an animal. It is an analogical use of the word to capture something of the immediate and nonverbal experiencing which is yet intelligent and involves awareness. To put words on this and become truly conscious requires a secondary act, a step-ping back from our immediate experiencing to articulate the pattern of meaning and value that is operating there. Kolb terms these two different modes of knowing apprehension and comprehension. The first relates to the ability to per-ceive meaningful patterns and forms within our immediate experiencing which is always unique and specific. The second relates to the ability to articulate to ourselves and others what that meaning is and then relate it to wider meanings. It is communicable knowledge, or knowledge in a communicable form. He writes:

Through comprehension we introduce order into what would oth-erwise be a seamless, unpredictable flow of apprehended sensations, but at the price of shaping (distorting) and forever changing that flow. Yet knowing through comprehension has other qualities that have made it primary in human society — namely that comprehensions of experience can be communicated and thereby transcend time and space (Kolb, op. cit., p. 43).

Studies into the structures and functioning of the brain are beginning to shed some light on this. It seems related to the integration between the right and left sides of the brain, with the first being concerned with spatial pattern for-mation in the here and now and the second being the seat of the ability to ana-lyze, conceptualize, and verbalize, drawing on the past and being open to the future. It also seems to be the link between the frontal lobes, the seat of purpose and intentionality, and the limbic region which is the seat of emotional respon-siveness and the relaying of data to the body structure.

But, whatever brain studies can tell us, there are some meanings that we discern in our experiencing that somehow become deeply embodied in the whole person such that the organism itself instantaneously formulates them and acts out of them in a whole person fashion. The process takes place at a point below that of intellectual thought; indeed, for the first five years or so of our lives, it takes place almost entirely without the ability of language, since the vocabulary needed to articulate or *comprehend* these meanings is simply not there. To a large extent our ability to comprehend our experience will always be inadequate in that it does depend upon the usage of words and the vocabularies available, as well as on my own knowledge of and facility in using those vocabularies, and this will always be limited.

Until we become conscious of these patterns of meaning in the actual moment of our experiencing, i.e., until we are able in some way to comprehend what the meaning of our experiencing is and the values they enshrine, and are able to see their inadequacy, we will continue to be dominated by them rather than by the more rational ways of knowing and acting that we may have formulated intellectually, or which may have been suggested to us either through education or expert guidance. When this happens, it has something of the character of waking up; we realize in a different and startling way what we have always been aware of. It is primarily in those moments of experiential *realization* that we achieve a real ownership of ourselves which makes available to us the ability to change ourselves. We can say that they are moments of objective clarity; we see ourselves objectively; we have become more objective about ourselves.

The Experiential Moment and Change

It is the capacity to discern IN THE MOMENT OF EXPERIENCING what our interpretations and goals are which frees us from them and makes it possible either to affirm them or see that our interpretations and behavioral reactions are inappropriate and so opens the way to the realization of more adequate constructs and responses. Education and the suggestions of experts can be valuable as different ways of interpreting our situation and its meaning; but they will not be effective until we have personally discerned their relevance in our own experiencing and have clarified and become conscious of those actual interpretations out of which we are operating which may be preventing us from incorporating the information. The ability to benefit from such information and so respond in more adequate ways is dependent on this awareness. Curran puts it this way:

> In proportion as he can free himself from prior unconscious selectivities in each new experience, he arrives at a certain primitive freedom which we call truth, and it is this truth that makes him wholly free (Understanding, p. 41).

The therapeutic emphasis, then, must be primarily on PRESENT experiencing. The person grows and develops insofar as he is able to be present and to articulate the meanings and values contained in his present experiencing. Counseling and therapy are not centrally concerned with the intellectual explanation of the origins of those present meanings in his past, nor centrally with the present social situation as it exists outside of the person, but on the discovery and articulation of the patterns of a person's experiencing in the here and now. All these other dimensions are important, but it is his ability to articulate his present experiencing of them that is the growth-producing element. His growth in this capacity in the process of counseling will enable him to achieve continued growth outside the counseling situation, thus rendering him more capable of owning and operating effectively within his on-going experiencing. Role-playing in therapy or in interpersonal training, such as Assertiveness Training, is an attempt to duplicate actual experiential situations so that one can become both more aware of the perceptual patterns out of which he or she is operating and thus realize more appropriate interpretations and behavioral responses and gradually form a new self-structure that will be available in the actual circumstances.

The point, however, in making these perceptual patterns conscious is to enable them to be modified and changed in a more useful direction and then to have them once again, providing they prove their effectiveness, sink back into prereflective state. The aim of self-consciousness is not to be always conscious of ourselves, examining our experience, articulating its meaning to ourselves, but in fact through the formulation of more adequate structures of meaning and value to become less self-preoccupied. We are most self-preoccupied in fact when we are in conflict, when the implicit meanings and values out of which we are operating are inadequate to living. In the reformulation of them and an increasing adequacy in living, we become less concerned about ourselves and more able to be fully present to the external realities of our lives.

Experiential vs. Intellectual Knowledge

Insofar as *counseling* as such aims to facilitate the process of helping the person to become more objective about his or her world, counselors are in a very different process from that of problem solving and advice giving. Practitioners of advice giving operate essentially on the level of the intellect, on the level of comprehensions. In both, counselors are primarily concerned with cognitive information ABOUT the meaning of the situation and what to do in it. As such, this process always has a degree of abstractness about it, and so, even if the cognitive understanding is good and the advice given theoretically sound, it will not of itself help a person to respond differently to the particularities of his situation. The client has still to *realize* its personal meaning and integrate that into a new operational self.

Although on occasion a suggested meaning on how to move forward may make immediate sense and become immediately operational, and hence bring about real change, generally this is not the case. The self-structure with its embodied meanings and responses resists easy change. Meanings become embodied, that is, written into the organism because they were seen, at least at one time, as being highly significant to the person in terms of his fulfillment. Until the person is able to become conscious of these embodied meanings and hence become conscious of his real operational self-investments, these will remain his operational framework of interpretation and the more theoretical understandings will remain simply that.

This is why so much of the popular advice, even when done by an *expert,* is usually quite irrelevant. Even if one is able to remember the advice that is given, it takes time to see personally the actual relevance of intellectual knowledge to one's real living. The extent to which one actually experiences its relevance, in contradistinction to the meanings and values one is currently operating out of, is the extent to which it becomes my understanding, fits in with my personal goals, and so becomes operative.

Advice, then, would be an effective way of helping someone only where in fact he was able to immediately see the personal relevance and value in his actual life and make it operational. Although on occasion this might happen, and our occasional success with this is what encourages us to rely on it, generally its likelihood is remote. The failure to realize the difference between the two processes involved and an overconfidence in simple abstract knowledge leads many counselors to the too-ready use of advice giving in helping relationships.

A Critique of Advice Giving

The Disparity in Client/Counselor Experiential Worlds

Advice, stemming from the abstract knowledge of the counselor is not of itself likely to help the person toward that self-transcendence and self-integration that is intrinsic to growth since it simply leaves the actual meaning and value patterns which determine action in the experienced moment unaffected. And this also holds true of that knowledge of the inner experiential world of the client gleaned by the counselor from the actual interview itself. One might come to a fairly clear understanding of where the person is getting into difficulties and what the *solution* to those difficulties might be. It would be unrealistic to say that those understandings should never be made known to the client. But such explanations and the advice that is derived from them will only be helpful to the client to the extent that he or she is actually able to accept them and invest his or herself operationally in the suggestions. The timing then of these suggestions is important. The clients must be at a point, as Curran says, of *guidance readiness,* if they are to be able to see and own the relevance of suggestions so that they can become part of their own meaningful world.

The Possibility of Sharing a Common World

The ability to come up with such advice, though not impossible, is only theoretically possible insofar as the counselor and the client are able to share in a common world of meaning and values. While on the basic level of human nature we undoubtedly do share a commonality of goals and values, on the cultural level, the form that the satisfaction of those goals takes can no longer be simply assumed today. In ages past when social life was more stable and whole communities shared a common understanding of the nature and meaning of life and the values to be pursued within it, this could be taken much more for granted than it can be today. There was a much more stable *objective* world in which meaning structures and behavior patterns were more objectively understandable. Today, however, especially in the Western world through widespread communication, increased travel possibilities and more extensive education, we have been exposed to a multitude of life visions and different value systems. This has encouraged individuals to formulate their own understanding of the meaning of their lives and the values they must live by. Today there is no one version of the *objective* world, either on the social or individual level. As Poole says:

> We are all conscious that there is only one world, but we are also quite sure that we all see it differently, we all interpret it differently, and we all attribute different meanings to it at various times (Towards Deep Subjectivity. London: Penguin Books, 1972, p. 90).

For the professional counselor in a secular setting, this disparity of worlds can be particularly acute. Dealing with a wide variety of people from every walk of life and social, ethnic, and religious background, these counselors are brought up sharply against the fact that the ways in which the overall meaning of life is formulated can vary greatly from their own, making it much more difficult to understand and appreciate what is really possible or desirable for the client. Because their ultimate goals are different, the counselor and the client might differ considerably on the meaning and significance of the various elements that make up the world of the client. However, for the reasons we gave in the first chapter, particularly in the objectivist approach, these actual disagreements can be masked over, and the therapist's meanings and values can be given a predominant status and hence a crucial element in the process of self-transcendence can be ignored.

If one of the essential ingredients of being a counselor is that he or she shares the same frame of reference and a similar set of values and goals with the client, this would seem to be a factor which renders advice giving within counseling as less possible today than it was when times were more stable and when there was a widespread acceptance of a common set of meanings and values. Because of this some would say today that perhaps counseling is best done by those who share a common framework of meaning and values. This work has come to be known as peer counseling. If counseling is to be seen as mainly an advice-giving process, then this would seem to make sense. To be able to advise how to achieve specific goals requires that one share in those goals.

Projection and Uniqueness of Client's World

However, even where the counselor and client do in fact share in a common world of meaning and values, the disparity of meaning-worlds is not total, otherwise we simply could not communicate. We still need to recognize that only when we really have shared in sufficiently similar situations to those of the client can we guide them in that territory.

If the advice is not to be simply beside the point or even totally misleading, then we have to be quite sure that we are able to understand the situation as it really is for the client. This condition is obviously extremely difficult, though not impossible, to meet. The closest we usually are able to come to realizing it is in self-help groups especially where the difficulty involved is shared among all the members, such as in Alcoholics Anonymous. But in the counseling situation, where we are dealing with clients whom we know mainly from the actual interview itself, we have to be wary of assuming because the situation seems familiar to us that, therefore, it is sufficiently similar such that the behaviors or solutions that worked well for us are really applicable to other clients. The dangers of simple projection are obvious here: The counselor does not know the situation in its interpersonal and historical uniqueness; only the client is sufficiently present to it in all its unique ramifications and possibilities to be able to decide what is the best solution at that moment. The counselor at best can only get an approximate understanding of the client's situation.

Language and Experiencing

As Allen E. Ivey and Lynn Simek-Downing point out, the inability of one person to clearly and precisely grasp the meaning of a situation for another, is partly a limitation intrinsic to language:

Language used by both clients and counselors can be only an approximation of reality. To describe one single moment's thought or experience may require thousands of words (op. cit., p. 177).

Human experiencing as such simply transcends or overflows language and can never be reduced to it. As Gendlin says:

Experiencing is capable of being differentiated so that units and content appear, but it is never itself these contents. Experiencing as a living process is always more and different than any such content (Gendlin, "Experiential Psychotherapy," in Current Psychotherapies, *Corsini, ed., p. 341).*

As a living process, experiencing is known by the person in its wholeness and meaning but in a prelinguistic way. Prior to the expression in language, as we have said, is a presence to that experiencing which is a real knowing and sensing of its personal meaning which even prior to articulation governs action. Only the client can be really present to this and differentiate in words or images what its content is and hence what is the necessary and best step forward.

Summary of the Limitations on Advice Giving

Advice giving, then, suffers from several severe intrinsic limitations. In the first place it is fundamentally based upon a cognitive understanding of the client's situation and what to do about it on the part of the COUNSELOR. It is knowledge ABOUT the client's situation, and as such is characterized by a degree of abstractness that inevitably weakens the possibility of its operational integration. Second, there is the likelihood today of there being a real disparity between the personal meaning structures and value systems of counselor and client, such that it cannot necessarily be assumed that they live in the same personal world. Third, there are intrinsic limitations on the counselor's ability to identify with the actual situation of the client.

The limitations, then, on the ability to help another through giving advice are not arbitrary but arise from the nature of the human situation. William Arnold puts it this way:

*Those limitations are broad based, extending to perception, ability to respond, ability to understand ourselves and others. . . . Such a general view of limitations has several implications. It means that we are incapable of always knowing exactly what we need for ourselves. Such an awareness of limitations raises serious questions about our attempting to "take over" another person's decision-making. It raises questions about how adequate we are to give advice in a demanding or authoritarian way (*Introduction to Pastoral Care. *Philadelphia: Westminster Press, 1982, p. 17).*

The Priority of Counseling

The Aim of Counseling

In our desire to help another we might be tempted to give a *quick fix* in the form of advice. But to really be of assistance, we need to take the limitations of advice giving seriously and find ways in which we can better strengthen the client's capacity to more clearly discern for himself the situation he is in, what he should do about it, and then discover ways in which he can integrate that knowledge into his own unique life situation in an operational way.

Changing the operational self is, in fact, out of the control of the counselor as such and is something only the client can do. It is the client who owns the perceptual world, who has generated it and is operationally present to it. If it is to change, the client alone can effect the change. Counseling, however, is an important aid to helping the person do this. It is not necessarily the locus of the actual change in the operational self of the client, but it can be a place where the groundwork can be done, making it more likely that the person can become aware of the meanings and values operating in his or her personal situation beyond the counseling situation.

The Priority of the Relationship

This highlights and makes central the QUALITY OF RELATIONSHIP that exists between counselor and client. The client is there prescisely because in some serious way, he or she is not present to the reality of who he or she is and the situation he or she is in. Indeed he or she may be quite self-antagonistic as he or she experiences inadequacy to act fruitfully to realize fulfillment. In order to discover what is wrong, the client needs to reestablish a positive and open relationship with his or her own inner and outer world and find the courage and ability to actually articulate what it is he or she finds there. The client needs essentially, as Curran puts it, to move from basic relationship characterized by *loving to hate;* to one characterized by loving to love oneself. The relationship with the counselor is how this is achieved. E. A. Edwin A. Burtt highlights the importance of this when he says:

> *True understanding of a person is gained only through the positive response to his presence. Only when one's interaction with him becomes an active participation in his growth towards fulfillment can one come to know his full self, because only in the medium of such a response is that full self coming to be (*In Search of Philosophic Understanding. *New York: Mentor Books, 1967, p. 238).*

We can gain real knowledge of another then, only through a relationship of love which respects the unique contours of his personal experiencing and affirms him in his ability to be self-transcending. Because, as we have said, the way in which we relate to phenomena dictates what potentialities are evoked in it. It is only by relating to the client in a way that is open to the reality of his subjective embodiment in all its uniqueness and is respectful and affirmative of his capacity for self-acceptance, understanding, and determination that these are evoked in the client and the client can haltingly begin to establish that sort of relationship with his own inner world.

Gendlin insists that this is crucial to the ability to actually touch and so change the meanings and values out of which the client is operating. He makes a radical connection between content and process. He writes:

> *They change only if the manner of the process of examining and becoming aware is new and changed. The eventual outcome of a process is like the manner of that process. . . . If one can give the other*

person room for whatever comes up, however unlovely, then what will eventually come up will be helpful. This is so even if the content of this moment is undesirable, threatening, disappointing, and even if intellectually one can see no solution (Corsini, Current Psychotherapies. Itasca, IL: F. E. Peacock Publ., 1979, p. 357).

In this type of relationship, then, the reality of the other begins to change in a way that enables him to bring to consciousness the meaning structures and values which are dominating his life and behavior. Through his developing self-respect and acceptance, he is able to gain a certain distance from them such that he can change and modify them in self-evaluated and self-determined ways in accordance with the data of his ongoing experience. There is then a process of self-integration going on which enables self-modification to take place.

As we have said, in the basic therapy which is emerging now in the psychotherapeutic world, it is being increasingly recognized that the knowledge and skills of the counselor are subordinated to this end and priority is being given more and more to helping the client come to deeper self-understanding and self-determination through a clearer grasp of the contours of his inner perceptual world and the basic meaning structures and value investments which govern his behavior. He might then decide for himself in which way he needs to change, modify, or abandon them in order to live more rationally and responsibly within the framework of his unique situation.

This is not achieved simply by diagnosis in terms of some abstract explanatory framework but through a quality of relationships that releases the person's own capacity to touch and articulate his unique self at the deepest level. As Burtt rightly says:

What can be known by objective psychology has its vital value, yet it is severely limited; the man thus known is a truncated man. But when two people are available to each other and realize unobstructed communion this limit is transcended; knowledge of self and other becomes possible (op. cit., p. 99).

The Central Skill of Counseling: Understanding

But, if we accept all the limitations on advice giving and discard it as the primary way of helping the client, what is left, we may ask. Arnold answers:

Seeking to understand becomes the first priority when we acknowledge limitations (op. cit., p. 17).

Seeking to understand, then, is at the heart of counseling skills. At first glance this can be interpreted to mean seeking to *figure out* on the objectivist mathematical model. In that the attempt to understand is aimed at the uniqueness of the client's intentional world, which is in and of its nature unknown to the counselor, understanding cannot mean trying to *figure out* the client. That would be to try to locate the contours of the client's inner world within some objective explanatory framework, given some absolute status. The *figuring out* connotation of *understanding* is a secondary and derivative meaning. Its primary meaning is the ability to symbolize accurately the world of the client as it appears to her. We still retain this usage of the term in our language in the phrase, *he or she was a very understanding person.* This conveys a very different sort of activity from the notion of *figuring out.*

In the first place *understanding* is a skillful way of relating to the person, creating for the person an environment in which she can gradually gain the confidence to explore her own inner world and behaviors and so begin to formulate a better understanding of her situation. It can also be a powerful instrument in helping the person clarify and understand her own inner world in all its uniqueness. It empowers the person's own rational reflective processes, freeing up her own dynamism for self-evaluation and determination. It harmonizes with that inherent dynamism within the human person for making *sense* out of herself and her experiencing and so be able to act more effectively within that experiencing: what we have termed rather abstractly as the subjective dynamism toward objectivity.

The Origins and Present Forms of the Skill

As a primary skill in the therapeutic situation, understanding was first articulted by Carl Rogers under the notion of empathy, i.e., the ability to enter into the world of the client as it is disclosed to him through the client's communications and articulating what the client's situation is and what it means to him.

This might, to those who are familiar with this notion, be rather a commonplace conclusion. But there are real indications today, both inside and outside the field of counseling, that in fact the nature of this skill is still not appreciated. Even more, it has in fact been distorted under the pervasive influence of the *objectivist* approach. Because of the latter's emphasis on the dominant role of the counselor as *expert* it has become either a way of putting the client at ease and establishing a relationship of trust that will render the client amenable to the counselor's advice, or as a way of manipulating the client into deep self-disclosure in order to get the necessary information the counselor thinks he needs in order to *solve* the client's problems. In this way the therapeutic power of this skill in and of itself has been watered down, mainly in order to safeguard the status and authority of the counselor. As a result, even in the professional field it is very often not really understood, appreciated, or practiced with any real skill.

Even where understanding is practiced, it is used as a technique in a sort of mechanical way, divorced from the quality of the relationship itself. Rogers himself has of late taken some responsibility for this development, attributing it to the original fascination of his team with the mechanics of the process itself. In a recent interview published in the *Journal of Counseling and Development,* he has said:

> *Frankly it becomes mechanical instead of really being present. I feel I'm partly responsible for the distortions that exist. . . . We became over-fascinated with techniques and that is what has been carried into the academic world ever since. And it was only gradually that I came to realize that, "Yes, what you say is important, but what you are in the relationship is much more important." And so I feel that I contributed to the distortion and misunderstanding by that real focus on technique (September 1984).*

The fact is that the use of this skill cannot be divorced from a fundamental commitment to the subjective nature and capacities of the client, a deep respect for the client's own innate capacity to articulate and evaluate the meaning of his own experiencing, and to decide for himself what best might be done to improve it. The skill of understanding demands on the part of the counselor a different set of basic beliefs as to the nature of the human person and a commitment to a different set of values as to what we are seeking to achieve. As we have seen, the intellectual and cultural environment within which we are functioning does not favor this perspective. Because of this, Rogers himself recognized that this was a revolutionary concept in psychotherapy, one which was extremely threatening to many in the field. It hit directly at their professional status as doctors of the mind after the model of medical doctors — experts in the control and prediction of the processes which bring mental and physical health.

It is increasingly being realized within the medical profession itself that the doctor is not in control of the forces of health; rather he assists the body to heal itself by removing blockages to its own healing processes. He is not the master of the situation but the servant of it. This is the revolutionary call that Rogers has been making to the psychotherapeutic community; to realize and act as servants of another's lifegrowth, rather than seeking to be master of it.

Immediate Goal of Counseling: Experiential Insight

What is aimed for in and through this relationship and process of understanding, then, is the sort of client *insight* which leads to client self-determination. Curran explains:

> The counseling therapy insight process aims at both self-evaluation and coordination of thought, desire and action. In this way the counseling therapy dialogue becomes also a diagnosis, that is a gain in inner operational knowledge and self-actualisation (Charles A. Curran. Counseling and Psychotherapy: The Pursuit of Values. East Dubuque, IL: Counseling Learning Institute, 1976, p. 156).

This is not simply intellectual insight. Many of the criticisms that have been leveled at *insight therapy,* as it is called, come out of a notion of insight as simple intellectual understanding, the ability to come up with a cognitive explanation of who one is and what one is doing. The labeling of this as *insight* is simply evidence of the Cartesian background out of which we are operating which makes a clear distinction between intellectual knowledge and bodily reality with neither experientially interrelated. On the contrary, the skill of understanding relates to a different level of insight: It seeks those symbolic articulations of a person's actual experiential patterns of operation. It seeks gradually to objectivize the operational patterns of meaning and value which are actually operating in the experiential life of the person.

These fundamental experiential meanings and values which constitute the core of the unique person are primarily made present to the person's affective responses to the situations she is in. The Rogerian process has been caricatured as being a process of *getting in touch with one's feelings* and so it is. But, unlike the popular misconceptions, it does not simply stay at that point. Especially in its later developments, as in the work of such people as Charles A. Curran, Eugene

Gendlin, and David Martin, that is only the entry, so to speak, into the discernment of the meaning structures and values which are actually operating in the person's life. Understanding, or insight, has not been achieved until these complexes are actually cognitively articulated and recognized. When they are and are fully accepted, then there is an inner intergration of the person. The person has achieved a self-understanding and the capacity to self-evaluate and self-determine which is freeing of her inner-life energies and the possibility of growthful change. Eugene Gendlin describes this process thus:

> When we differentiate and symbolize a felt meaning by using words (just those words which, at the moment, feel exactly right), a physically felt change or referent movement occurs, indicating that one alters the felt meaning by accurately symbolizing it. Similarly, when another person responds accurately to my felt meanings, just by his doing so, I feel an increased aliveness and bodily sensed release which of course constitutes a change. Language symbols are similar to interpersonal responses in human interaction: both are modes in which felt meanings become symbolized and thereby carried forward (The Goals of Psychotherapy. Mahrer, ed. New York: Appleton-Century-Crofts, p. 189).

The point that Gendlin is making here is that when a person is able to symbolically capture the meaning of his actual experiencing, either through his own searching for the *right word* symbol, or through the response of another, there is a bodily release of tension which, so to speak, clears the mind and enables further meanings of experience to emerge. The inner intrinsic dynamism within the person for intelligibility and significance is released, or unblocked; and the person increasingly gains the ability to make sense of his situation and hence becomes better able to see what it is that he needs to do within it.

Curran has detailed the evidence that in this process a person usually moves through fairly predictable stages, characterized in the beginning by negative emotions, through increasingly positive emotions to decision and choice as to new value possibilities (see *Counseling and Psychotherapy: The Pursuit of Values*). Carl Rogers has detailed the movement from rigidity of thinking, stereotypical behavior, and paucity of emotional responding to a free-flowing capacity to articulate the experiential moment and operate effectively within it (see *On Becoming a Person*).

Understanding and the Growth Process

This process, then, is far from being a simple affirmation of the person which, while letting him know he is being empathically listened to, at the same time leaves him essentially where he is. Done over a period of time, the raising to symbolic clarity of the essential contours of the person's experiential world is a confrontative process of holding up to the person in clear relief, in a way which is capable of being owned by the person, who he really is in the patterns of his intentional living. It meets the criterion of what Lock Land has posited as being the one essential type of feedback from the environment that enables growth to take place. This type of feedback he calls positive/nutritive. He explains it thus:

It means that in responding to an act of another person something in that act is seen and responded to in a positive way — that the tone or character of the response is positivistic. Then, in supplying nutrition, information, this can contain data that actually serves to correct the non-useful parts of the perceived act (ibid., p. 93).

The affirmation is contained in the way in which the counselor conveys, through his efforts to understand, that what the person is trying to say has importance and, furthermore, that he as a person can make sense to another human being; that in her uniqueness she is not alone. Thus one is enabled to enter into that interpersonal dialogue which is so essential to feeling of value and worth. The nutrition is contained in the fact that the counselor, in his verbal response, actually does *understand*. This does not happen if the counselor simply mirrors back what she hears. Repeating does not convey understanding; it simply says that one heard the words and sentences much as a tape recorder might. We get closer to it in the notion of paraphrase, but this, too, can simply be evidence of a certain intellectual cleverness. To understand, however, is to really see what the client is trying to convey in a way which expresses the uniqueness of the counselor. In other words the counselor is embodied in the response; the client hears the counselor as a real person, and what she hears, though accurately embodying what she was trying to convey, looks new and fresh and different. The client then is enabled to see herself in a new and different light. Something new then is contained in the response which is nutritive. This newness can be owned by the client because it essentially links up with what he or she already owns.

This skill is complex and not easily learned, though not beyond the capacities of any ordinary person. However, the effects of this on a person in aiding her growth into a deeper and more objective grasp of who she is was well put in an editorial in the magazine *Revision* in which the writer, commenting on the work of Edgar A. Levinson, who operates out of what we have termed the emerging paradigm, says:

But there is a strong feeling when therapy is going well that an elusive pattern is emerging, a powerful central theme evident on all levels at once. The therapist is saying nothing new to the patient "but resonates with something the patient already knows and brings it into clearer focus. The change results as a consequence of the expansion of configurational patterns over time. . . . It is not so much that a therapist is correct in his formulations but that he is in harmony or resonance with what is occurring in the patient. "It is as though a huge, three-dimensional, spatially–coded representation of the patient's experience develops in therapy, running through every aspect of his life, his history and his participation with the therapist. At some point there is a kind of overload and everything falls into place." The pattern or theme has emerged dramatically for the patient (quoted in the editorial, "A New Perspective on Reality," Revision. Summer/ Fall, 1978: p. 60).

Understanding and Confrontation

Furthermore, it emerges within a constant process of self-evaluation. Far from being a comfortable, supportive experience it can be a painful and disturbing one, though one in which the person is able to experience a deep respect and security through the quality of relationship the counselor offers. New connections of hitherto disparate data tend to come together into new configurations which as a whole were never recognized before. The person may discover that in many ways he is not who he thought he was. His self-concept is disturbed, emotions are increasingly experienced in greater variety and intensity and around surprising areas; game playing and self-deception are revealed. But amid the disturbances comes a deepening sense that he is in fact capable of deeper self-knowledge and self-determination without being destroyed or rejected and also relief that he is able to see himself and his life as it is and so make more realistic and more satisfying choices.

Conclusion: The Role of Advice Giving in the Helping Process

The objective knowledge of the counselor however can be of great importance in this process by sensitizing him to what is emerging in the client's process and in giving him the capacity to articulate it for the client. It enables him to make suggestions as to possible ways forward, avenues that might be explored, activities that might prove beneficial. It is at this point that the counselor might be able to offer specific skill training of one sort or another or offer other advice as to what to do. But such advice giving, if offered at all, would be minimal and would come only at the end of the process, after the person has achieved a clearer self-understanding and capacity for self-determination around the area of concern and when the counselor and client are in clear agreement with regards to the values to be realized and the goals to be achieved. John Pietrofesa *et al.* sum this up when they say:

> Whether or not to advise depends on the persons involved and the type of advice requested. The counselor's experience and knowledge should be made available to the counselee, but only as far as the counselee is able to incorporate this into his own decision-making *(The Authentic Counselor. Chicago: Rand McNally, 1971, p. 176).*

With the development of the skill of understanding, we have been enabled to put the guidance mode of helping another into a wider perspective and into a different and sounder context. It was the absence of the knowledge and development of this skill which gave *counseling* in the past such a predominantly guidance tone. Until recently, we had no other way of seeking to be of help to another. For those who have not had any exposure to the nature and dynamics of this skill, it still remains of necessity the only way we have to help others through their difficulties.

The development of this skill then has not as such vitiated the guidance mode of its relevance; we do not, in other words, have to abandon the place of guidance or advice giving altogether. In and of itself, it can be a further step in helping another see himself and his situation in more objective terms and discern different ways of behaving than he has hitherto adopted. But especially in the area of personal difficulties which is so dominated by the uniqueness of meanings and values of the individual person, advice giving does of necessity occupy a lesser place than *understanding.* This means that the advice given has to be done in much more limited terms and without the sort of dogmatism that can come from thinking one is an expert in the personal world of the other.

Advice giving would, as a first approach, seem to be most appropriate when a person is in some severe crisis and momentarily incapacitated in some emotional way and needs someone to take over the running of his life for a short period in order to accomplish some necessary goal. The risk of not advising then outweighs the risk of doing so. In this case the counselor should, if at all possible, remain close at hand in order to monitor the effects and results until such time as the person is able to assume personal responsibility for the running of his own life.

Under normal circumstances, however, advice giving is only appropriate when the person has already come to a certain clarity about herself and relates it to her own individual circumstances with a certain discrimination. When, through the counseling process, the person has come to realize and accept primary responsibility for assessing and deciding what can and ought to be done, then she is in the position of making the best and most judicious use of the suggestions. Advice, in fact, as we have said, can only really be assimilated and applied in a fruitful way by someone who has the ability to really understand what is being said and how it might apply in her circumstances. The key is the capacity and willingness of the person to be responsible for her own behavior. Suggestions as to the best way forward, if the counselor honestly judges that he has such and that they are relevant at that point, might then aid a person in her independent evaluation process and maybe increase her ability to act more effectively than previously. It gives the person other options to weigh, other avenues to explore, and different ways of construing her situation and its possibilities. Such advice or guidance should be offered to the person not in any dogmatic or coercive fashion but in humility and tentativeness, with full recognition of the subjective limitations on the counselor's ability to really discern the best way forward for the client and with full recognition that it is the latter who has to bear the consequences for any behavior she adopts. Care, too, needs to be taken that the client understands that this is accepted and respected by the counselor and that noncompliance with the advice would not bar the person from returning for further exploration.

Once a person understands and is facile in the use of the skill of understanding, his awareness of the dynamics of the integration process within the client becomes much more acute and comprehensive. He is then in a much better position to assess the relevance of the suggestions being made and their effect on the client. Guidance, given by one who knows how to relate to a person in this way, if the counselor genuinely believes that he or she has the guidance to give, can be far more growthful than if given by one who does not have this skill, or has some knowledge of it, but has not made it central to their work with the client. The skill of *understanding* will modify both the amount of guidance given, the way in which it is given, and the awareness of how it affects the client.

Part II Advice Giving and Pastoral Counseling

6 Moral Directives in Pastoral Counseling
Distinctive Nature of Pastoral Counseling

So far we have been dealing solely with the use of advice giving in counseling as such and, insofar as pastoral counseling utilizes the psychological principles involved, it applies there also. The limitations on the possibilities and value of giving advice, in that they are based upon the nature of the human being as a unique subject, living in situations which have their own unique characteristics, must apply also in the sphere of pastoral ministry which is explicitly concerned with helping the individual realize his personal destiny from within the historical context of his social and cultural situation.

However, in saying this we involve ourselves in something of a problem. It might be generally accepted that PSYCHOLOGICAL knowledge about human functioning might have intrinsic limitations; that while it might be valuable and necessary in helping us to be sensitive to and understanding of the individual's situation, it will not of itself help the person to move beyond the situation. Furthermore, it might also be possible to accept that there is always a danger of projecting our understanding onto the other in a way that prevents us from actually discerning and respecting the uniqueness of the individual. However, those in pastoral counseling may find it more difficult to accept that they might not share in the same normative objective world of meaning and values as the client does. Is this not what is meant by belonging to a faith community? In a church or religious setting, is there not a rightful presumption that the counselor, as pastor or parish worker, would share the same framework of goals, meaning, and values, as the client such that, depending on the knowledge and expertise of the particular worker, advice giving is more clearly a rightful expectation and a desirable possibility?

This raises the question of the distinctive nature of pastoral counseling over that carried out in the secular world. If there is something distinctive here, it would seem to lie precisely in the sharing of a common world in which there is agreement as to the ultimate *objective* meaning of human fulfillment and how best to realize it. As we have seen, all counseling and psychotherapy presumes an ultimate rationale concerning the nature of man, his destiny and hence what constitutes healthy functioning. Whereas, however, in *secular* counseling this can and does usually remain implicit, in the Christian faith of its very nature it cannot. This is the *raison d'etre* of Christian faith, its starting point. The very existence of the Church is based on the claim to have objective knowledge of what constitutes the total and ultimate nature of human reality and fulfillment, and, hence, on how to achieve it, and those who belong to it do so because to some significant degree they share in that belief system.

Belief in the possession of this definitive knowledge, gained primarily through Revelation and passed on with divine authority, has inevitably influenced the way the Church has understood and practiced *counseling,* giving it a strong bias toward guidance in which the individual's understanding of the meaning of his or her situation has been subordinated to the explanation of the Church. Hence, the dominant mode of pastoral care up until now, as Clebsch and Jeakle have shown, has been *inductive guidance,* i.e., the derivation of behavioral norms from a conceptual framework accepted as objectively true. Consequently, what is known as pastoral counseling has been seen primarily as an indispensable way of guiding people toward realizing the objective ideal presented by the Church community and then actualizing it through their attitudes and behavior. The pastoral counselor, then, because of his position in the community, has usually been considered to have much more authority to direct people into a particular way of being and acting than the secular counselor, particularly in the spheres of moral behavior and spiritual growth. The Church's manuals of pastoral care down through the centuries have been compiled to help the pastoral minister carry out his guiding function in the best way possible.

Inasmuch as we now have a way in which we can powerfully help a person to come to deeper self-understanding and self-determination, can and should this still be the major connotation to the use of the word *counseling* in pastoral life? Is pastoral counseling primarily an objectivist endeavor, or can and should it now become primarily a subjectivist one as has been claimed here for counseling in general? In what way can these two dimensions be combined in pastoral counseling?

Jeakle and Clebsch believe that what they term *eductive counseling* has, since its development by Rogers and his colleagues, been adopted as the primary way of relating. It is difficult to decide this factually and discern to what extent pastoral counseling still shares in the predominantly objectivist perspectives current in secular counseling, and it is, for our purposes, unnecessary to do so. More importantly, we need to see how the approach suggested here can fit with the pastoral and theological context within which pastoral counseling takes place.

To see the primary issues clearly, we will look first at that area of pastoral counseling where the discrepancies between what has been said so far and the objective content and authority which the Church claims for itself might show up most strongly, i.e., the area of spiritual and moral direction. And we will look at it mainly from the perspective of the sort of client who wishes to formulate his own understanding of what is true and right to do. In looking at it in this way, we will be able to highlight clearly the tensions involved in a situation in which what the client believes and wishes to do is in conflict with the counselor. Then we will look at the opposite side of the coin, so to speak, where the client comes clearly and insistently asking to be told what to believe and how to act. In doing so, we are taking a somewhat extreme position, not because this is necessarily the typical client the pastoral counselor deals with, though they are certainly far from rare, but, again, in order to show the issues more clearly.

Recent Moral Theology and Objectivism
Predominance of Inductive Guidance

Although Clebsch and Jaekle have shown that the more subjectivist *eductive guidance* has never been absent from the Church's practice, nevertheless in recent years, especially in moral matters, the bias has been predominantly toward *inductive guidance* as the dominant mode of pastoral care. The primary reason for this was the fact that intellectually the Church shared in a similar emphasis on the objectivist framework of thinking that was present in the secular sphere. This has been termed by Lonergan the *classicist view* of culture. Keith Seasoltz describes it thus:

*The classical view of culture then maintains that there is but one cul-
ture which is normative, universal and permanent. The values it em-
braces and the meanings it communicates are universal in scope and
claim. It appeals to an abstract ideal and its concerns are unchanging
and universal. It is informed by classical philosophy, structured according to Aristotelian logic and issues laws which are universally applicable and truths which are eternal. Circumstances of place and time
are accidental in a classicist matrix. Humanity itself is a universal concept reflecting an unchanging reality. . . . When a classicist understanding of culture prevails, theology is looked upon as a permanent
achievement; theologians simply discourse on its given nature ("From
Liturgical Reform to Christian Renewal,"* Clergy Review, *March 1982:
p. 90).*

Out of this classicist view of reality, it was believed that human reality, especially in its spiritual and moral dimensions, could be *figured out,* its principles
of operation clearly outlined, and the results codified into generally applicable
laws. The contents of this natural law were viewed as the moral equivalent of
those invariable laws which governed physical reality. As such, they were seen
as escaping the exigencies of subjectivity and, regardless of history, governed
the whole of human reality, so that the individual, notwithstanding the particularity of his unique situation, was subordinate to them. Robert Springer has described this *objectivist* situation in recent times in these words:

*Concretely the fixation of moral was evidenced in that it had become
a code morality. Instead of a flexible set of moral rules going beyond
the basic principles in the area of morality, these rules were elevated
to the status of universal, unexceptional principles. In theory they re-
mained rules and, therefore, had exceptions, as Aquinas had taught.
But in practice, in pulpit and classroom, in the lives of the faithful, they
were the predetermined and predetermining norms of behavior. They
should have been guidelines for decision allowing for the particularity
of each moral choice, the* contingens singulare *of St. Thomas, and the
changing situation of mankind. Now conscience had only to apply the
right rule and the answer was almost automatic, a kind of computerized morality. You feed the data into the machine (object, purpose,
and circumstances) and conscience selects the pertinent norm.
Whereupon out comes the answer* (Absolutes in Moral Theology,
Charles E. Curran, ed. Washington, D.C.: Corpus Books, 1968, p. 20).

Changing Perspectives on Objectivity

Theology today, however, through an intense dialogue with the emerging
philosophical and scientific consciousness of our generation, especially, but not
only, in the matter of moral principles and behavioral norms, is moving away
from that excessive objectivism without, however, seeking to discard its value.
According to Lonergan, the movement now is to what he calls an empiricist view
of reality which brings more clearly into relief the subjectivity of human knowledge. Seasoltz explains his view thus:

*Unfortunately classicist culture has failed to realize an important factor
which relativizes its normative value for people today. It has not been*

sufficiently aware of its own historical conditioning as well as the historical self-making of individual persons and social groups. . . . The contemporary empiricist approach to culture acknowledges that there are as many cultures as there are distinct sets of values and meanings. Articulated in a variety of sociologies, anthropologies, and social psychologies, contemporary culture recognizes the historical and relative character of the means by which it communicates meanings and values. It is concerned with the particular rather than the universal, and it sees each human institution as the product of a specific history of efforts to satisfy human needs and wants and to sustain what is deemed worthwhile. . . . When an empiricist notion of culture prevails, theology is conceived as an ongoing process to be carried out in the context of modern science, modern philosophy, modern history, and modern scholarship (op. cit., p. 91).

Although some view this dialogue with suspicion as a pandering to secular thought, in one way or another a dialogue with contemporary thinking has always been part of Catholic tradition. This tradition has always acknowledged that its religious understanding of man could never be entirely separated from that pervading the world in which it functioned and that tradition could be enriched by the dialogue. Without *selling itself out* so to speak, it has always been willing to enter into dialogue with the prevailing philosophical and psychological views on the nature of man. In doing so, it modified the secular perspectives to fit into the ultimate framework that it brought to the dialogue from its originating experience of Jesus Christ and in turn it was modified, sometimes consciously but very often unconsciously, as in the strong objectivism outlined above, by the secular thinking as to what precisely ultimate salvation might mean and how to achieve it.

The uneasiness that some feel about this current dialogue is understandable since it involves the very notion of objectivity itself. In theology as a whole we question what the fact that all knowledge is intrinsically influenced by historically conditioned subjectivity means for our understanding of the objective content of Christian Faith. Is there any part of that content which escapes this conditioning? If the answer is *yes,* then, precisely how much; if not, then what does this mean for the objective content of Christian Faith? Precisely what *objective content* must be accepted by the individual before he or she can be considered to be a member of the faith community?

Theological Objectivity and Subjective Growth

The theological and moral sciences as sciences share in the relativity of all scientific findings: They are created points of view that enable us to integrate the data of our experiencing as it unfolds before us. They are not absolute but must be open to creative reformulation as we reexamine the data of our experience. The degree of objectivity they attain is dependent on how closely they conform to and lead to a continual realization of the created structures of human being.

This is simply an application of the principle that grace builds on nature, that redemption is the realization of human beings in their fullness; it perfects what was given in creation. The objective content of Christian Faith today will be judged by the extent to which it is able to account for and harmonize the various polarities and tensions that make up the human being, particularly those between the individual and the community and between our current meaning structures and our ongoing experiencing. It must be able to take into account, and lead us to a deep respect for and enhancement of, both human subjectivity and uniqueness, as well as the intrinsically communal nature of human being. Moral thinking, especially, must be able to take into account the tensions involved in this dialectic between the process of future-oriented, subjective self-transcendence, and past-oriented tradition.

We need, then, to ask to what extent the Christian *story* supports the process of self-transcendence. The logic of the argument necessitates that we examine in a deeper way the relationship of the development of the individual person in his subjective self-determination to the content of ultimate salvation as formulated in moral theology. Does that tradition include subjective self-determination or does it exclude it? The answers we arrive at will have important consequences for the activity of pastoral education, care, and counseling.

Relation Between Subjectivity and Objectivity in Moral Thought

De facto Effects of Theological and Moral Pluralism

The first consideration is simply a practical one: the fact that people in the Church are claiming for themselves a right to self-assessment and determination around the areas of spiritual and moral concern. While undoubtedly there is still a closer identity between the pastoral counselor and the client in terms of the ultimate meaning of life and the hierarchy of values that will realize it than there is very often between a counselor in the secular sphere and his client, it is clearly evident that it is far less so today than in former times. The social mobility, increased education, and the exposure to widely differing lifestyles and value systems referred to before have also made deep inroads into the social cohesiveness and identity that characterized church communities in the past. Theological pluralism which, in the past, was usually intercommunally based, today is intracommunal. It is more deeply present within the same religious community than it ever was in the past.

Not simply waywardness, this is to some extent the result of the Church's own commitment to religious and moral education, developing against a background of increased general education. This pluralism seems likely to increase as both general and adult religious education continues to develop and people are given more and more of the theological tools whereby to come to personal assessments of their religious faith and experience. Our very pastoral commitment to education on all levels is developing the subjective self-determination of church members. If this trend continues, and it seems evident that it will, the days of simple doctrinal and moral uniformity will have passed and, within the Church, the variations in the meaning of the gospel message and what it requires in concrete behavioral terms will continue to show more divergence today than it used to. The question is whether this will result in an added richness or simply chaos. The answer would seem to depend on the extent and depth of dialogue within church structures on all levels. If there are no structures of dialogue then subjectivism and pluralism will undoubtedly result in fragmentation and loss.

This growing variety of views is increasingly present, and especially notice-able in the Catholic Church probably because, more than any other communion, it has been socially very cohesive and has had a strong tradition of carefully thought-out moral laws and doctrinal statements. The Protestant communities have always been less socially unified, and moral theology as a science has, until recently, been less well developed. These *de facto* influences have important implications for the practice of counseling. However, what Don Browning says of the Protestant communions is true of the Roman Catholic Church too:

> The public world is increasingly made up of individuals and groups of diverse faiths, different moral commitments and conflicting life-styles. This is the way the public world is outside the church — and increas-ingly, we must admit, inside the church as well. . . . This pluralism makes consensus, both inside and outside the church, difficult to achieve . . . it also complicates the way we care for and counsel one another *(Don Browning. Religious Ethics and Pastoral Care. Philadel-phia: Fortress Press, 1983, pp. 13–14).*

One result of the commitment to religious and secular education is that the sort of religious and moral authority based on knowledge of the corpus of tra-dition and confined to clerical circles is weakening, and people are not looking at authoritative pronouncements in the same way they used to. Especially in the areas of personal spirituality and morality, people are beginning to claim the right to formulate their own understandings of the meaning of their experience and develop their own assessments of what the gospel requires.

Changing Attitudes toward Authority

In this the Church is simply part of a wider social trend as regards authority. Increasingly, people are no longer taking one perspective on the meaning of life and how to live it as being a privileged one, nor are they looking to particular persons, i.e., priests, parents, teachers, as being in a position to tell them *the way things really are.* Today, for instance, young adults do not automatically see their parents as reliable guides in the business of living since the particular world they live in is no longer the same as that of their parents. Undoubtedly this is used by many as an excuse simply to go their own way and do *their own thing,* but it does highlight the fact that parents, educators, and clergy cannot simply take their position as authoritative guides for granted and that the way in which moral principles are passed on to people today must change to account for this desire for personal decision making.

De facto in its pastoral practice, the Church has no option today but to acknowledge and reckon with the fact that many of the faithful are claiming a right to a self-assessment and self-determination in the area of moral and spiritual behavior. What the Church's response to this ought to be is a debatable point, but, particularly in the realms of personal relations, sexual morality, business ethics, family life, and social issues, pastoral counselors are likely to find an increasingly wide variation among their clients in the assessments of what is ideal and there-fore of what one must, or can, do. This was summed up by a man who said that when he went to confession, the first thing he said was: "First I want to tell you what you think I have done wrong, then I will tell you what I think I've done wrong." *De facto* priest and client may not be able to agree on the real meaning of a situation and hence of what ought to be done in it. Even if we do not agree with this as a development, as pastoral counselors, we have to be prepared to take it into account. Realizing that on a practical level it renders the advice-giving mode in the pastoral care of the individual less of an option and highlights the necessity of counseling as I have defined it as the dominant way of ministering to people.

Negative Consequences of Moral Objectivism

But the reason for seeing advice giving as being of less value today in pastoral counseling needs to go deeper than a simple practical necessity. The question arises as to whether this is a trend that should be encouraged or combatted. Generally speaking, especially in the Western Church, there has been a strong movement to encourage it. On the one hand, this is based on the developing recognition within the Church itself of the necessity, for the sake of its own moral and spiritual health, of developing people who are able to personally own and live the values of the gospel. It acknowledges the fact that the days of simple social cohesiveness, and the conformity to commonly accepted values that it made possible, are over, and that the complexity of social issues demands of the Church members that they be able to discern for themselves how the gospel applies in their situations. It has been recognized that it is no longer sufficient simply to tell people what to do; they need to know why that is so and to be able to discern the validity of those reasons for themselves. In the multifarious situations and problems of today, it is more than ever clear that the official Church is no longer able simply to do this for them. Pauline Mulligan expresses this well when she says:

> The pluralism of our modern society resulting from the ever-accelerating pace in the use of mass media has brought about a cleavage within our outlook, so that today there is more tolerance for the open expression of views which are in contradiction with Christian values. Our Christian standards of morality are openly controverted, various trends of thought are constantly modifying the atmosphere in which we have to live out our Christian life, modern scientific development brings with it a trail of problems which are a never-ending challenge to the Christian. Under these conditions the individual must be sufficiently equipped to make and defend his own decisions in moral matters, i.e., he must aim at an ever-growing spiritual maturity which will enable him to react personally in all the circumstances of life. He must know, not only the "How" of his moral decisions, but also the "Why" ("Personalist Orientation in Moral Catechesis for School Leaders," Lumen Vitae, 23(2), 1968: p. 265).

On the other hand, there is a growing realization that this situation is simply bringing to light something that in fact was always part of man's ontological condition: a personal responsibility for one's meanings and values and the behavior that flows from them.

The *objectivist* understanding of morality that predominated until recently tended to hide or render somewhat unconscious this basic ontological fact that no matter how clear the *laws* we were still personally responsible for our actions.

This led to a situation which we are now beginning to recognize as being psychologically and morally unhealthy. With regards to the growth and development of Catholics, this was referred to in an article in *Theological Studies,* 30(3): p. 473.

> *A psychiatrist can often observe that Catholic patients are really unable to experience the real nature of their hard-heartedness, vanity, self-satisfaction, etc. Often they are unable to see what makes such conduct wrong. They immediately leap to the general explanation that such conduct offends God. One has the impression that by seeing the reality almost exclusively in this way they have allowed their real sensitivity to values to atrophy.*

Essentially what the author laments is that because Catholics were taught that morality was mainly a matter of obedience to *objective* law which they violated only at the expense of incurring God's wrath, they lost their capacity to be consciously and rationally present to their actual experiencing and to be sensitive to the actual consequences of their behavior. They abrogated their responsibility for these either to God or to the Church, maintaining for themselves a rather self-centered security against the fear of rejection or disapproval by God or the community. It led to a lamentable lack of moral sense, especially in those areas not covered by explicit laws.

The Necessity for Personal Appropriation

This sort of result is inevitable when values are lived only for extraneous reasons. It is a feature not just of Catholics but also among any group which places responsibility for the rightness or wrongness of their actions on an extraneous authority, be it society, a church, or even simply on the authority of a book such as the Bible. However, although undoubtedly still widely prevalent in religious communities, both Catholic and Protestant, it is less easy today to avoid the challenge to be personally responsible for one's moral position and its consequences than it was in the past. A major cultural turning point in our realization of this came with the Nuremberg trials after the Second World War and more recently with the trial of Eichmann in Israel in which it was held that obedience to the dictates of legitimate authority could not relieve a person from personal responsibility for his actions. Simple unquestioning obedience to the moral dictates of another was clearly rejected as a valid moral stance. So, even where we espouse certain social meanings and values, and it is of course still perfectly valid to do so, today, culturally, we are more likely to be held personally accountable for that acceptance and the results of it than we were in the past.

Vatican II and Personal Responsibility

The call today simply from our historical situation is to a personal appropriation and accountability for the meanings and values out of which we operate. It is a call the Church, in its developing understanding of the gospel message is, in fact, taking seriously and at the present time is seeking to understand and respect.

In recent years in moral theology, there has been a radical movement away from a simply individualistic ethic in which one was concerned mainly with obedience to law so as to safeguard one's personal rightness with God, to a realization that the quality of one's personal relationships, both in depth and in extension is central to one's moral status *vis-a-vis* God. It is movement away from a rather cerebral *objectivism* to a more sensitive, experientially based subjectivism.

In the Catholic Church, the basis for this movement can be clearly discerned in the Church's teaching on the relationship of the Christian to the world. There is a radical shift in perspective away from an understanding of spirituality as being a flight from involvement with the world and a fear of contamination from it. Hence, the Vatican Council could say:

> The Christian who neglects his temporal duties, neglects his duties towards his neighbor and even God, and jeopardizes his eternal salvation (Gaudium et Spes, par. 43).

The task of the Christian is to help in the process of revealing the face of God himself to the world through his personal, intersubjective relationships, a task that demands a more personal sensitivity to the quality of moment-to-moment experiencing and its intrinsic demands. Hence we read:

> This result is achieved chiefly by the witness of a living and mature faith, namely, one trained to see difficulties clearly and to master them. This faith needs to prove its fruitfulness by penetrating the believer's entire life, including its worldly dimensions, and by activating him towards justice and love, especially as regards the needy. What does most to reveal God's presence, however, is the brotherly charity of the faithful who are united in spirit as they work together for the faith of the Gospel and who prove themselves a sign of unity (ibid., par. 21).

The centrality accorded love here has several important implications which are now in the process of being worked out. In the first place, love cannot be commanded from the outside but depends on a personal conviction and appropriation of the values to be realized in one's present situation. In this task of personal appropriation and conviction, we are primarily alone before God, and it is this essential aloneness before God which, with regards to the appropriation of meaning and value, in terms of moral decision making, grounds the primacy of the individual over the collective in Christian Faith.

Gospel Perspectives on Moral Development

Love: The Response to the Will of God

A personal response to God's will, it would seem, is central to the gospel message of Jesus Christ in his injunction to *seek first the reign of God,* and not to be afraid of what others can do to you. In making the personal discernment and response to the will of God paramount in human life, Jesus called on the individual to respond to a relationship above and beyond that of the social group. In his practice of what he preached, he revealed what was already at the heart of created reality; he was elucidating and grounding that necessary dimension of human life, the fact that one can relate fruitfully and in a life-giving way to others only when he or she is willing to respond to the absolute and transcendent values of truth and love as he or she personally discerns them in the present experiencing of these values.

104

This, then, is the second implication: that the demands of love coming from the uniqueness of the present moment cannot simply be read off from abstract laws. One does not love simply by doing what is right according to external norms but only by seeking to do what is personally understood to be good in this particular situation. This does not mean of course that there is never a correlation between external norms and the existential "good," only that there is not a necessary link, and in terms of priority our discernment of what is best in the present situation must take precedence over the generic formulations of the law based on previous data. This is that indispensable obedience to the will of God which Jesus himself manifested and lived by. Günther Bornkamm in his profound analysis of the person of Jesus, maintains rightly that this obedience characterized and was at the core of Jesus' personal *authority*. He writes:

> Their (the rabbis' and scribes') authority is always a derived authority. Jesus' teaching, on the other hand, never consists merely in the interpretation of an authoritively given sacred text, not even when words from scripture are quoted. The reality of God and the authority of his will are always directly present, and are fulfilled in him. . . . This is true to such a degree that he even dares to confront the literal text of the law with the immediately present will of God (Jesus of Nazareth. *London: Hodder and Stoughton, 1960, p. 57*).

Bornkamm goes on to say:

> The immediate present is the hallmark of all the words of Jesus, of his appearance and his actions, in a world which . . . had lost the present, because it lived between the past and the future, between traditions and promises or threats, in security or anxiety, conscious of its own rights, or under sentence for its own lawlessness (ibid., p. 58).

As we have seen in our discussion of psychological health, to live in the immediate present is to be utterly open to our present experiencing and to respond to it out of its own meaning. To live merely out of *objective* law is to live out of the community's past, out of the way in which it formulated the meaning of its experiencing and its embodiment in law; to live simply out of the fear of punishment for breaking that law is to live out of the *future* in which that punishment will be meted out. This does not in itself devalue either those past formulations or remove consciousness of the future judgment, but it puts them in a different perspective and opens us up to the present where, for Jesus, the reign of God was being revealed and realized. It would seem for Jesus that past formulations of God's will were brought to fulfillment precisely in the fact that the person was able to respond in his or her own unique way to the demands of the will of God as these were made known in and through the present.

The Relativity within the Law

This focus in the gospel on the necessity of determining the will of God in the present moment is being increasingly highlighted today, as through the work of scripture scholars and moral theologians, we become more aware that there is a relativity within the law itself. In the first place, the provisions of the law itself were not simply handed down by God intact and unalterable. Through biblical research we have been made aware of the fact that the concrete moral prescriptions that are given, such as the Ten Commandments, show evidence of growth and development as the moral consciousness of the community grew (contrast Ex. 20:17 with Deut. 5:21 *vis-a-vis* position of women).

Second, neither are laws capable of simply being read off in detail from nature and hence essentially unchanging and applicable in the same way in all times and places. The question here is centered around the existence of negative moral absolutes. Are there any laws which are applicable in the same way, at all times for everybody, no matter what their circumstances? The growing consensus seems to be that there are not such laws. There is a hierarchy of absoluteness in moral principles, ranging from the most general to the most specific. In one sense the relativity of the law has always been recognized in Catholic moral philosophy. It was St. Thomas Aquinas who maintained that the farther we moved from the general principle *do good and avoid evil* toward its concrete requirements the less sure the law becomes. John C. Milhaven, in his admittedly preliminary study of the presence of negative moral behavioral absolutes in Thomas, has concluded that:

> What emerged progressively from the analysis was that the moral center of gravity for Thomas did not lie in the act itself and in its physical effect, though these were relevant factors. As long as the acts contributed to some good purpose, the crucial question to decide the legitimacy of a given means was the authority of the person acting: not what was to be done but who would do it (Absolutes in Moral Theology. *Washington, D.C.: Corpus Books, 1968*).

It would seem then that even St. Thomas, whose theological system has been so influential in forming the Church's objective understanding of moral law, did not give any absolute status to its more specific negative provisions. To recognize this is to see the detailed applications of the law in a different light, as being rather the articulation by the community of what it considers at this moment to be ideal, given the historical situation it is in. Laws are subject to the essential historicity of all human reality.

Implications for Pastoral Practice

The Development of Personal Conscience

Acceptance of this in pastoral practice means an acceptance of the necessity for the individual in dialogue with the community in its understanding of what the gospel demands to formulate his or her personal understanding of what the gospel values mean in his or her life and situation. Essentially, this means that all our pastoral ministry, especially that of counseling, must serve and support the development of personal conscience, so that the individual is able to discern for himself the right thing to do in the unique situation he is in. Hoffman describes conscience thus:

> A careful analysis shows that in conscience man has a direct experience in the depths of his personality of the moral quality of a concrete personal decision or act as a call of duty on him, through his awareness of its significance for the ultimate fulfillment of his personal being ("Conscience," Sacramentum Mundi, *London: Burns Oates, 1975, p. 287*).

He goes on to detail the relationship of personal conscience to *objective* norms and laws thus:

The relation of objective norms to conscience cannot be understood as the meeting of two competing values. The objective law is the will and order of God in his creation and this is made known in the conscience of man who carries on his life within this creation and its plan of salvation. Its place cannot be taken either by moral knowledge or by opinion or by direction from another. The judgment of conscience is the ultimate definitive norm for the individual, but it does not thereby become a general norm for people faced with similar decisions (ibid.).

With the emerging emphasis on personal conscience, then, we are discerning a distinction between *objective* codes of conduct, applicable on the level of the human community as a whole, and *subjective* moral demands coming from the unique particularity of the individual's situation — demands which are applicable to him alone at that moment. Although both objective codes and subjective moral demands are essential, today it is the latter that needs most to be developed.

Conscience and Church Authority

One of the Church's primary tasks today is to foster the development of personal conscience. And it is on its teaching on conscience that the Church in recent years has most clearly sought to incorporate the modern understanding of subjectivity. Springer describes this development thus:

Subjectivity also means that man in part escapes objectification. . . . But to conceptualize is to objectify, to find concepts with a formal object to express what man is and should do. Therefore there is a limit to our ability to conceptualize, to formulate, the objective demands that rest upon us. This greater awareness of the subjective in modern philosophy, counterbalancing an earlier overemphasis on the objective, is reflected in the teaching of Vatican II on conscience. Instead of a doctrine couched solely in terms of response to objective norms, it recognizes a depth in the person that defies objectification: "Conscience is the most secret core and sanctuary of a man", it says in one place; in another it speaks of "unsearchable depths of the human soul" (op. cit., p. 23).

Joseph Ratzinger describes the shift that took place in Vatican II as it sought to incorporate the central role of the subjective into its moral thinking. He comments as follows on Vatican II's teaching concerning marriage.

The procreative view is here supplanted by a personalistic view . . . the text points to conscience, to the Word of God, to the church interpreting the word of God, as proper guides for morality in marriage. . . . There is a decided difference between a total moral statement based on the concept of the race and the propagation of the race and on the concept in accordance with nature, and a view which focuses on individual conscience and, on the Word of God and on responsibility towards children, towards the husband or wife, and to-

*wards the community of mankind. The context within which con-
science operates, the entire atmosphere in which all decision and moral
commitment is made, differs radically in these two cases. It is simply
not the same, whether a person asks himself if his actions are responsible actions in view of other persons with whom he is in accord
with or whether he must ask whether his actions are related in the
marriage community and whether his actions are responsible in view
of the Word of the Personal God who has indicated the fundamental
pattern of conjugal love by comparing it with love for the Church as
exemplified in Christ. [Eph 5:25–33]* (Theological Highlights of Vatican
II. *New York: Paulist Press, 1966, pp. 166–67).*

This emphasis on the development of personal responsibility and the subjective assessment and the personal appropriation it necessitates is most clearly
expressed by the Church in its teaching on the moral development of youth:

*This Holy synod likewise affirms that children and young people have
a right to be encouraged to weigh moral values with an upright conscience, and to embrace them by personal choice, and to know and
love God more adequately. Hence, it earnestly entreats all who . . .
preside over the work of education to see that youth is never de-
prived of this sacred right* (Declaration on Christian Education, *par.
1).*

Personal Investment and Objective Norms

To be able to embrace values by personal choice necessitates an ability to
differentiate in our experiencing the meaning and importance of the various values
proposed to us and the ability to own them as our own, such that we act them
out from personal conviction. This does not mean the abandonment of teaching
specific moral injunctions nor does it demand that each person formulate the
corpus of moral teaching for himself from the beginning. Such would be both
impossible and unhealthy. The idea of personal conviction places a barrier against
seeking to impose value conclusions on the basis of authority which pressures
people into living values simply out of fear of others, the need to be accepted,
the fear of responsibility, or any other motive which might result in outward conformity in terms of behavior without the inward commitment of some personal
conviction as to the importance of such values. The Vatican Council strongly
underscores this when it proposes that:

*Authentic freedom is an exceptional sign of the divine image within
man. For God has willed that man be left "in the hand of his own
counsel" (Sir 15:40) so that he can seek his Creator spontaneously,
and come freely to utter and blissful perfection through loyalty to
him. Hence man's dignity demands that he act according to a knowing
and free choice. Such a choice is personally motivated and promoted
from within. It does not result from blind internal impulse nor from
mere external pressure* (Gaudium et Spes, *par. 17).*

Personal Conscience and the Prudential Process

Although this may sound new and revolutionary, in fact it rests upon a solid
if somewhat neglected dimension of Catholic tradition, especially around the virtue

of prudence as it was formulated by St. Thomas Aquinas. Commenting on Bult-
mann's moral theology, Christopher Keisling O.P., highlights this neglect. He writes:

> It [Bultmann's theology] does serve to focus attention on a critical facet
> of the ethics of Aristotle and the moral theology of St. Thomas Aquinas:
> the indispensable activity of prudence in the moral act. By prudence
> man decides and orders himself to act now, in this situation, in this
> way, in order to incarnate in concrete action the will of God for these
> circumstances. Catholic moral theologians have generally paid little
> attention to prudence and its acts of counsel, judgment and com-
> mand. Failing to do this, they have failed to focus sufficient attention
> on and bring to awareness in others, the role of personal responsi-
> bility in Christian existence. . . . Without a developed doctrine of
> prudence, responsibility is shifted from the individual to law and leg-
> islators. By their very nature, these cannot determine concrete acts
> apt for every particular situation (Theological Studies, 30(2), June 1969,
> pp. 236–237).

Benedict Ashley suggests how this got lost;

> In the second phase, from the founding of the universities at the end
> of the twelfth century to the Reformation, the scholastic doctors de-
> veloped a systematic Christian ethics as an integral part of a total sys-
> tematic theology. . . . Both models stressed the perfecting of human
> nature ("character") by the cardinal virtues of temperance, fortitude,
> justice and prudence elevated by grace through the specifically Chris-
> tian virtues of faith, hope and charity, with charity as the unifying prin-
> ciple. In this scholastic theology the themes of wisdom and of the
> New Adam or the Image of God still predominated, and we may well
> speak of this as a sapiential Christian ethic. At the end of the Middle
> Ages, however, especially through the influence of the great doctors,
> Duns Scotus and William of Ockam, a radical shift began from this
> sapiential model to a voluntaristic one in which the stress was no longer
> on Christian character but on obedience to the sovereign will of God
> expressed in the biblical commandments. The causes of this shift are
> complex, but it can be seen as a reflection of the rapid social changes
> produced by urbanization and the formation of strong national states.
> People lost faith in the possibility of achieving order in social and per-
> sonal life through a wisdom achieved by reasonable discourse and
> placed their hope in inculcating obedience to legitimate, indisputable
> authority (Moral Theology Today: Certitudes and Doubts. St. Louis:
> The Pope John XXIII Center, 1984, pp. 47–48).

It is, then, to this lost tradition of the prudential process that we are now
returning. If we are to help develop a personal conscience in people, we need
to develop the virtue of prudence, with its other attendant cardinal virtues of
temperance, fortitude, and justice. It is the way in which we move out of mere
subjectivity in moral and spiritual matters toward greater objectivity. It parallels
in the moral sphere the process we outlined as necessary in the psychological
sphere.

The Role of Prudence

For St. Thomas the virtue of prudence is that virtue or capacity to decide wisely what one should or should not do in the unique circumstances of one's life. As such it is the art of right living and the pathway toward moral and spiritual maturity. This is quite a different view of prudence than that which was commonly taught until recently. This view had never entirely been lost but had become somewhat distorted by the objectivist framework that had come to predominate our thinking; it came to mean simply being cautious and taking the safe, i.e., the socially approved way. In other words it lost its note of personal decision making and was subordinated to the virtue of obedience to those who were expert in moral science. Thomas Gilbey, commenting on St. Thomas's treatment, shows how different the proper function of prudence is. He describes it thus:

> *Consequently the morality of a human action in the concrete, which is the proper interest of prudence, cannot be comprehensively defined by common and general rules of law, or even by delicate refinements of them. Indeed prudence may often be engaged where there is no operative and relevant law. Not that prudence is antinomian, but simply that its precise concern as such is not to be resolved into keeping a law, though often, or even usually, this in fact may be involved. Its function is to put right reason into human deeds by translating our deliberations and choices which otherwise would remain arrested at an internal or immanent attitude in the* order of intention *into effective practice in the* order of execution *(Blackfriars, 1974, p. 174; Summa Theologica, vol. 36 (2a 2ae, 47–56), Appendix 1, "Prudence and Laws, p. 176).*

Reliance simply on the teaching of moral doctrine, the grammar of right and wrong, so to speak, was one of the major effects of living in a cultural milieu formed and molded by a Cartesian-Kantian outlook. Looking at reality from the outside as a realm of fixed objectivity, it first of all promoted an exaggerated view of the possibility of conceptualizing that reality and discovering the universal laws that governed its operation; then, under the influence of Kant, it created an exaggerated equation between clear abstract knowledge and operational competency which can be summed up in the phrase: when you know clearly and precisely what you should do then you should be able to do it. It is merely a matter of the clarity of intellectual knowledge and the application of willpower, with the intellectually clear understanding being discovered through the sciences and the willpower being activated from within by simple decision. This tended to encourage the individual to place the major authority, as to what to do, in the hands of others, considered expert either by virtue or status or knowledge.

The older medieval position, on the other hand, accorded far more freedom and respect to the individual to discern, judge, and decide for himself what needed to be done because it seemed not to have had such an exaggerated view of our ability to clearly conceptualize reality and its dynamics; it saw the study of being as much more a study of the way in which the subject operates. Writing of the early Scholastics, Malcolm Clark notes:

Living before the rise of science, they did not regard it as evident that to be is to appear as an object. Hence all talk of being was taken as belonging, not to a study of what is common to objects of observation, but rather to an inquiry into what it means to be as a subject (The Need to Question. Englewood Cliffs, NJ: Prentice-Hall, 1973, p. 98).

The earlier Scholastics had, then, it seems, a greater appreciation of the role of the living embodied subject in the formulation of knowledge and, hence, a greater awareness of the limits of conceptual knowledge to encompass the unique particularities of human existence. The study of moral being then could incorporate a much greater emphasis on the development of the moral character than could the later emphasis on simple obedience to moral laws.

One cannot rule out here, either, the simple historical circumstance that on the whole the ancient and medieval world lacked the exaggerated view of the power of law itself to mold virtuous subjects. There was no system of law enforcement which could keep in place that sort of social influence. They did not look then to law as such to bring about virtuous citizenry: They had to rely much more heavily on the education of moral character. Whatever the reason for this, the development of moral character occurred prior to the development of a simple law-abiding mentality.

This does not mean that in themselves the sciences, especially the moral sciences, are unimportant, but rather that they are not the only or even the dominant factors in the attainment of virtue. Curran describes the relationship between them in this way:

Moral science, as science, still says what is to be done in an abstract and general sense. But prudence determines what is to be done by the individual person himself in all the extremely complex concrete circumstances and conditions that are involved in even one completed action. The moral virtues are the resources he calls upon within himself to bring sufficient order within his many conflicting urges, so that he can carry out what moral science in general, and his own prudence in this particular case, determine he should do. Confusing moral science with prudence and moral virtue can perhaps cause a person to overlook the highly difficult process that is still necessary even after we have clearly determined in principle what should be done (Counseling in Catholic Life and Education, p. 433).

Distinction: Best as Ideal, Best as Real

There is an important distinction here between the best as ideal and the best as real. The two are not always synonymous. In forming our understanding of ideals we necessarily have to abstract from our historical and cultural and personal particularity. Through the formulation of ideals as to what is best, we try to discern what is ultimately and generally desirable for everyone based on an analysis of a common human nature. Such formulations are necessary in order to give us the *long view,* so to speak, the ultimate directions in which we can and should move. But growth and development can only take place in the here and now particularity of experiencing. The best as real, therefore, concerns what is actually possible for me here and now. The one abstracts from historical, psychological, and cultural limitations and the other acknowledges and works within these limitations.

These two realms are not necessarily opposed but are in a sort of dialectical tension with one another. The prudential process is where we work with this dialectic tension. Although decisions made at this level will take into consideration the discerned wisdom of the community as to what is ideally best, they will not necessarily be bound by it in their formulation of what is best in these particular real situations; and, although thoroughly objective, the decisions arrived at here will not necessarily be generally applicable to everyone.

The Prudential Process

The importance of the prudential process lies in the fact that it seeks to delineate those operational capacities that enable a person to act in a personally effective and rational way within the particularities of his unique experiencing in order to realize his fulfillment. It has three main parts: COUNSEL, DECISION, and COMMAND. We need to consider each in turn.

1. Counsel is the act of surveying all the relevant aspects of the situation that we are in. It is the willingness to step back from our immediate experiencing and seek to get as objective a view of it as possible, both internally and externally. It involves looking back to the past to see how we came to this point, the experiencing and factors that have formed us to be the way we are. It seeks to pay close attention to the elements of our present experiencing, especially the feelings and emotional components of our inner life, in which our present meanings and values are enshrined and make themselves known. It looks to the future to see what our actual goals are and what the consequences of our actions and way of being might be. The ability to take counsel with ourselves is itself a virtue, a capacity that has to be developed through action. It grows in its effectiveness to the degree that the person becomes secure within his own reality and unafraid of what might be found and/or of what the process might eventually require of him.

2. The process of *taking counsel* merges into the second stage, that of judgment or evaluation, assessing and deciding about the meanings and values discerned, and, where necessary reorganizing, changing, or abandoning some, modifying and strengthening others. This depends radically on the ability to trust ourselves, and our own capacity to be reasonable and come to our own decisions, to take responsibility for our meanings and values. It grows in proportion to our experience of success in acting in satisfying and productive ways. This evaluative process is not simply an intellectual exercise; it is the discernment of meanings in which we wish to be actually invested. It is decision then around what one's real values are and how to actually put them into operation in this particular situation.

3. Decision, therefore, is intrinsically linked with the final part of the prudential process, that of command, the actual putting of ourselves into the act of doing. This is not the simple Kantian notion of willpower, a forcing of oneself to an obedience to law but more an allowing of our intrinsic desire for what we discern to be good to become operative in our lives. Hence, Jacques Maritain writes:

*There are objective norms of mortality, there are duties and rules, because the measure of reason is the formal constitutive element of human morality. However, I neither apply them nor apply them well, unless they are embodied in the ends which actually attract my desire, and in the actual movement of my will . . . in order that a man follow them, at the moment of temptation they must not merely resound in his head as mere universal rules which suffice to condemn him though not to set him in motion; but he must recognize in them . . . an urgent demand of his most highly individuated, most personal desire, for the ends upon which he has made his life depend (*Existence and the Existent. *New York: Image Books, 1956, p. 61).*

This view of command as against the Kantian notion rests on the fundamental view of man as actually oriented toward being *reasonable* in his deepest desires. At a lesser level it presumes that one who is willing to engage in the prudential process is to some extent consciously invested in seeking the highest good. St. Thomas would consider an essential ingredient in sin to be an unwillingness to engage in this process. Although the prudential process may not in any specific instance result in conformity with a particular provision of a specific moral code, nevertheless, it is ultimately oriented toward the realization of the best psychological, moral, and spiritual ends. It will move toward the realization of goals which are of individual and universal value. Maritain, for instance, points to the saints who in many instances have seemed to act radically against what in the common view might be considered *morally* correct. He writes:

The saints always amaze us. Their virtues are freer than those of a merely virtuous man. Now and again, in circumstances outwardly alike, they act quite differently from the way in which a merely virtuous man acts. They are indulgent where he would be severe, severe where he would be indulgent. . . . What does that signify? They have their own kind of mean, their own kind of standards. But they are valid only for each one of them (ibid., pp. 63-64).

In them the very highest universal goals are united with an intimate presence to the particularities of the present situation, producing actions which escape conformity to the abstractions of law.

The prudential process, then, is aimed at enabling the individual to understand and integrate his various desires around his intrinsic dynamism toward his ultimate fulfillment and to operationalize himself within his own unique situation toward the achievement of his reasonable goals. These goals are of two basic varieties: easy goals and difficult goals and for each there is a corresponding virtue that needs to be developed. With regards to easy goals there is the virtue of TEMPERANCE, and for difficult goals the virtue of FORTITUDE.

Easy goals are those for which we already possess an operational competence and which produce immediate satisfaction. Some of these we are simply born with, they are written into our animal natures, developed to ensure the survival and maintenance of our physical being. They are the tendencies toward pleasurable things, eating, drinking, relaxing, reproducing; others develop out of our idiosyncratic capabilities, music, or some other innate talent. The virtue of temperance does not seek to annihilate any of these but enables us to integrate them into an overall plan of life through helping us to see them in their proper perspective. It enables us to resist simply being locked into them and using them as a refuge, a retreat from having to tackle difficult areas or projects.

Psychologically, C. A. Curran relates this virtue to the Freudian defense mechanism of compensation, in which easy goals are substituted for difficult ones. The presence of easy goals readily realizable is the basis for this mechanism. When faced with a difficult situation which we do not want to face, we can often take refuge in something which is easy for us and seek our total fulfillment through that. He would see alcoholism and drug addiction as such compensatory mechanisms. Indeed, it is probably this which lies behind what is called the addictive mentality as such. It narrows down our search for fulfillment to an identification with and immersion in that which is easy for us. Eating, for instance, might be a substitute for self-acceptance and nurturance, or masturbation a substitute for sexual relationships. Our culture generally tends to play on this in its attempt to make happiness something that is easily obtainable without a great deal of personal effort. Indeed, the less effort required to achieve satisfaction, the better. It is, for instance, a great deal easier to take a pill in order to get to sleep than look at the sort of lifestyle or personal anxieties that need to be dealt with in order to sleep easily. The main purpose of temperance then, as Curran says, is

> . . . to restrain this urge towards the easy goal, to keep us from seeking more from any easy goal than it can actually give (Inst. of Spir., p. 60).

Fortitude, on the other hand, is the ability to tackle necessary goals which are intrinsically difficult for us because in some way or other they threaten us with loss. Here we are faced with barriers which have to be overcome if we are to realize what we discern as reasonable goals. Whereas temperance regulates goals to which we are operationally determined by our evolutionary, cultural, or personal past, fortitude looks to future goals toward which we must yet direct ourselves in order to achieve fulfillment. Fortitude is the way in which we combat the compensation mechanism and hold ourselves to the realization of difficult tasks. Following Thomas, Curran relates this virtue to the overcoming of the fear of death. He writes:

> This virtue primarily concerns the fears of death and secondarily all fears concerned with these barrier goals and our urge to recoil from those difficulties. . . . St. Thomas points out what modern psychology has more recently come to, namely that all our fears, even our fear of any particular failure or difficulty, are ultimately related in some way to the fear of death or annihilation (ibid., p. 58).

Fortitude more generally then is related to the fear of entering into the unknown in which we are uncertain of our ability to control the outcome for our benefit; it might result in a loss of being. Hence it concerns also the fear of failure, failure which in some way is catastrophic. This tendency can color what in themselves are inconsequential goals, goals which might legitimately entail the possibility of a certain failure but not in any way a loss of being. Two attendant virtues connected with fortitude are patience and encouragement. The first accepts the fact that success may take time and effort, the second holds up to us previous success or the evident possibility of success.

Justice, the third cardinal virtue, is the capacity to give others what is due them as human beings of equal status and dignity. Temperance and fortitude relate to the individual in his dynamism to achieve goals which are for his individual benefit, while justice relates to those which concern others too. It is the ability to recognize the limitations imposed upon us by our communal nature as that which meets us in another individual or as it manifests itself in the community as a whole. To be just is to be able to recognize the reality of the other and actively respect and further her basic rights. Just what these might be constitutes in large measure the body of moral doctrine developed by the Church.

There are, then, three major virtues or operational capacities which are essential to growth into integration and wholeness: temperance, fortitude, and justice. These three are linked together operationally by the fourth, the virtue of prudence with its three stages of counsel, decision, and command. Through the operation of the prudential process, a person is able to achieve that articulation of who she is and the contours of her personal world such that she is able to gain a clearer grasp of it, and integrate herself around values which she has rationally discerned to be more adequate to the realization of her fulfillment — values which, in her heart, she really wishes to realize.

7 The Pastoral Relationship: The Environment
Guidance and Counseling in Pastoral Ministry

Promoting Personal Responsibility for Moral Decisions

In itself the virtue of prudence cannot be taught; it is acquired only through experience in which one acts out of one's own sense of what is right here and now. It is, however, developmentally dependent upon an environment where one knows that one's personal decisions and actions are respected and supported, even though not necessarily agreed with. As we have seen, this has not always been the case in Catholic life and practice due to the *objectivist* framework out of which we operated. If we accept the general conclusions stemming from the work of Piaget and Kolburg on moral development, we have tended to try to fix people at a rather childish level of obedience to rules. However, now, with the acceptance that the higher level of moral living demands personal assessment and appropriation, we are being called to reorient our thinking and practice.

We are not successful as ministers of the gospel simply if people conform to certain behavioral norms but only if, through the environment and relationships we form, they are personally able to come to an understanding and acceptance of themselves so that they are able to act out an inward conviction that the values they adopt are the best ways to relate to themselves and the world. We are essentially servants to our people in their personal articulation and appropriation of the requirements of the gospel message for their lives. The task for pastoral ministry now is to create the sort of environment in which people are enabled to come to a personal, experientially based understanding and appropriation of moral convictions. It is this personal appropriation that counseling, as we have defined it, addresses, and hence is the reason why it should be paramount over simple guidance or advice giving in pastoral work. Curran sums this up when he says:

> Giving advice has great limitations, therefore, because it does not of itself take the place of counsel and prudence. While we have experiences in common with others who share in general the same life vocation, activities and occupation, there is a point at which the singular events of our life are unique. No one has experienced them before and no one will experience them again. These individuating aspects of each of us are the things that make us distinct, separate persons. At the same time, we have a common humanity and we live in a common material world. Principles and laws we usually learn from others. These make up the valuable deposit of natural and supernatural knowledge which mankind has received and achieved through the ages. . . . But, in the day-to-day experience of the flux of events as we meet them, our judgments must be our own. We alone undergo

that singular experience and we, better than anyone else, if we think clearly, know all the factors which induce our own particular judgement. . . . No one can do this for us. Like the virtues of courage and moderation that go with it and are founded on it, prudence is acquired only by action (Counseling in Catholic Life and Education. New York: Macmillan, 1964, pp. 28–29).

In our pastoral practice then we need to be sure that we are not relating to the individual in such a way as to hinder the emergence and action of personal prudence. Hoffman makes this explicit when he says:

The training of conscience, the aim of which is the fully developed conscience functioning in terms of autonomy (independence), intensity (depth, immediacy, vitality of experience), and extent of moral knowledge at one's command, is only partly the result of moral instruction and incomparably more the result of the encouragement of genuine activity of conscience implemented throughout the entire field of personal experience. Its aim is the fullest possible exercise of conscientious decision, and therefore the opportunity of adopting a personal point of view must not be taken away ("Conscience," Sacramentum Mundi. *London: Burns and Oates, 1975, p. 284).*

Intrinsic to this environment is the freedom to raise questions about what is currently proposed as objective meaning and value. By raising questions we do not mean the negative *putting into question* that can simply be a stubborn refusal to entertain seriously views other than one's own, but the sort of questing which is indispensable to exploration and personal integration. Such questions come from and carry forward that questing for the fullness of being which is constitutive of our reality as human beings and leads to health, both psychologically and morally. Michael Novak puts it this way:

*Elementary health and morality . . . are measured by a person's achievement in raising questions about the myths into which he was born, weighing them, sifting them, until the myths by which he lives have been chosen by himself (*The Experience of Nothingness, *p. 87).*

Distinction: Pastoral Care and Pastoral Counseling

Lest this all sounds too individualistic, it is perhaps necessary to point out that we are here dealing with the individual counseling relationship, not with the overall pastoral care of the community. The community still has the obligation to reflect upon the Gospel and formulate objective guidelines as to its central values and behavioral expressions, and as ministers we need to work to create structures whereby people are able to learn what these are and so share and benefit from one another's faith.

But even here these value conclusions need to be presented in a way that enables personal appropriation. This essentially entails the offering of *wisdom* in which the intrinsic value is shown forth in such a way that it will appeal to the intrinsic subjective desire for what is good rather than being imposed with authority and demanded under some sort of implicit penalty. This is likely to either simply arouse and strengthen the inner resistance to subordination that is inherent in individuality or produce external conformity.

The Obligation to Seek Guidance

However, there is also a corresponding obligation on the individual in his or her prudential process to take advantage of the community wisdom concerning moral matters so as to be able to make the best informed decisions, especially concerning those areas which relate to the good of the community as a whole. We are never simply autonomous individuals but always *individuals-in-community,* and the community as such can never be indifferent to our personal moral decisions. In one way or another and to varying degrees our personal decisions as to what is good or bad do affect one another. The community itself, then, has a stake in what individuals discern as right and wrong and, as a community, it has the obligation to reflect upon the generalities of human behavior to discern their overall acceptability. As individuals we have the obligation to reflect on what we do in the light of its conclusions. This is an intrinsic necessity on the part of the individual for achieving that authentic objectivity which is obedience to the will of God.

In our personal counseling of others, we are concerned to create the environment that will enable them to do this. Counseling is not aimed simply at the development of a subjective point of view, but at a subjective assessment and appropriation that is able to take into account the *wisdom* of the community around important issues. In our emphasis on creating an environment which fully accords the individual freedom to arrive at personal conclusions, we are implicitly assuming an inner orientation to realize the best they are capable of which will lead them to an openness to that wisdom.

Tensions Involved in Pastoral Counseling

Commonality of Meanings and Values

We can, in fact, rely on this goodwill. In spite of the fact that we cannot simply assume an identity of meaning structures and values in all who come to a priest, minister, or parish worker, generally there is more likelihood that they will share a basic common framework of meaning and values than would be the case in the secular sphere. If people know that their own values are severely at odds with those of the minister, it is unlikely that they will come to him or her for counseling when they are wrestling with some moral dilemma. When people come to a minister or priest for consultation over some moral issue, it is usually because they are confused about it in some way: They may sincerely believe in the moral principles espoused by the community but be very troubled as to how to live them out in their own lives; they need assistance in deciding how to relate the teaching to their concrete situation. The issue, as such, is not ordinarily simply a matter of needing information, but one of how to put into practice the knowledge they already have, or a confusion as to how to apply it in their situations. Such a situation might be over the use of contraception, or the necessity for sterilization to safeguard either a marriage or the life of the wife, or it might be over a particular business situation, or political, or social dilemma. They are wrestling with the tension between the ideal as best and the ideal as real.

Possibility of Disagreement and the Pull to Advice Giving

However, whenever a person engages in the prudential process, there is always the possibility that the person will come to a conclusion that clashes with the priest's or minister's own assessment of what would be right. This is intrinsic to the process of personal appropriation. The pastor who is wedded to an advice-giving model might at this point be tempted to use his moral authority to ensure that his perspective prevails. To have a counselee come to moral conclusions which are at variance with the moral conclusions of the pastor, and which the pastor wants others to know that he stands for, can be very threatening. The pastor runs the risk of being interpreted as agreeing with or approving of the client's decision. This is a vulnerable position to be in and is undoubtedly one of the major pressures on a pastor to see the counseling situation as mainly one of giving advice or moral exhortation, especially when dealing with people who have been brought to him by others, or whose behavioral decisions will affect others, so that others have a vested interest in seeing a particular outcome for which they may hold the pastor responsible. Advice giving, persuasion, moral exhortation, or direct pressure is then an understandable attempt to safeguard one's own reputation as the guardian of particular community values.

Consequences for Moral Maturity

Such a strategy can in fact, at least in the short term, be successful, but it comes with a price, as Gendlin points out:

> Value conclusions can be adopted without the experiential process leading to them, but [will be] accompanied by feelings of confusion, denial, conflict, and surrender of certain areas of enterprise. Such adoption usually makes it less likely that the individual will ever obtain the experimental process leading to these values (The Goals of Counseling. p. 197).

Even where the values themselves are good, they remain the prudential judgment of the one giving them. As such the person's own growth in prudence has been blocked. Furthermore, to rely on advice giving is to run the risk of deepening the alienation that might already exist in the person between her *inner* real self, the one that stands open before God in her personal responsibility for living the requirements of truth and love, and the outer *social* self which seeks the acceptance and approval of others. As such advice giving can hinder the development of personal psychological, moral, and spiritual maturity.

Responsibilities Involved in Advice Giving

Depending on the level of sophistication and independence of the person concerned, it might in fact be fairly easy to pressure a person, especially one who is confused and uncertain and maybe fearful of the responsibility facing him or her, or of what others, particularly the minister, might think of them, to adopt a particular line of action which would satisfy the moral consciousness of the counselor. But, simply on a practical and emotional level, it is salutary to remember that it is the client who has to live with the ultimate decision, not the one who is giving the advice. If advice givers do decide to pressure the person in one direction or other, then they ought to be prepared to help her carry out that decision and to live with the consequences. Simply to pressure her into a particular line of action and then distance themselves from the results would evidence a real lack of responsibility and care for that person.

In recent years the churches have been challenged on this, particularly over the matter of abortion. It has become clear that, if they were going to strongly advise against abortion or even bring pressure on a member not to have an abortion, and in moments of crises and panic such action might be deemed prudentially necessary, then they should also be committed to helping the person both through the pregnancy and beyond, especially when the person was a minor or had been sexually abused or was living in difficult family circumstances. Such a line of action has, of course, gone beyond a counseling situation, even understood as advice giving. There may indeed be circumstances in which such action would be necessary, particularly if the life of the person or of others seems to be immediately at stake. Just when the minister has to shift from a counseling situation and take a stand for or against a particular decision is a prudential decision on the part of the minister. It is usually applicable when dealing with a minor or when the person shows definite evidence of being incapable of rational decision making. The details of this, however, are outside the range of our discussion here.

Locus of Accountability

However, this sort of situation does constitute a real moral and theological dilemma for the pastor. It is one, however, which is common to all who accept the burden of counseling others. It is sometimes posed in the form of the question: *Whose agent are you?* Are you, *vis-a-vis* this person, the agent of the community or are you the agent of the person? If the former, then one's thrust will be to get the client to conform to the behavioral norms which the community has formulated as desirable; if the latter, then one serves the individual in discovering what he or she thinks is desirable. Some systems of counseling, as we have seen, especially those employed by social agencies, see their work as aimed at the former and would generally favor behavior modification techniques. Others would definitely see themselves as the agent of the client, and these would favor the more humanistic, self-actualization perspective.

The priest or minister shares in this dilemma in an acute way. In a real sense the pastor is the agent of the community in its promotion of the values and behaviors which the community has discerned as the valid interpretation of the gospel message, and, as a purely social entity, the church has always demanded that its ministers *stand for* those values and behaviors. The pressure to be the agent of the community *vis-a-vis* the client, then, can be very strong. It has in the past been seen as the main work of the minister and in a somewhat crude and unreflecting way the Church has often simply engaged in behavior modification through the use of fear and guilt. How to combine these two roles, however, is the dilemma.

Theological Guidelines for a Resolution of the Tensions

Justification by Works or by Faith?

Of central importance here is the pastoral theology out of which the pastor operates, in particular whether or not he sees his task of mediating to the individual an experience of justification by faith or of justification by works. Although, as formulated, this is primarily a theological question, it seems that in fact it is a crucial question in all attempts to promote human growth. It is one of those critical elements of the Christian story that supports and promotes that process of personal self-transcendence that we have referred to as intrinsic to human growth. In its theological form it relates to the grounds on which we are found acceptable to God; in its psychological form, it relates to the grounds on which we are acceptable both to ourselves and to others. It wrestles with the tension between who we are at the moment and the ideals proposed to us either out of our own personal discernment or by the community as to how we ought to be; in psychological language, the relationship between our actual self and our ideal self. It is concerned, then, with the grounds on which we can achieve integration: integration between the human race and God; integration between the individual and society; and integration within the individual in the dynamic movement to realize the fullness of our humanity.

The relevance of justification to pastoral care, therefore, centers around the question of "on what grounds is a person acceptable to the community of faith?" Is it on the basis of not violating the law as articulated by the community at that time, or is it on the basis of a sincere questing to realize one's personal best, even when that results in actions which differ from the community norm or when one consistently fails to realize it or is incapable of living it in some way or other? Is our relationship as ministers to those who come to us based upon the former or the latter?

Justification by Works

Justification by works essentially means that we can, through our own efforts, through doing certain things, achieve that integration between God, others, and self. The *right* things are usually specified in a body of law: The ideal is made specific and understandable in behavioral terms, and acceptability is determined by how well we realize these behavioral dimensions. If the balance is positive, then we feel we merit acceptance; if negative, then we expect rejection. The ultimate responsibility is ours. In Scripture this mode of achieving acceptability characterized the Pharisees, and they have become the paradigm for this perspective in Christian tradition. Luke describes them thus:

> And here is another parable that he told. It was aimed at those who were sure of their own goodness and looked down on everyone else (Lk. 18:9).

What follows is the parable about the Pharisee and the publican. Although the picture given of the Pharisees in the gospel is undoubtedly colored and overdrawn by later Christian experience, nevertheless, the seeds of such a portrait would seem to have been contained in their theological tradition. Alan Richardson writes:

> In rabbinic Judaism a man was dikaios (counted righteous) if his merits outweighed his transgressions; if he tried hard, he could eke out his barely adequate merits by drawing on the superfluity of merits piled up by Abraham, Isaac and Jacob and other heroes of Israel (An Introduction to the Theology of the New Testament. London: SCM Press, 1958, p. 81).

He was able to draw on the merits of the great Saints because the primary work of justification was membership in the community of Israel achieved through acceptance of the *yoke of the law* and circumcision. As a member of Israel a person was automatically justified by God. By justification here is meant being judged as righteous. John Robinson explains it thus:

> It refers to the corresponding right-standing or faithfulness to the demands of the covenant-relationship from the other side. It is the status or position of one who can stand before God in this relationship, who can face God on his own terms. Such a man is righteous before God. Of course in order to stand before the holy God on his terms, certain moral conditions are implicit. Yet righteousness *does not primarily designate the ethical standard but the religious standing, the status of being right with their God. It is not so much goodness as God-acceptedness* (Wrestling with Romans. Philadelphia: Westminster Press, 1979, p. 40).

Robinson goes on to explain the Judaic understanding of how man achieved this:

> . . . his (God's) justification must have respect to ethical realities. And conviction is expressed by saying that a man is justified by observing the law. For it is thus that a man fulfills the demands of the convenant relationship and acquires a righteousness *corresponding with them* (ibid., p. 41).

The Core Meaning of Justification by Works

Although primarily formulated within the context of certain important theological disputes, as a fundamental principle of acceptability, justification by works of the law can be seen as operating wherever the grounds for acceptance are delineated by certain behavioral norms which we feel obliged to realize, whether these be moral norms or simply social mores and customs. As such, the idea of justification by works is one manifestation of a tendency which runs throughout human social life. We are constantly sending messages to people that they are acceptable only if they mirror the ideals that have been formulated and proposed by the community, if they conform to what we have called the communal objectivity. These criteria have to be spelled out in behavioral terms, since it is only external behavior that can be seen and judged. These complexes of behavioral expressions of the ideal then take on the force of law. To be acceptable means to portray in our lives these behavioral patterns.

The Church is no exception to this dynamic. Practically speaking, in a rather negative fashion, it has operated out of a justification–by–law perspective: that our ultimate salvation depends upon the avoidance of certain behaviors. To attain heaven, there was a certain minimum acceptable moral behavior. On a more mundane level it was also extended to social mores, and, like the rest of society, in our community life we formulated various images of the acceptable or righteous person on the basis of which we determined acceptability or nonacceptability. Hence, we have various images of the *good* Catholic, the *good* religious, the *good* priest, etc. Not to exemplify these ideals was to court rejection or social disapproval.

Behind this lay what has for centuries been the predominant model of the Church, that of a city. Seeing the Church as a city caused us to emphasize primarily behavioral obedience to authority. In terms of city life what is of primary concern is correct behavior. As members of a city we are not so much concerned with the inner life of a person as with what he or she does, and the main concern of authority is that of regulating behavior through the clear delineation and proclamation of law and its enforcement.

This is, at root, a form of *objectivism*. It shares with the objectivist approach a primary concern with behavior. It seeks to delineate the right or correct behavior which will produce the desired results. As with the objectivist approach, the essential weakness of the justification-by-works modality is that it judges the inner person by his external actions. It tries to read off the internal state of the person from external behavior. It is not primarily concerned with the meaning of that behavior within the perceptual field of meaning and values of the individual.

It is not that this is wrong in itself. There are many realms of life where a person can be judged as acceptable only in terms of behavior. These are the areas where particular behaviors are essential to the person's position in that particular group, especially where the group is task-oriented, as in the workplace. This kind of judgment becomes inappropriate and iniquitous when it is extended to encompass the person in her core reality, such that in her essential being she is judged as acceptable or unacceptable on the basis of certain external behaviors. It fails to recognize that behavior in and of itself is ambivalent. Its meaning derives from the internal perceptual world of the person and this cannot be gauged simply from the outside. The meaning of behavior can be known only through the self-disclosure of the person who engages in it. Recognition of this fact lies behind the Church dictum that one can hate the behavior but should love the sinner, a dictum that stems from a central and much insisted upon aspect of the message of Jesus himself: the injunction not to pass judgment on the moral standing of another before God.

Justification by Faith

Jesus' central concern was the salvation of the person in his essential being. In his message and actions he therefore espoused an attitude of justification by faith and made this paramount over justification by the works of the law. Justification by faith reaches beyond external behavior to the person simply as a human being. Although St. Paul was the first and undoubtedly the greatest theologian to wrestle with the relationship between these two dynamics of law and faith, he was simply developing the central teaching of Jesus himself. To quote Richardson again:

> The Pauline doctrine of justification is simply a way of expressing the truth which Jesus himself had taught, that salvation is the result, not of our own meritorious works, but of the outgoing righteousness of God, which brings salvation to sinners who could not have attained it for themselves (op. cit., p. 233).

The parables of the prodigal son (Lk 15:15) and of the pharisee and the tax collector (Lk 18:9–14) illustrate this clearly. The core of the revelation of Jesus as to the nature of the Father and his relationship to us is precisely that we are acceptable to him through our faith and trust in his love for us, not through our ability to keep the law. The law is undoubtedly necessary and Jesus himself had great respect for it; it embodies the community's best understanding of what the will of God is in terms of social and personal behavior, but it is not the ultimate basis on which a person can be deemed as acceptable either to God, others, or self.

St. Paul came to see the law as essentially belonging to the level of immaturity when we needed education and discipline. But, as he rightly says, it cannot itself motivate us to grow and develop into mature human beings. As Paul saw it,

> The age of world history from Adam to Moses was the age of innocence, the infancy of the human race. Then, as the divine education of mankind continued, the Torah was given through Moses at Sinai. Law was a stage on the road to salvation, but it could not itself confer salvation. It taught God's people in what righteousness consisted, but it contained no power that enabled man to attain it (Richardson, op. cit., p. 234).

On the contrary, its main thrust is to reveal to us our inadequacies and the fact that we are *sinners*. Of itself this can lock us into a sort of death posture in which we feel increasingly dispirited and less able to make the effort needed to change. Our self-condemnation, our sense of alienation from God, others, and ourselves is deepened. St. Paul himself knew this experience and in his desperation cried out: "Who can rescue me from this body of death?" (Rom 7:24). His answer was Jesus Christ. Through him we come to understand that the exact keeping of the law is not the basis on which we are acceptable to God but rather our acceptability is based on our willingness to live and trust in his love for us: salvation is an act of grace. St. John sums up the whole process of redemption thus:

> . . . for while the Law was given through Moses, grace and truth came through Jesus Christ (Jn 1:17).

Our faith, then, is the ground which makes possible the appropriation of this unmerited justification offered us by God. Commentators are at pains to emphasize that this faith is not another work, but something evoked in us by God himself through the event of the death and resurrection of Jesus. In this event God has revealed to us his faithfulness to his promises; he has proved to us that his love for us is true and enduring in that he was prepared to suffer and die for us while we were yet sinners.

To perceive the event of Jesus' death and resurrection in this way is to have our faith and trust evoked and to enter into life. During his life Jesus sought to make this faith possible through the signs of this ministry: his way of life, eating and drinking with sinners, his cures of those bound up in sickness by sin, his preaching, and his fundamental attitude to all. Some allowed the meaning of these acts to penetrate their lives and change their inner attitudes and hence their behavioral responses to life; others fought to prevent this and distorted the meaning of their experience in order not to be changed.

Justification by Faith and the Moral Quest

Justification by faith is indispensable in the search for moral and spiritual maturity. This necessitates the introduction into our pastoral practice something that we as Catholics are not overtly familiar with though, in fact, it has permeated many of our practices, especially that of the sacrament of Penance. Ashley writes:

> This teaching of Paul was, of course, accepted by the Catholic Church from the beginning, but as the Reformers were to point out, its implications have not always been fully implemented. Even among the Fathers of the Church St. Augustine had to battle to have it recognized, and the earlier scholastics did not always appreciate it. In reaction to the Reformers, the post-Tridentine moralists, while strictly adhering to its dogmatic truth, seldom allowed it to shape their moral treaties. In the light of Vatican II we should be able to surmount these inhibitions and fully recover the Pauline and patristic awarenesses that the supreme principle of Christian morality is not the Law, not any law, even the great commandment of love of God and neighbor (Mk 12:28–34), but faith in Jesus Christ, who thus himself is that supreme principle, the New Law itself (op. cit., pp. 50–51).

Penance and Justification by Faith

This has always been present at least in its core meaning in the sacrament of Penance in which one could always receive forgiveness for one's sins, no matter how many or how grave, upon recognition of their sinfulness and the desire, not the ability, to leave them behind. True reception of the sacrament, in fact, depended radically upon one's faith in the love of God for us and the capacity to receive that love in the form of forgiveness. This alone and not the ability to actually not commit the same sins again, formed the basis for one's acceptance by and reconciliation with the community and with God.

However, our experience of forgiveness and reconciliation tended to be confined to this situation and that in a rather hidden unarticulated way, since the practice itself took place in an *objectivist* framework in which the individual simply detailed his violations of the objective, behavioral expectations espoused by the community and submitted himself to the assessment and judgement of the confessor.

The Effects of Justification by Faith

In the practice of this sacrament, therefore, we need to make overt its intrinsic basis in the justification-by-faith mode of salvation and out of our practice of it there, extend it to all personal pastoral counseling. However, one of the inhibitions that might continue to prevent us from really incorporating it into our pastoral practice is the fear that it might lead to moral license. Given an *objectivist* environment such as we have described, such a danger is a real one. True appreciation of the inner core of the Sacrament of Penance does depend on a change in the way we view personal decision making in morality and educate our people toward it.

However, in itself, to know that we are acceptable to God apart from the exact keeping of the law is not, as Paul himself was charged with advocating, to be given permission to indulge in moral license but to be freed to quest and search for the best that we are capable of; it makes possible the better keeping of the Law since we need fear no longer that the failures and inadequacies and mistakes which are inevitable in such a search will stand against us and alienate us from God in any ultimate way. It is to know and rejoice that God is with us in our questing for the best. It increases human freedom and the actualization of our personal potential for self-direction and responsibility. It makes possible that radical self-acceptance which is the foundation of our continued growth into the realization of the reign of God over us and our lives. It is this environment as a whole that we need to create. Out of that will come a better understanding of the nature of the Sacrament of Penance and the counseling that might take place within it.

This acceptance, however, not being based on our accomplishments, cannot be earned but only given and received as a gift. On the part of the giver it is an act of grace. On the part of the receiver it is appropriated by trust and confidence in the love of the other for us. It therefore opens us up to community with ourselves, with one another and with God.

Justification by faith, then, is intrinsically necessary to the creation of that environment which enables us to achieve integration on all levels, with God, others, and ourselves because it enables us to accept ourselves in our full humanity with all its inadequacies and failures. Justification by works makes our inadequacies and failures a threat to our very fulfillment and hence leads to a rejection of those unacceptable areas and we tend to hide them both from ourselves and others.

The Necessity for Moral Guidance

As such justification by faith does not annihilate the need to formulate the best behavioral components of the ideal. The formulation of behavioral principles and ideals will alway be an indispensable part of the Church's service to mankind. Without them we would be at a severe disadvantage in trying to delineate the necessary steps to achieve human fulfillment. As St. Paul pointed out, behavioral principles and ideals do have an important educative and restraining influence on us. They call us to serious reflection on how we live, to that objective search for those meaning structures and values which will actualize our being, and they offer us tried and tested ways of acting which can help us realize our fulfillment. If we do decide to act differently, we need to have good reasons for doing so. The danger is in absolutizing them and making obedience to them the only virtue. This is to subordinate the individual again to abstractions, in this case moral abstractions, and to vitiate the possiblity of the person being present to, evaluating, and articulating his own experiencing, without which he cannot attain to any real maturity.

Justification by Faith and the Prudential Process

In our pastoral ministry we need to be committed to the justification-by-faith mode of relating in order to create an environment which aids the person in engaging in the prudential process. As we have said, in itself the virtue of prudence cannot be taught; it is acquired only through experience in which one acts out of one's own sense of what is right here and now. It can, however, be immeasurably aided by an environment within which one knows that one's personal decision and action are respected and supported, even though not necessarily agreed with. The development of the virtue of prudence can only take place in an environment in which the person, through the counselor, experiences a justification by faith such that he really begins to appropriate the fact that God is with him in his wrestling and respects and supports his personal responsibility to come to his own assessments of what he can and ought to do without fear that this will result in rejection.

Experiencing it through the counselor, the client can gradually begin mediating it to herself and begin to overcome the self-rejection that might lie within herself at her failures to meet the ideal. It opens the person up to what is there in her inner and outer situation and enables the person to grow in that indispensable self-acceptance without which she cannot truly *take counsel with the self.*

Justification and Advice Giving

It is easy for a minister to manipulate the client to adopt his solutions or perspectives through a subtle threat of moral or social rejection. Creating guilt in another is a time-honored method of inducing conformity. To engage in this sort of dynamic is to be operating out of a justification-by-law model. Advice giving can be one such mode of manipulation. Strongly given, it can in the mind of the client have the force of an imperative without the form of it. *What will the pastor think of me if I don't do as he suggested?* is the question the client will inevitably go away with. To mediate a justification by faith, then, takes a positive commitment. It must be something the pastor himself deeply believes in. The skills of counseling are the potent means whereby such justification can be mediated.

8 Pastoral Relationship: The Dynamics
The Tension Between Guidance and Counseling
Bases of Acceptance in the Community

As pastoral ministers given this understanding of the gospel message, it is our responsibility to mediate the experience of being justified by faith and trust so that the person who comes to us knows and realizes that acceptance and community with God and the Church is not based simply on obedience to those behavioral prescriptions which the minister and the community advocates as ideal, but on the fact that they are human beings wrestling with the human situation with all its attendant risks of mistakes, inadequacies, and failures. They should be able to experience that they are respected for their humanity as it is with all its powers and capacities as well as its limitations and inadequacies.

This does not mean agreement with them in whatever solutions they come up with, nor does it obviate challenging them and offering differing perspectives or relevant information drawn from community tradition or personal conviction. Such may all be necessary, and the conditions for the most effective offering of such information will be looked at later, but it does entail on the part of the minister, not only a deep respect for persons in their struggle but also a positive willingness to work with them in such a way as to maximize their capacity to freely formulate and act upon their personal assessment and evaluation. Only in this way can a person grow and develop beyond the childish fear of authority and obedience to other's rules and prescriptions and grow to the maturity of adulthood in which she is capable of deciding for herself and taking personal responsibility for her life.

This is of paramount importance if the freedom that the individual has today to decide for himself what his values are and how he should live is to be used to the fullest advantage both for his own good and the good of the community. In our present world, Teichtweier considers this to be essential. He writes:

> A moral code which appeals to the human conscience, and trusts a man to make responsible decisions for himself, is not following an extreme ethics of individual situations, but is in accordance with the biblical and traditional testimony to the dignity and significance of the conscience. The appeal to individual conscience sets up an absolutely indispensable bulwark against modern mass processing, ruled by slogans and prefabricated solutions. Of course after a brief period of morality maintained chiefly by rules imposed from without, much genuine effort and great patience will be needed in order to lead members of the congregation to the true liberty of the children of God (The Crisis of Change, Allen, TX: Argus, 1969, pp. 85–86).

Implicit in this is the suggestion that if the churches had spent more time in developing people who were capable of taking personal responsibility for their decision making and in providing them with the environment in which they could safely do this, there would not be the present susceptibility to the influence of *cults* and *religious demogogues*. These groups depend heavily upon people who lack the inner ability to formulate their own personal meanings and values and hence are vulnerable to stronger personalities with a superficially coherent message and the ability to provide psychic and social security. And there is evidence to suggest that Catholics in particular are vulnerable to such people.

Standing for Ideals; *Understanding* Persons: a Tension

The priest or minister is in fact in a unique position to mediate the experience of the gospel justification by faith with all its growth producing effects in a person's life, precisely because he is established in the community as the one most identified with the proclamation of the ideal. He stands for the ideal in a way that no one else does. It is his ordained duty to proclaim and promote the value system that the community has identified as being of God. The question that now arises is the relationship between that dimension of his position and his work as a counselor.

Some ministers might in fact see their role as being mainly one of standing for the community norms and underrate their work with individuals in the depth of their inner life. This they would want to leave to specialists. While it is true that each has to find a level of comfort in dealing with individuals and not go beyond what he feels competent in doing, nevertheless to deny that he is called to minister to the individual as such in his process of sanctification would be to go against a longstanding tradition of priesthood in the Church which charges the minister with the *cure of souls*. Oden has pointed out that this is a literal translation of the Greek *psychotherapy* (see *Kerygma and Counseling*. New York: Harper & Row, 1978, p. 146).

In Catholic tradition the primary structure in which this is carried out is in the Sacrament of Reconciliation; this is intrinsic to priestly duties and not something optional. Work, then, with individuals in the depths of their personal striving for wholeness through community with God and the Church is a major dimension of the Catholic ministry of priesthood. It is precisely in this context, as well as in their work with individuals in wider contexts of counseling that justification by faith is most clearly mediated.

In the counseling relationship, whether it be in the confessional setting or simply in general consultation, we are not, as we have seen, the agent of the community *vis-a-vis* the client but the agent of the client *vis-a-vis* his wrestling with the call of God to him in his situation. (Of course, in a more fundamental sense this is also to be an agent of the community in its role as reconcilor.) Although there may be legitimate occasions in a primarily counseling situation where information may be necessary and desirable, it seems Oden is quite correct in advocating that in this area the overt standing for the community norms should remain in the background. It properly belongs to those community activities which directly involve preaching and education. He writes:

> Our stronger intuition, however, is to advise against frequent proclamatory intrusions in counseling. For our temptation is very much more to become moralizers, judgers, and answer-givers, introjecting our viewpoint and imposing it on troubled persons, often ineffectually, rather than allowing them to discover the freedom to discover the covenant at the center of their own personal existence through dwelling in the presence of a person who mediates the reality of God's

acceptance relationally rather than verbally (Oden. Kerygma and
Counseling, *pp. 30–31).*

Given what we have said above about the place of advice giving in counseling, such information would best be left until the primary counseling relationship has been established and the person's own prudential process has gained
strength.

Resolution of the Tension: Jesus as Model

But there is undoubtedly a tension here that is not always easy to live with.
On occasions it will take a great deal of courage to walk the line between standing
for the community values and being a servant to others in their prudential struggle
to relate those values to their lives or discover that particular complex of values
that they need to live by in the unique circumstances of their lives. However, it
seems clear that it was a line that Jesus himself had to walk in his ministry. While
standing for the highest ideals of the kingdom, he yet laid himself open to the
charge of being a *friend of sinners.* It might be said that walking that line is what
finally led to his crucifixion. It enabled the Pharisees, who have always exemplified
the justification-by-law syndrome, to be clear in their own mind that this man
could not be of God. As one of them said:

> *If this man were a prophet, he would know who is touching him and
> what kind of woman she is — that she is a sinner (Lk 7:39).*

In response to the charge he asked: "Who can convict me of sin?" In him
the two polarities were united: a total identity with the values of the kingdom
together with the ability to meet the sinner on his or her own level in a totally
accepting and understanding way. There seems to be no alternative way to dealing
with this tension other than an internal integration in the pastor between the
values he is personally and publicly identified with and the willingness to meet
the *sinner* where he or she is, with understanding and compassion, though not
necessarily with agreement. If others choose to misinterpret that, as the Pharisees
did with Jesus, then, like him, it is something that simply must be accepted as part
of one's vocation.

Incarnation-Redemption: The Pattern of Salvation

The Servanthood of God

However, it is precisely against the background of standing for the ideals
of the community that, in his meeting with and respect for the other where they
are, he is most able to mediate and live the image of the God of Jesus Christ,
who redeems us not by standing over against us as a demanding, critical lawgiver
and judge whom we can never satisfy but who has incarnated himself in our
world, dwelling among us, participating in our life and its uncertainties and confusions, living the human struggle and bringing it to fulfillment in the resurrection
so that through union with him we can be raised up to share eternally in his life.
This is most clearly expressed in the Epistle to the Hebrews:

> *The children of a family share the same flesh and blood; and so too
> he shared ours, so that through death he might break the power of
> him who had death at his command, that is the devil; and might lib-
> erate those who, through fear of death had all their lifetime been in*

servitude [2:14-15]. . . . And therefore he had to be made like these brothers of his in every way, so that he might be merciful and faithful as their high priest before God. . . . For he himself had passed through the test of suffering, he is able to help those who are meeting their test now [2:17-18] . . . [therefore] ours is not a high priest unable to sympathize with our weaknesses, but one who, because of his likeness to us, has been tested in every way, only without sin (4:15).

Jesus, then, is the paradigm for all priesthood or ministry.

For every high priest is taken from among men and appointed their representative before God, to offer sacrifices for sins. He is able to bear patiently with the ignorant and erring, since he too is beset by weakness; and because of this he is bound to make sin-offerings for himself no less than for the people (5:1-4).

On this model the minister, while standing for the ideal, needs to be able to come down and live his participation in the humanity of those he is serving. This means becoming incarnate in one's historically conditioned subjectivity with all the limitations that that involves. Especially in his dealings with people in their human weakness, he needs to be able to own and accept his own.

The God-Project and the Ministerial Position

This is by no means easy, especially for those in the community endowed with moral authority. Their very position calls for a public identification with the communal *objectivity* as that is formulated in its abstract conceptualizations and ideals and concretized into certain behavioral forms. This can lead in various ways to a certain denial of the limitations inherent in one's subjectivity; one either gives the status quo an absolute and transcendent status and hides behind it, or abrogates to oneself a like transcendent status. Both exclude from consciousness the limitations in thinking and knowing inherent in human historicity and individuality and the moral inadequacies that are intrinsic to embodied, developmentally conditioned humanity. The one identifies God's voice and will with that of the community, deifying it and sharing in its transcendence through identification of the self with the institution; the other identifies that voice and will with the self, deifying the self and, by extension, those who are identified with him. The one is familiar to us as the exemplar of communal respectability and righteousness; the other as the charismatic figure who gathers around him followers and disciples.

This is one manifestation of what Satre referred to as the God-project in which the tension between subjectivity and objectivity can be resolved. Its resolution here is located in the human person, not as being God in and of himself, but as being the authoritative spokesman for the transcendent Being. It is in fact located in the human person but is rationalized by referring it primarily to the transcendent Being; it is appropriated through identification in some way with that Being.

However, the notion of God that generally speaking we have inherited from our Greek philosophic heritage is primarily characterized by the notion of transcendence, possessing the totality of absolute knowledge, power, and value. This is essentially a non-Christian notion of God as one who is intrinsically beyond and unaffected by human history. Although such a philosophical view of God derived from Greek philosophy has in fact been very influential in Christian thinking for many centuries, and obviously has its value, it is at odds with the biblical, particularly the New Testament, understanding of God as one who is radically involved with and concerned about the human person in his historical journey, and who, through the Incarnation, has chosen to both participate in and be affected by that history.

Its roots, however, lie deeper than simply rational philosophy; it is a notion that lies deep in the human psyche. Its origins seem to be linked with the primitive narcissism of the child with its originating experience of being whole and entire, omnipotent in its ability to manipulate its environment to satisfy its simple needs for physical satisfaction, security, and order. In the first place the child experiences itself as having a Godlike centrality and power; later as it becomes more aware of its vulnerability and dependency on another, it deifies its parents and beyond them the adult world, retaining its own deification through identification with them. The progress toward maturity is, in large part, a coming to terms with one's God-project both by being able to distinguish ourselves from it and by being able to locate it beyond ourselves. In biblical terms it is continual movement out of the tendency toward idolatry to the worship of the true God.

Ministry: The Sacrament of God's Salvific Activity

The danger inherent in institutional religious authority, precisely because it is expected in some way to stand for and speak for God in the community, is to seek to appropriate God to oneself through identification. Ownership of the inherent subjectivity of human nature with the limitations which that involves, therefore, can be especially difficult for religious authority figures. However, the call of the gospel is precisely to this acknowledgement and acceptance if we are to image the God of Jesus Christ, who was willing to leave behind the glory of transcendence to participate in the historical struggle of humanity toward its unique fulfillment. The biblical image of God, while not excluding the notion of transcendence and absoluteness, has radically modified this notion, and with it the notions of power and absoluteness that it brings. The biblical story has revealed God as one who out of love has voluntarily shared his power with man and made the accomplishment of his purposes dependent on dialogue and cooperation. This risk bore fruit, and his purposes for man were realized totally and completely in and through the process of incarnation in which, in the man Jesus, God was able to bring about the perfect response and thus realize human fulfillment and redemption. Only insofar, then, as they are able to do likewise can the ministers of the gospel be truly understanding of and redemptive to others. Insofar as they give way to the tendency to confuse their abstractions with reality and their ideals-as-best with the ideals-as-real, and seek power over others, they remain unable to appreciate and work with the meanings contained in the unique particularities of human life and unable to help others discern for themselves what is really possible there. Insofar as ministers opt for authority, they become increasingly irrelevant, and indeed harmful to people in their growth and development toward the realization of their subjective personhood. To avoid this, their model must be the form of ministry adopted by God himself as we understand this through the experience of Christ: a personal participation in the human drama.

The Word Made Flesh

The early tradition of the Church, embodied in the apostolic *Kerygma* (see Acts 3:13f, 4:10f, 5:30f) tended to concentrate the redemptive activity of God into the death and resurrection of Jesus. By the time of the Johannine writings, however, this redemptive activity had been extended to incorporate the whole process of Jesus' life, including its historical antecedents back to the moment of creation. "The Word became flesh and dwelt among us," is, for John, the heart of the Gospel message and he saw this as the divine way of healing or redeeming mankind.

Oden has called on Christian counselors to see their work in the light of an *analogia fide* in which, out of our faith in the ultimate saving work of God as portrayed in the whole life of Christ, we model our own saving and healing work. Whether or not the *analogia fide,* following Barth, is quite as simple as Oden makes out, nevertheless, our faith does call us to examine our own work as healers of the human psyche in the light of what we see as the ultimate saving method of God, revealed in the total event of Jesus Christ. This reflection will show that the Christian *story* does indeed back up the process of subjective self-transcendence that we have outlined as intrinsic to human growth and development.

The Incarnative-Redemptive Approach to Counseling

The most profound and detailed work on this in recent years has been done by Charles A. Curran, who was largely responsible for introducing counseling to Roman Catholic circles. He explicitly called his approach an *Incarnative-Redemptive* approach to counseling. He writes:

> Incarnation and redemption can be viewed not only in a religious sense but also as a description of a psychological relationship and process. This is demonstrated in counseling and psychotherapy, and one can pattern educative relationships from his model (Religious Values in Counseling and Psychotherapy. *New York: Sheed and Ward, 1969, p. 175).*

Recently, the same theme has been taken up independently by David Benner but from a different angle (see "The Incarnation as a Metaphor for Psychotherapy." (Journal of Psychology and Theology, 11(4), 1983:287–294).

The central process that embodies and recapitulates the incarnative way of redemption, for Curran, was precisely that central skill of counseling that we have referred to as understanding, in which the counselor enters into the client's inner world, as this is made known to him through the client's communication, and articulates for the client what is revealed in it. Through his symbolization of it, he is able to help the client objectify himself and so gain a deeper understanding of himself and what it is he needs and is capable of doing. The counselor thus serves the client's own prudential process and growth into maturity. We need to look now at how, on the individual level, this recapitulates the process of redemption on the universal level which was realized by God in Jesus Christ.

Jesus Christ as the *Word:* The Realization of Human Being

In Jesus Christ, the writer of the Gospel of John discerned the ultimate perfection of human reality, the embodied actualization of the ultimate meaning of human life, the Word which articulates who we are as human beings. C. H. Dodd explains:

> Throughout the gospel Christ is spoken of as Son of Man, which as I have shown is best understood as the virtual equivalent of anthropos alethinos, the real or essential man, or the Idea of Man (The Interpretation of the Fourth Gospel. London: Cambridge University Press, 1980, p. 279).

As the real and essential man he embodies completely and has actualized fully the purpose of God in creation and in this is the revelation of what that purpose is, and hence of who God is and how he regards his creation and what he wishes for it. As embodying and revealing the purpose of God in creation fully Jesus is *Logos* the *Word* of God. Dodd describes its core meaning as:

> the rational principle in the universe, its meaning, plan or purpose, conceived as a divine hypostasis in which the eternal god is revealed and active (ibid., p. 280).

For John it is the same *word* which came through the prophets of old and, even farther back, the *word* through whom creation was brought forth. He was the Wisdom which was with God before the world was and through whom creation was made. The *word* in Scripture is that which brings order out of chaos. In Genesis God spoke and the chaos was ordered. It is a word of meaning, that which renders something intelligible, an effective word. It is not just a bare concept but that which effectively evokes a result, accomplishes God's purpose of bringing life (Is 60:10-11). It is a meaningful word, one which is intelligible to man, which renders his experience meaningful. The *word of the Lord* which came to the prophets was that which rendered intelligible the people's historical experience. Indeed this is its primary usage, as Dodd goes on to say:

> The idea that God similarly addresses a word to what we call inanimate things, and by means of such a word He called the ordered universe out of primeval chaos, is a refinement upon the idea of the word that came to men through the prophets, to bring order and justice into human affairs under the rule of Torah (ibid., p. 264).

As the word of God, Jesus of Nazareth is the way God himself, out of deep and faithful love, acts definitively among us to bring order out of the chaos, rendering human life intelligible and effectively bringing it to the realization of its full and intended perfection, the capacity, in communion with the Father, to enjoy the fully personal life of God himself. In thus linking ultimate meaning with the person of Jesus, and identifying the fullness of life with personal community with God, John takes salvation out of the realm of simple reflection of a conceptual pattern and locates it firmly and fundamentally in a relationship characterized by faith and love. He raised it beyond the keeping of the law, which is the conceptualization of moral realities, with which the word of God had been identified in Judaism, to the entering into of a relationship of personal communion. In the "Word" the paradox of subjectivity and objectivity is resolved, not in a conceptual way, but in the existential living reality of a human/divine person.

Ultimate salvation, therefore, is realized only through a personal relationship with God based on faith and love and realized through interpersonal communication: This is made possible through an incarnative process in which the perfect person of God acts out of love to enter into the embodied, historically conditioned, chaotic life of man and through involvement and dialogue with him speaks a word that renders that life intelligible and makes possible the actualization of its potential. In John, all the words and acts of Jesus are part of this fundamental process, but the giving of himself over to death is the ultimate act of love and the Resurrection, the final *word* which reveals human life's ultimate meaning and potential and guarantees its ultimate *realization* through the return of Jesus to full communion with the Father.

Jesus Christ, through his active involvement with his world, enters deeply and fully into its historical process and speaks the *words* which reveal its meaning, bringing human life out of the isolation of meaninglessness. The disciples, those who receive *the Word* and the *words* he utters are brought into intimate communion with Jesus and the Father and are to recapitulate this process with one another and so mediate life to one another. I have used the word *entering in* here. Raymond Brown would query this. He writes:

> *The Prologue does not say that the Word entered into flesh or abided in flesh but that the Word became flesh. Therefore, instead of supplying the liberation from the material world that the Greek mind yearned for, the Word of God was now inextricably bound to human history* (The Gospel according to St. John. *London: Chapman, 1966, p. 31).*

The word *become* is, of course, much stronger and does in fact add an important and indispensable element: the fact that one is intimately affected by the relationship, changed by it; one is informed by that to which one is related, while yet remaining the same person. In the Incarnation God is informed by humanity, affected by it, suffering from all its limitations, voluntarily participating in its becoming while yet remaining God, capable of bringing it to its full and complete integration and value.

The incarnative process is above all one in which, out of love, one is prepared to in some way become the other. It is a *knowing* of the other in the biblical sexual sense of that word, which is used by John, especially in the epistles. We become that which we know in that sense without, however, ceasing to be ourselves. In *The Word* God knows human reality, without ceasing thereby to be God. The *Word* knows the human world in which he lived, with all its negative and positive realities without thereby ceasing to be the *Word*. This incarnative process is also redemptive because in becoming the other and being informed by the other, God also draws the other into his own being which is the fullness and perfection of life, bringing humanity to a level of *realization* not otherwise possible. Through his relationship with his disciples, and all those with whom he came in contact, especially the outcast and sinner, Jesus lived the same process, entering into their lives and drawing them upward to participate in his own life.

Mediating Salvation: Recapitulation of the Pattern

The disciples are called to likewise recapitulate this process with one another; to *know* one another, become affectively involved with one another in the historical process of realizing their fulfillment; becoming one with one another in the way Jesus is one with them and with his Father and thereby becoming redemptive to one another. We find this descending pattern throughout John in which incarnation as the way of redemption is recapitulated at each level of reality. In John: 15:9,12. we read:

> "As the Father has loved me, so I have loved you. . . . This is my commandment: love one another, as I have loved you." so that "they may be one; as thou Father art in me, and I in thee, so also may they be one in us. . . . The glory which thou gavest me I have given to them that they may be one, as we are one; I in them and thou in me, may they be perfectly one" (Jn 17:21–23).

We find the same descending pattern though in a slightly different form in the great commandment, which is of course much earlier than John and seems to be unique to Jesus Himself:

> "Love the Lord thy God with your whole mind . . . and your neighbor as yourself" (Mk 12:28–34, Mt 22:34–40, Lk 10:25f).

This descending pattern is also an ascending process. Through loving one another in the way that Jesus has loved us we come to know God as incarnative and redemptive, not just cognitively but experientially. We learn about God and are informed by him in and through our relationships with one another. Indeed this is the only way we can come to know and be united with God.

> Dear friends, let us love one another, because love is from God. Everyone who loves is a child of God and knows God, but the unloving know nothing of God. . . . If he does not love the brother whom he has seen, it cannot be that he loves God whom he has not seen (1 Jn 4:7–8, 20).

The writer of the first epistle of John, meditating deeply on the meaning of the Resurrection, came to see that this process is redemptive only because the higher is willing to love first and reach down and incarnate or become the lower, thus validating, confirming, and affirming the value and dignity of the lower.

> The love I speak of is not our love for God, but the love he showed to us in sending his Son. . . . If God thus loved us, dear friends, we in turn are bound to love one another (1 Jn 4:10–12).

Implicit in this is the notion that the lower cannot redeem itself but needs the higher to reach down and be with it and establish a personal relationship with it. Mankind could not redeem itself, could not give itself ultimate meaning and value, but must await it in the act of personal love whereby God reaches down to establish a personal relationship.

The Necessity of a Personal Response to the Salvific Action

But this personal act is redemptive only in so far as it is met with faith which allows its validating power and intelligibility creating potential to work its transforming way into our lives. Brown describes Johannine faith thus:

> This pisteuien eis may be defined in terms of an active commitment to a person and, in particular to Jesus. It involves much more than trust in Jesus or confidence in him; it is an acceptance of Jesus and of what he claims to be and a dedication of one's life to Him (The Gospel of John, 1).

It involves, then, a commitment to the person of Jesus and to the relationship in real openness and trust and a willingness to be radically changed in one's inner perspectives on who we are as human beings and the nature of reality as a whole, and, consequently the value system that we adopt and the sort of actions that result from it. The radical change is called in Scripture "metanoia." In John it is the passing out of death into life, out of darkness into light.

He is saved, therefore, who is able to discern in Jesus the meaning of human existence and is actively able to entrust himself to the love of the one in whom it is revealed, and live out the meaning that he has discerned. The word is not just the sound but the meaning that the sound conveys; one receives the word when one recognizes its meaning, both the meaning of the word and the meaning of the one uttering it. Dodd writes:

> Thus logon akouein is not simply to receive with the sense of hearing a connected series of sounds, but to apprehend the meaning which those sounds convey. . . . Thus the Logos of Christ is the sum total of his spoken words regarded as containing his thought and meaning but his uttered words nonetheless. . . . It is clear that for the evangelist the uttered words of Christ, constituting his logos, his total message to the world, are in a specific sense a life-giving power, and the medium through which he gives himself to men (op. cit., p. 266).

The word apprehend here is important, it means not just a cognitive comprehension but an experiential realization of meaning. It has the connotation of recognizing the intelligibility of immediate experiencing, such that it is illuminated and brings about behavior change.

Redemption, therefore, takes place when – out of a love that seeks a personal relationship and an involvement that includes the possibility of being affected and changed – the words that are uttered in some way render our experience intelligible to us, bringing order into the chaos of our lives and making possible the appropriation of the convalidation as a person which the words convey. They effect a real change such that we are recreated.

> But to all who did receive him, to those who have yielded him their allegiance, he gave the right to become the children of God (Jn 1:12).

The Incarnative–Redemptive Pattern in Counseling

Such a relationship is the heart of the counseling process, as it is of any life-giving relationship. It is mediated in the relationship through the understanding responses which are the core of the counseling skills. For Curran it is this recapitulation on the level of actual human relationships of the pattern of God's relationship to mankind that forms the basis of what he calls correspondence, the fact that human relationships mirror and point beyond themselves to patterns of relationships both within the Trinity and between God and mankind. Curran sums this up in his meditation on the contribution that St. Augustine has made to our understanding of the relevance of the notion of the Trinity to human growth and development:

> There is a separation of persons, but they are so totally understanding of the otherness of each that they are one. There is a total fusion of the two (Father and Son) in love (the third, the Holy Spirit) and so we

speak of the triune God to capture their oneness. . . . This, of course, is consistent because as understanding proceeds between two persons they become more and more alike. We say that by deep understanding we get into another person's skin. If, then, we could understand perfectly, there would be a becoming — like that would be total, and yet we would also remain one and other as well. . . . This is our model of belonging. Augustine never strayed far from the scriptures; he helped us to understand in the scriptures the mystery of the triune God and the Second Person becoming incarnate. . . . This provided an incarnate-redemptive relationship and gave us the right to be considered sons and daughters of God, to be part of the magnificent image of the Godhead. The indwelling of the Holy Spirit gave us a special, unique kind of divine love that binds us more powerfully to God. One might say that the family of humanity is a notion now possible of realization in our time if we understand that the family of humanity is the shadow of the sunlight of the family of God ("The Rediscovery of Person in the Age of Science," Pastoral Psychology, 31 (4), Summer 1983: p. 254).

Oden has a similar position in that he sees the counseling relationship, whether secular or pastoral, as finding its ultimate justification in what God has done for mankind in Jesus. What all good therapy or counseling, whether secular or religious, does is live out this relationship, and it is precisely this which renders it healing (see *Kerygma and Counseling.* New York: Harper paperbacks). For Curran especially, though, the counseling relationship should incorporate all these same dimensions that are found in the theological concept of incarnation-redemption. On this paradigm the counselor loves first by actively committing himself to a real and deep relationship with the client, and through his attention and sensitivity incarnates himself in the cognitive and affective world of the client with all its inner chaos and disorder without thereby losing himself or being absorbed by it. Through that active commitment, out of love, to incarnation, he seeks to render the chaos of the person's affective, cognitive, and volitional world intelligible through understanding words, those which bring the bits and pieces of the person's communication into intelligible patterns thus bringing order into that chaos. Thus Curran writes:

Interwoven and mutually dependent are the understanding process itself — the dialogue — and the deepening relationship it produces — the commitment. Together, relationship and dialogue aim at greater self-understanding, orientation to more adequate goals and values and more complete operational integration and efficiency (op. cit., p. 199).

In doing so the counseling relationship also overcomes the sense of isolation and loneliness that is intrinsic to being a unique individual. In rendering the other's world intelligible, it brings the person back into community with others in the person of the counselor and, beyond him, to the possibility of realizing and internalizing what it means to be in community with God. In this it is *redemptive.* Andre Fossion puts it beautifully when he says:

The word brings into play what it signifies; subjects are born in the fabric of the countless relationships of intercommunication. Thus, on every verbal exchange that establishes, even obscurely, a relationship of mutual acknowledgment, the work of the resurrection leaves its mark: the triumph of life over death, of meaning over non-sense, of relationship over isolation. Every word that initiates a covenant stands in the salutary space between death and the resurrection. In every exchange it is the risen Christ who stands in-between and forges the ties of human alliances ("The Word of God and Human Speech," Lumen Vitae, *30 (4), 1977).*

Toward the client therefore the counselor is Logos, reaching down into his or her unique world, affirming the person in all her unique affective confusion, with its failures and limitations and its historical becoming as something of value and significance and rendering it intelligible through the words he speaks, bringing the person back into communion with himself and others. The effect of this, as Curran says, is that

*gradually — through reaching such core-concepts which fit the person's groping self-understanding — the person comes to see himself, others and his particular life situation more clearly. At this stage he or she seems to have more control over their whole person and so make better choices (*Understanding: Essential Ingredient in Human Belonging. East Dubuque, Ill.: Counseling-Learning Institute, 1978, p. 17).

In other words, the counseling relationship works to bring about the integration of the person: It affirms his uniqueness and value as an individual while at the same time bringing him into relationship with another; it acknowledges that there is chaos and limitation in that world and faces it squarely and nondefensively yet affirms the intelligibility of his world and encourages the capacity to understand it and bring it into more conscious harmony.

Benner adds another possible dimension to this as a healing process by suggesting that in thus incarnating himself in the client he recapitulates the redemptive work of Christ by offering himself as the locus whereby the person's negative dimensions are drawn out and absorbed by the counselor in the same way that Christ on the cross absorbed the evil of the world without thereby being destroyed by it completely. He explains:

He [Christ] did not solve our sin problem at arms length but took us into himself and purged our sin from us. Our sin taken upon him, was overcome by his grace (op. cit.).

This, on the model of Incarnation, is what the therapist does.

In more concrete terms this is seen when the therapist accepts the projections and transferences of the patient and bears them patiently. Sometimes the anger received in such encounters causes pain. However, out of a position of strength, the pain is absorbed without retaliation or defensiveness and eventually the patient stops projecting and can begin to own the projected material (ibid.).

This likewise is part of the healing process but only when, as Curran insists, such feelings and projections are cognitively understood, that is, given adequate verbal symbolization by the therapist such that the client can recognize it and own these feelings and projections.

Recapitulation of the Pattern within the Client

As also with the incarnate-redemptive process, this redemption and healing takes place only to the extent to which the client is able to commit herself to the relationship in faith, gradually perceiving the meaning of the therapist *vis-a-vis* herself in her limited, inadequate and confused condition and give herself over to the counseling relationship in faith and trust. And, out of this experience, the client is able to increasingly mediate it to herself, not standing over against herself in a disincarnate, demanding, or condemnatory way, fearful and resentful of her confusion and inadequacy but gradually with increasing love and respect incarnating herself in her own actual human historical condition with its inevitable limitations, weaknesses, and struggles, mediating to herself significance and understanding, recognizing and accepting, both her real inadequacies as well as her actual possibilities, working from within to modify the one and enhance the other to achieve a personal best as against an ideal best.

The Incarnative-Redemptive Process and Moral Dilemmas

Translated to the situation in which the client comes to us concerning moral dilemmas, precisely because the priest is identified by his function with the moral ideal, in his ministry to the individual he is able most closely to imitate the God who came to dwell among us while we were yet sinners. Through his fundamental love and respect for the person in his actual condition the priest counselor makes possible the gradual realization of the best of which the person is capable. Out of his inner sense that as an individual he too is a struggling *sinner* the priest dwells with the other in nonjudgmental acceptance and understanding.

Where people are able to experience this environment of acceptance and noncondemnation, especially from one who is most identified with the ideal, the hope is that they will also be progressively freed up and encouraged to explore their situation more openly and objectively and hence realize the requirements of the moral law more adequately. First, it mitigates the almost automatic response of self-assertion over against the demands of others which can lock a person into an inadequate position; second, it removes the fear of rejection that might come from formulating a position different from that of others or because of one's inability to live those community ideals one does hold and believe in; and, third, it in fact enables the person to be more open to understanding and appreciating the community's position on the relevant issues.

These community positions can be made known to the person, if that is necessary, through the counselor himself. In and through the counselor, then, is made possible that dialogue between the individual and the community which is essential to the ongoing process of becoming more objective. The wisdom of the community then becomes available to him in a way that strengthens his own prudential decision-making process. Instead of being a threat and a reproach to him, the ideals held by the community, and the Ideal that is God himself, become a valued resource in his quest for true fulfillment. God and the Church then cease to be tyrannical and oppressive forces which deny mature adulthood, but valued and sought-after guides on one's journey toward maturity. The true incarnate-redemptive relationship creates the conditions whereby the person can grow in the capacity to respond positively to the moral demands that face him, utilizing all the resources available to make the best decisions possible for his unique situation.

9 Trust and Distrust in Human Growth and Development

Human Nature: Trustworthy or Untrustworthy?

Trust and Clinical Evidence

Implicit in the approach we have been taking is the assumption that the human person is capable of being trusted and that the counselor must make a radical commitment to the person's own ability to come up with the best solutions for her difficulties. But, especially in terms of moral decision making, is this not too optimistic? Is it not rather naive to think that, if people are presented with the right environment of acceptance and affirmation, they will thereby choose solutions which are positive and morally sound? It was one of Carl Rogers' most central beliefs, derived from his wide clinical experience that, where clients experience this type of relationship and atmosphere, they can be trusted to move of their own accord to ways of thinking and acting that are both personally satisfying and morally positive. It does not issue in license (see *On Becoming a Person*. Boston: Houghton Mifflin, 1961, p. 184). In this, of course, he has been accused of being naively optimistic about human nature and of overestimating the capacity of the individual to choose well.

The charge does have some foundation in that it might be inappropriate to generalize from the sort of people who benefit from the client-centered approach to human nature in general. There is some evidence that the people who most benefit from the client-centered approach are those who are already in some way seeking to improve their lives, who already possess an implicit commitment to seeking something better for themselves, emotionally or spiritually. In other words, the people who really benefitted from Rogers' work were those who were already positively oriented toward improvement.

Reasons Not to Trust

However, even where we might be able to accept that people who, however weakly, are committed to personal realization of the best they are capable of, can be trusted to arrive at responsible decisions as to what is right and necessary to do in their situations, it is still not easy for us to act out of this belief. Our first tendency is to seek to control and direct. There are two fundamental reasons for this, one positive and the other negative. The positive reason is the belief that the community, out of its many centuries of reflection on human life and the Gospel, has gained a far sounder understanding of what is best than the individual can gain in a short lifetime. The community possesses, in other words, a more objective view, whereas the individual is more likely to be governed by short-term aims and narrower concerns. Out of this, ministers and pastoral counselors might genuinely feel that the individual is not essentially trustworthy, not because of bad will, or the lack of a genuine desire to improve but because of an inevitable shortness of vision as to what is truly good in the long run both for himself and others in the immediate situations and for the human community as a whole in the long term. Their work, then, as the experts in that tradition and public guardians of the communal good should actively seek to ensure that the individual in his decision making bring solutions into line with what is proposed by the community, and to do so for the good of the person involved.

The second reason is more negative and derives from the fact that much of our pastoral outlook in the past has been *sin-dominated;* that is, we have presumed that, because of the power of original sin, the human person is fundamentally untrustworthy and, if not controlled and directed from the outside, especially by those with the God-given social authority to do so, will automatically tend toward a life of aggressive selfishness. So deep is this belief that as counselors we will probably operate out of it quite unconsciously. Our whole cultural context is one which takes this perspective as axiomatic: It lies behind the desire to *figure out* the dynamics of human functioning, both psychologically and morally so as to be better able to control and direct it effectively. It permeates the belief that law and the threat of punishment is the one proven way in which the citizens can be controlled and order maintained for the common good. So much are we dominated by this attitude that at the present moment we are in real danger of becoming a law-bound society in a somewhat analogous way to what used to be called muscle-bound, — so constricted that it is impossible to respond adequately to the requirements of the moment. In medical and health-care facilities, for instance, there is a real danger of the breakdown of the system so surrounded by laws and regulations are they in the name of protecting the client. The need to conform to the letter of the law in many instances is making it impossible to give the real individual care that is actually necessary. The fundamental premise seems to be that those offering these services cannot be trusted and need to be controlled from the outside.

The Self-fulfilling Prophecy

There is undoubtedly much evidence that could be adduced to warrant this belief; human history does not give much indication that people are essentially trustworthy. However, the question at its root is not simply an empirical one. As I have emphasized previously, one of the most fundamental features of human nature that complicates the situation is that we ourselves create to a large extent the sort of world we live in and hence what will be found in it. The data that we find empirically in our world are in fact dependent largely on how we structure our world through our belief systems: We will find there what we expect to find. It is the ground of what is known as a self-fulfilling prophecy. A self-fulfilling prophecy might be defined as an evaluation of a situation which evokes particular behavior, which in turn enables the original prophecy to come true. Jack Gibbs has done much to elucidate this dynamic especially with regards to the effects of distrust in organizational management. He writes:

> We see how the cycle is set up: hostility and its inevitable counter-part, fear, are increased by the distrust, distortion, persuasion-reward and control systems of defensive managing. And the continuing cycle is reinforced at all stages, for as fear breeds distrust, distrust is rationalized and structured into theories which sanction distrustful managing practices. The practices reinforce distrust; now the theorist is justified, and latent motivation to continue the cycle is itself reinforced (Science and Human Affairs. Farson, ed., pp. 203-204).

Gibbs believes conversely that the only way in which we can bring about a world in which people are trustworthy is to make a radical commitment to the belief that they are so and organize our relationships and community structures accordingly. The results of this in his experience are startling. He writes:

*It is possible for people to create communities that have caring, inti-
macy and depth, that differ dramatically in these characteristics from
the institutions we encounter in our daily lives. Our fear/distrust assumptions allow us to see most communities as frightening and un-
changeable. When the trust levels change significantly and we make
new assumptions, the effects upon our community life are startling.
We can create ongoing communities that will significantly reduce the
alienation, unconnectedness, and superficiality of modern life* (Association of Humanistic Psychology Newsletter, *January 1980*).

Theological Considerations

Meanings of *The World* in the Gospels

This belief that it is possible to bring about a new world in which fear and
distrust are eliminated is central to the Christian gospel. First of all the notion that
the *world* is primarily a creation of man is reflected in the Gospel of John in the
way the writer uses the word *world:* the world is both what God created and
also what man has created by his attitudes and behavior, though usually he uses
it in the latter sense to refer to the world of sin and negativity that man creates.
Thus in the prologue we read:

*He was in the world, and though the world was made through Him,
the world did not recognize Him (Jn 1:10).*

Here both senses of the word *world* are used: The world as created by
God is good and to be loved, "God so loved the world that He sent his only-
begotten Son" (Jn 3:16). But the world is also that realm of sin and death brought
about through human rejection of the light. "If the world hates you, it hated me
first, as you well know" (Jn 15:18). The world so constituted is the realm of darkness, but with the advent of Jesus a new *world* has been created or brought
into being, a *world* characterized by *light* and *life.* In him the *world* as created is
brought to its fulfillment and mankind has the possibility of entering into that new
world and experiencing the fullness of life. For John, this was Jesus' central challenge to people: to enter into a way of being in which the fullness of life in community with God and one another was possible not just beyond death but here
and now. *Eternal life* for John was something experiencable here and now through
faith in Jesus.

This is essentially the same picture as is found in the Synoptics. There we
find Jesus challenging people to radically change their understanding of human
life and its possibilities, to look at themselves and their lives from a different perspective, one that would change the empirical data of the way they lived and
related to one another. He himself was the evidence that human beings could
be different and a new world, the kingdom of God, could be realized among
them: the change of heart that the prophets longed for which would make possible a different world was now realizable through the experience of Jesus in
whose human reality it was already being made manifest. He was Messiah precisely in this sense, that in him the reign of God was being fully realized and made
possible as an experiential reality through him. Through his different approach to
sinners, he himself lived this belief and hence began to bring it about. To those
who were willing to be touched and moved by him, he drew out new and more

positive potentialities, making possible an experience of a higher, more life-giving personal and communal life. He promised those who fully incorporated him that they would do new and more creatively life-producing things than he himself had done. After Pentecost and the in-spiriting that it brought, his promise was realized in a new and vivid way.

Creation of a New Humanity

The apostolic Church, especially in people like St. Paul, was dominated by the possibility of the creation of a new humanity, the creation of a different person and hence a different world under the influence of Jesus. Hence Paul writes:

> You were taught . . . to be made new in the attitude of your minds and to put on the new self, created to be like God in true righteousness and holiness (Eph 4:22).

Rudolf Schnackenburg, commenting on the vision of Paul, writes:

> The formation of a "new" man who regains and surpasses the glory in which he was created — a man "conformed to Christ" — is of course a process that will reach completion and achieve its manifest and perfect realization only when the Lord returns "who will change our lowly body to be like his glorious body" (Phil 3:21). But this new eschatological creation begins even in baptism, and expresses itself even in the Christian's life on earth, when he becomes Christ-like and shares in Christ's death in order to live with Christ. (Schnackenburg. Christian Existence in the New Testament. Notre Dame, Ind.: University of Notre Dame Press, 1966, p. 15).

Behind this, is the fundamental belief that this new creation is not simply an imposition on human nature, so to speak, but something intended as a human potentiality from the beginning, that Christ through his presence and work is bringing human nature to the fulfillment that it was created to enjoy. This is contained implicitly in the apostolic teaching that as human beings we were created in the image of Christ. He is the one we were created to be like and are positively oriented toward recognizing and resonating with him. In the famous passage from the Epistle to the Romans we find the clearest enunciation of this:

> Indeed the whole created world eagerly awaits the revelation of the sons of God. Creation was made subject to futility, not of its own accord but by Him who once subjected it, yet not without hope, because the world itself will be freed from its slavery to corruption and share in the glorious freedom of the children of God. Yes, we know that all creation groans and is in agony even until now. Not only that, but we ourselves, although we have the spirit as first-fruits, groan inwardly while we await the redemption of our bodies (Rom 8:18–23).

For Paul, that destiny for which the world was created has been brought to completion in the resurrection of Jesus. Robert Faricy comments:

> For Paul, as for John, all that exists comes from God, but all things come to be through Christ and remain in existence through Christ (1 Cor 8:6). The doctrine of the first three chapters of Ephesians is that God's whole creation-salvation plan has from the beginning been

centered on Christ. That plan is to bring everything together under Christ as head (Eph 1:10), for Christ is the ruler of everything and he fills the whole creation (1:23) ("Dimensions of Salvation," Theological Studies, *30(3), September 1969: p. 468).*

Essentially, in the Gospel of John we encounter the same basic thought. In the Prologue we read:

All that came to be was alive with His life, and that life was the light of men. That light shines on in the dark and the darkness has never mastered it. . . . He entered his own realm and his own would not receive him. But to all who did receive him . . . he gave the right to become children of God (Jn 1:4, 10–12).

and C. H. Dodd observes:

Thus it is quite consistent with his thought to interpret the tekna theou *of 1:12 in the sense that already before the coming of Christ there were in the world those in whom the divine Logos was present, and who therefore had the* right *to be children of God (op. cit., p. 282).*

It is this, he believes, that lies behind John's title of Jesus as the Son of Man. He brought to full realization what was present in human reality through creation. Other scholars, such as Raymond Brown, agree that, in John, there is the sense that Jesus, to use scholastic terminology, was the final or exemplary cause of creation. Although we do not find in the Scriptures the modern psychological belief that there is a positive inner developmental thrust or dynamic toward a condition of wholeness or self-realization, which if only it is given the right psychological environment will flower naturally, in John we come close to it in his exposition of sin which for him, fundamentally is one of unbelief. Because of Jesus' connaturality to humanity in its striving and growth the natural response to Jesus was one of recognition and faith. Unbelief had to be deliberately chosen. Essentially, we were created for the light; we have to choose the darkness.

The Trustworthiness of the Redeemed Christian

There is always the option to choose the darkness and so live in ways which contradict and distort our growth and so create a world in which we can find the distortions created by fear and distrust. This is the mystery of sin, and the world that we know is radically and inexorably infected by it. And the fact that we are born into a social environment which is so distorted by sin does mean that at a very fundamental level we are all infected by that environment such that there can never be any natural conditions which would render our progress toward that self-realization automatic. The pressure to sin and its psychological and environmental consequences are always there such that the values of the kingdom have to be actively and continually chosen, and their realization in our lives constantly struggled for. But the light remains and, where one lives in the presence of and in dialogue with God revealed to us in Jesus Christ, then the Gospel seems to be saying to us that we can have faith in that light both in ourselves and others to lead us to realize ways of thinking and acting that will be positive and fruitful. It is this, it seems, that Jesus himself appealed to in his own ministry and, following him, it is our faith in this God-given dynamic that we are called to respect in our dealings with those who seek counseling.

Trust and the Presence of the Spirit

This dimension of the gospel tradition is also deeply related to the presence of the Holy Spirit at work among and within us. Talking about the role of the Holy Spirit in the creation of human identity, Enda McDonald writes:

> In the more conventional distinction between objective standards of living and subjective efforts and achievements, Jesus and his life-style offer objective challenge and pattern, while the Spirit provides the subjective enlightenment and capacity to respond to challenge and attempt the pattern. It is the enlightenment and capacity provided by the Spirit which enables the disciple to find his own differentiated and creative way while recalling and remaining in solidarity with the historical achievement of Jesus and his pattern ("The Holy Spirit and Human Identity," The Irish Theological Quarterly, 49(1), 1982: pp. 45–46).

To trust in the redeemed Christian is, therefore, also to trust that in her innermost being the Spirit is at work guiding, teaching, and developing the person toward the realization of the pattern of Jesus in her life, in accordance with the unique circumstances and potentialities that are hers. This trust does, however, presuppose the indwelling of the Spirit, that through faith in Christ, the person has somehow been fundamentally changed and has really become a new creation. In St. John's terminology such an attitude assumes that one has through baptism passed over from being a child of the darkness into one who dwells in the Light. Of such a person John can say:

> A child of God does not commit sin, because the divine seed remains in him; he cannot be a sinner, because he is God's child (1 Jn 3:9).

This is a strong statement and one which must be taken seriously, but it needs to be balanced by the fact that John was clearly aware that the redeemed Christian does sin. He writes:

> My children, in writing thus to you my purpose is that you should not commit sin. But should anyone commit a sin, we have one to plead our cause with the Father, Jesus Christ and he is just (1 Jn 2:1).

What the apostolic church seems to be pointing to is that in the conversion process a fundamental change does take place in the person such that he is new while recognizing that the process of sanctification does take time and effort, with many failures along the way. The redeemed Christian then can be trusted because of this fundamental change in outlook and direction. Through his conversion he has laid hold of a core understanding of what constitutes true life out of which he can draw his understanding of how to relate the Gospel to his daily life. St. John points to this when he says:

> You, no less than they, are among the initiated; this is the gift of the Holy One, and by it you all have knowledge . . . the initiation which you have received from him stays with you; you need no other teacher, but learn all you need to know from this initiation, which is real and no illusion. As he taught you then dwell in him (1 Jn 2:20, 27).

This echoes the admonition of Jesus himself to his disciples to "call no man your teacher. You have one teacher, the Christ and you are all brothers."

The Essential Goodness of Humanity and Catholic Tradition

Despite the practical belief that, because of Original Sin, human nature is untrustworthy, theoretically the Church has never lost sight of this more basic tradition of the essential goodness of human nature and its orientation toward Light. We find in the Thomistic tradition that although this orientation has been weakened by sin it has not been lost. Original Sin weakened the human will to good but did not destroy it; it clouded the reason but did not annihilate it. Furthermore, the Thomistic tradition would maintain that even in choosing something evil the person would do so because it is seen as good. At his core the human being is essentially good and seeks to realize what is good in order to attain the fullness of being.

Psychological Tradition and Human Goodness
Positive and Negative Perspectives

Freud and the psychoanalytic tradition did much to deepen the suspicion of the intrinsic evil in the person, as did in some ways the Darwinian tradition that we are evolved from the lower animals and still retain *animal-like* tendencies. Freud firmly believed that the forces of the *id* were fundamentally selfish and needed social constraints and channeling. Today, however, psychology is recovering something of the more positive understanding of the essential goodness of human striving with the notion of self-actualization begun by such people as Goldstein and Maslow. They fostered the belief that there was in humanity a positive striving upward toward a higher state of being which, given the right environment, would reveal itself and demand realization. For Maslow, this was not a strong drive but one which, because of social environmental conditions which distorted and inhibited it, was somewhat weak and unclear. However, it is also stubborn, persisting in its demand for realization. Everett Shostrom has explicitly formulated an understanding of this process which is remarkably close to the perspective of the Thomistic tradition. He has written, for instance, that

> In a general sense, actualization may be defined as a sense of relatedness to the world based on genuine interdependence. Psychopathology may be described as limited or distorted attempts to actualize ("From Abnormality to Actualization," Psychotherapy, Theory, Research, and Practice, *10, Spring 1973: p. 39).*

In both humanistic psychology and Catholic tradition, there is general agreement that man in his essential being is good and is oriented toward the good. In all that he does he is seeking the realization of his essential being. The corollary to this is that if a person can gain an articulated and conscious presence to the actualities of his being, he is then in a positive position to take those steps that will more adequately realize it, and he is more likely to take them. Insofar as he is alienated from the essential contours of his being, inaccurately reading and articulating it, then he will be more likely to involve himself in self-defeating behaviors.

Both, too, would locate some of the reasons for man's failure to realize his own goodness and fulfillment in the environmental conditions, that self-defeating ways of being have become culturally institutionalized such that from birth they constitute a distorting environment. It is possible, then, from both perspectives to see psychopathology as resulting when the basic drive to actualize is distorted by ways of perceiving and behaving which are in contradiction to the essential nature of man. To be mentally sick then is to be living in ways which are self-contradictory, and the degree to which we are doing that will dictate the degree of pathology. The healthy person, on the other hand, is one whose perceptions and behavioral patterns are in harmony with that essential being such that these perceptions and patterns are the channels whereby he can continue to grow and develop in both inner and outer unity of life.

Maslow and others would maintain that the human person is trustworthy in her actual decision making to the extent that she is characterized by these inner attitudes. The more they characterize the inner life of the person the more trustworthy in their decision making they will be. The inner pressure from a person's being to realize these characteristics is there. Although Rogers in much that he says seems to think that, given the right conditions, the process of realizing these characteristics is somewhat automatic, like the growth of a flower planted in the right soil. Maslow himself who did most to establish the psychological notion of self-actualization came eventually to realize that progress to the B-level of living, as he calls it, was radically dependent upon a person's perception of the importance of harmonious patterns and commitment to actively choosing them in specific circumstances of life (see *Toward a Psychology of Being*. New York: Van Nostrand, 1968, p. 175).

The Human Person: Potentially Trustworthy

In this Maslow is much more in harmony with Catholic tradition which locates the origins of sin in the world, and also in the conscious choice of the human person who is able to refuse to live in harmony with the call to holiness. From neither perspective, then, can the human person be considered *de facto* trustworthy, despite an internal pressure to seek what is good, but only potentially trustworthy insofar as there is a core harmony with that internal pressure. In our pastoral practice, it is this potentiality that we seek to further. We cannot do that if in our actions we assume that untrustworthiness. To do that would be to be involved in a negative self-fulfilling prophecy. People tend to define themselves in terms of others' expectations of them. If we begin with an expectation that the other is untrustworthy, then we bring on a pressure for that person to actually *be* untrustworthy.

The same seems to be true on the social level, pointing to the fact that, despite the many evidences of abuse between persons, for a healthy society to develop the primary emphasis should always be on trust, with a minimum reliance on law. Rather than seeking to totally remove the possibility of abuse through law which is the present situation, society needs to be able to accept and live with its possibility and deal with it on a more *ad hoc* basis. There is obviously a risk here, but at a very basic level it is a risk that has to be taken. At some point or other we have to trust another human life. This would be totally impossible without trust. A fundamental stance for distrust is ultimately self-contradictory and self-destructive. Trust or distrust of oneself or others is a radical fundamental choice in human living and one which we are faced with in all human relationships. Which we choose will dictate the quality of potentialities that are evoked in life, qualities which enhance living or qualities which restrict living.

Elements of a Growth-producing Environment

Whether a person chooses well or ill, therefore, is dependent upon a fundamental choice for growth, and this is essentially outside the control of the counselor. But, beyond the necessity of personal choice, what is needed to actualize that potentiality is an environment and a relationship that will encourage the choice of those characteristics which lead to growth to be realized. There are two dimensions to this. The first is the encounter with one in whom those characteristics are exemplified, and, second, the experience of a relationship which actually develops those characteristics.

1. As we have said, being born into a world in which one is surrounded from birth with distorted perceptions and behaviors means inevitably to participate in that distortion and so be alienated from one's true being and fulfillment. One can move out of that environment, be saved from it and become more trustworthy only if one encounters someone whose ways of thinking and relating are in harmony with that essential nature. The ideal has to be in some way actually experienced; it has to be perceived as a human possibility. Through the work of Bandura of the behavior modification school we are more aware today of the psychological importance of modeling as a way of growth. It is not a new idea, of course; it is contained in the thought of Aristotle: that one learns what it means to act justly through seeing what a just man does, and the age-old importance accorded to the idea of giving good example. The human person becomes more and more trustworthy then to the extent that he encounters experientially and begins to internalize the qualities that characterize a self-actualizing person. This is a process that goes on in the deepest recess of the person's heart, and is to a large extent unpredictable and uncontrollable.

2. However, encountering such a one who relates to him out of the belief that he is at his core trustworthy and can become more and more so encourages this internalization and nurtures the growth of this inner potentiality, where it has been interiorly chosen. It was through the work of Carl Rogers that modern psychotherapy was made clearly aware of precisely what behaviors and attitudes actually develop and encourage this dynamic in relationships. At the heart of it is the mediating of what he calls an unconditional positive regard for the other which is revealed in and through a deep acceptance and understanding of the world of the other. This the therapist articulates to the person, activating and encouraging self-reflection and deeper self-understanding, acceptance and responsibility. It is based upon the fundamental attitudes of genuineness and respect which allow the other full autonomy to come to her own conclusions and decisions about what is the best way forward for her. His central point is that if we wish to develop people who are mature and self-directing, growing into their own individual powers and potentialities for inner and outer integration then, as counselors, we must relate to them in a way which both assumes that this is what they are capable of becoming and enables them to realize it. This, as we have seen, is reflected in the theological sphere by the doctrine of justification by faith.

The Gospel and the Actualizing Relationship

Salvation, then, is mediated to us first through the encounter with one who is self-actualizing. In the first place, this ought to be the counselor, and through him in the pastoral setting the client should be able to encounter the person of

Jesus himself. The pastoral counselor will be effective in helping people become more trustworthy in their moral decision making to the extent to which he is able to mediate to the client the qualities which characterize Jesus himself so that through the counselor the client encounters Jesus himself.

Second, salvation is mediated to us through the experience of a special quality of relationship. Although Rogers disclaimed any reliance on the Gospel, it has been long acknowledged now that the quality and characteristics that he proposed are basically the same as those contained in the Gospel and are exemplified most fully by the work and character of Jesus Christ. Through his incarnate relationships and the unconditional positive regard that is conveyed, he related to people out of a deep sense of genuineness and respect for their freedom and autonomy, in no way forcing belief in them or the values he espoused. Indeed, the temptations in the desert can be seen as his personal battle against the pull to use his powers and popularity to manipulate people into adherence. To the end, on the cross, he refused the challenge to win converts through psychological pressure. At his very core, he believed in people and lived this out. The cross is the symbol of that powerless position and the ultimate refusal of God himself to try to force or manipulate a person into faith and love.

Pastorally then, we need to recover the courage to act out of the perspective that human beings are essentially trustworthy because they are in the depths of their being oriented toward a being like Christ and have the Spirit of God within them. We accept the belief not simply on the basis of empirical evidence but programatically, so to speak, in the hope that the acting out of this belief will create a different psychological world which will unlock this will for good and help to uncloud the reason so that people will gravitate toward making good decisions, not evil ones: the empirical data itself will change.

Conclusion

This answers also the first objection to the idea that people should be considered trustworthy: the fact that they lack the breadth of vision that the community possesses and are more likely to be governed by narrower and more short-term aims that ultimately are not socially beneficial. This is undoubtedly true. In conditions of stress and confusion, people are governed more by their emotions than by their reason. However, if the understanding process aims at giving those emotions and the meanings and values that they enshrine clear symbolization, then there is a release from their domination and the person's capacity to reason becomes increased. Through the understanding process there is a gradual movement out of short-sighted and inadequate responses to more rationally considered ones. There is much clinical evidence for this though the actual process remains something of a mystery. Brain studies suggest that it has something to do with the integration of the left- and right-hand sides of the brain and the hypothalamus which is the seat of basic emotional responding. Whatever the neurophysiology of it, symbolizing emotions, meanings, and values does produce a release of emotional tension and a capacity to think more clearly and rationally. There is a broadening of the capacity to think beyond the immediate situation and take in wider factors, to bring the whole picture into focus.

When a person has achieved this ability to look at the self and its situation in a wider, more comprehensive way, he then becomes more capable of weighing and deciding about any input that the counselor might deem necessary or valuable. Furthermore, as we have pointed out before, people are more likely to be open to considering the broader vision offered by the Church if they are treated with a respect that affirms their dignity as responsible, trustworthy persons. Where they have experienced this and grown in their trust of the counselor to respect and affirm it, then it would seem that a challenge to see other aspects of the situation, especially what the community has discerned as good for the community as a whole, and therefore for themselves as individuals within it, can be offered. In the counseling situation especially, the way this is offered is important. Offered respectfully with the freedom to decide for or against it clearly left in the hands of the client without threat or rejection, it is likely to be a valuable way of helping the person towards greater objectivity. Offered punitively, however, it will likely reduce the possibility of acceptance and indeed probably destroy the ability to maintain an ongoing relationship.

The ability to benefit from challenge seems to depend radically on the level of trust and security that the person has in herself. Until this inner self-trust and security is present in the person, challenge will be seen as threat and the inner forces of defense will be mobilized to keep it at a distance. The contours of this can be seen clearly in those who in fact come looking for information and advice, who are seemingly most open to being advised on what to do. We will look at this under the heading of the dependent person.

10 The Dependent Person and Counseling
The Present Situation
The Effects of Objectivism

Despite what has been said above about the different relationship to social authority figures that is prevalent today, there are still many who in crisis situations will come to the priest or minister, or some other socially authoritative figure, seemingly open and eager for advice or direction. They find the situation they are in so painful, confusing, or frightening that they are desperate for someone to tell them what to do, to show them the way out of their dilemmas. The instinctive thing to do is to run to someone, like a psychologist or minister, who *has the answers.* Implicit in this is a mentality which is deeply dependent. This dependency has many different origins but, as we have already seen, psychologists have encouraged this dependency by the belief, at least on a popular level, that they are in a position to give people sure ways out of their difficulties. People have been educated to believe that only the expert has the knowledge necessary to be able to function adequately: that knowledge as to how to live effectively is something that is primarily dependent upon theoretical education which they themselves do not have.

The result is that we are finding more and more people acting and relating in stereotypical ways based on those simplistic psychological notions which have achieved some general popularity. What this objectivist environment has done is encourage a tendency in people to be and remain childish, unable and unwilling to decide for themselves what they need to do and to take responsibility for it. The emphasis on *science* as the only real way to discover the truth, while it has not necessarily created the dependent personality, has helped to vitiate the development of the ability to be present to one's personal experiencing and able to make sense of it.

What has been lost is that capacity which Kolb refers to as experiential learning, the capacity to learn from personal experience, which in former ages was known as prudential wisdom. Put in terms that we have used, people have become radically dependent on the prudence of others. This is essentially the condition of a child. But reliance simply on the prudence of others leaves us alienated from, and unable to cope with, those situations in which there is no readily available theoretical knowledge.

Seen from this point of view it is possible to make sense of a good many of our social ills, e.g., the fact that so much crime in society and disharmony in social relationships seems to be a result of simply childish behavior in an adult form. It is the result of a lack of ability to be really present to and understanding of the data of immediate experiencing and able to assess and act within it out of a sense of our own rationally discerned long-term interests. Lacking this ability we remain victims of our own immediate emotional responses, especially those which have been denied because they do not fit the popular notion of the ideal. The result we increasingly find is that people who on the surface seem to fit *the ideal* and seem to be thoroughly rational people, can on occasion act in devastatingly irrational and antisocial ways. When that happens, society confesses itself bewildered, as happened recently when a highly effective and intellectually bright government official was revealed to be a wife beater in private life. He was very competent intellectually at tasks which demanded theoretical knowledge but quite incompetent in those areas which demanded experiential knowledge and wisdom.

The Social Response

Society's response to this at the present moment, over a whole variety of social ills, is education, and in this we can see the same overemphasis on theoretical knowledge which is producing the ills in the first place. Again the belief is that what is lacking is theoretical knowledge and that giving people theoretical knowledge about the situation will alter the behavior. Without decrying the value of education, this is still a somewhat *neurotic* response in the sense that it is simply the intensifying of a form of response that has already shown itself to have limited value. There seems to be little evidence that education about sex or drugs, for instance, has done anything to mitigate the problems in these areas. This is being gradually realized and the way in which education is being resorted to as the means of preventing the social problems that we are encountering is itself showing a sort of desperation rather than a firm conviction about its value. We do not know what else to do. In our desperation we are turning to the experts, especially those in psychology, who out of their superior knowledge of human functioning can tell us how to resolve our difficulties.

Dealing with Dependency in Counseling

The Need for an Expert

What is happening on the social level is also happening on the individual personal level. There is in all of us at certain moments, when our world threatens to collapse in some way and we become really anxious, a sort of regression to childhood in which we turn to a parental figure for assistance as the best way to resolve our difficulties. In the first instance, this may be the ultimate parental figure, God, but, then, along with him, we may also turn to those who seem to possess some of God's own qualities of knowledge and operational competency. Among these especially, are those we see as being his representatives among us, the priest or minister. People in this sort of condition come to the pastor projecting onto him something of the same qualities and expectations that they project on to God, and he often finds himself in the prestigious position of being the one who knows the answers and has the capacity to rescue people from their dilemmas.

Parent/Child Syndrome

It is difficult for those in ministry to resist this projection. Transactional analysis has shown us how the child and the parent are psychological complexes which exist within all of us and which in our relationships call one another forth. One dominated by the child complex will project the parent complex onto another and bring it out in him and, vice-versa, where one acts parentally toward another, it will tend to evoke the child in the other. The dynamics that result will depend on how each relates to that child or parent within. If one approves of the parental role in himself, then one is likely to find the projection both natural and satisfying, at least in the beginning. One might even, as a minister, only function well with people who evoke and support that role. The question has often been raised as to what extent people who take up counseling do so precisely to act out this parental role; to what extent do the counselors need the clients? It can also be raised with regards to ministry: to what extent in those who seek the ordained ministry is there a need to feed this paternalistic or messianic image of themselves? It is probably considerable.

But, even if we are not in the grip of this particular dynamic and do not wish to be seen in a paternalistic or messianic role, genuine compassion for the suffering and anxiety of the other may easily lead us into an immediate attempt to rescue the other person by trying to give advice or answers that will solve his difficulties. We likewise resort to education and guidance.

Problem/Answer Modality

This sort of response at least has the virtue of giving us the feeling that we are doing something positive and in today's world where *doing something* is considered to be a paramount virtue, the need to do something that will be immediately effective can be very strong. What is at stake here is our own sense of competence and our status and value in the eyes of others. In Maslow's terms we are dominated by our need for self- and other-respect. In theological terms it is the need to be justified by our works, with the hidden law that is operative: we are acceptable if we are effective in solving the other's difficulties.

We have already discussed in detail the intrinsic limitations of advice giving generally, the first one being that it is abstract. Not being in living contact with the particularities of the situation, the counselor's understanding of what is possible within it can only be approximate. We have also criticized the perspective that develops from this of seeing the person who comes to us in terms of *problems.* We pointed out that, while not denying that there are many commonalities in the sorts of difficulties people meet in life, there is in fact no such thing as *a problem* apart from the unique perceptual world of the person. *Problems* are only such from within the meaning structures and values or goals of an individual person in all her particularity. To talk of *problems* outside of this context is to talk about abstractions. Problems are the obstacles that we meet to the achievement of our goals. Precisely what the problems are then will depend upon the goals, values, beliefs about self and the world, and their particular gestalt in the consciousness of the individual.

The danger in thinking in terms of problems is that it can lead us to ignore the subjectivity of the person who has them and the unique perceptual field that constitutes his situation as problematical. It also has the disadvantage of trying to compartmentalize a person's life into carefully delineated areas. Life is undoubtedly problematical in that we seek fulfillment and do not know precisely how to realize it. Within life, and as a consequence of trying to realize our ultimate fulfillment, we set up more specific goals in accordance with our value systems. Problems arise when we either encounter barriers to realizing those goals, or where we find that our goals do not bring us the desired satisfaction, or where we discover a conflict in our goals. Life is then *problematical* in so many different ways which are intertwined with one another that clearly to delineate a specific, concrete problem can be quite artificial and can do violence to the complex, personal striving of the individual.

Furthermore, although counselor and client may share many common goals, it is not, as we have said above, by any means certain that there will always be an identity. We have already mentioned that there is a tendency to set up a specific, normative set of values with their correlated goals which is given some privileged position of authority. If both client and counselor agree on these normative structures then it might be possible for both to delineate quite clearly the goals to be achieved and the barriers which are preventing their realization. The danger is that, on the one hand, the counselor might assume that the meaning structure and its complex of values that he himself espouses and believes in are subtly imposed on the client; and, on the other, where made explicit, might be intellectually accepted by the client out of respect for the psychological or moral authority of the counselor.

As we have seen, this can in fact render the counseling process ineffective since the client's own experiential and operational values will not have been made conscious and reassessed and, hence, will not have been changed. The result is that essentially they are likely to remain as the primary determinants of his behavior. Values cannot be imposed on another or assumed and hence *problems* as such cannot be deduced from abstract schemes but only from within the client's own experiential striving. It is important to emphasize, therefore,that the counselor does not deal with problems as such but with persons in the dynamics of their experiential striving to realize their fulfillment. It is the person he is concerned with, not the *problem*.

The essential weakness of education or guidance as a solution to problems lies precisely in the fact that it will not of itself change the operational goals and values of the person. Change in one's operational self-system will occur only as one experientially discerns the value of other goals over one's present investments. Education itself is important in that it offers us other ways of looking at life and what might be valuable to pursue, but it will not of itself affect the change in the operational self-structure. Awareness of that self-structure and the goals it is designed to realize are an essential "infrastructure" to the incorporation of new knowledge.

Key Modality to Problematic Situations

Where goals are agreed upon, however, it may in fact be possible on occasions to help a person substantially through showing the way to overcome certain external obstacles or to achieve certain external goals, but in many of life's problems, particularly those concerning interpersonal relations or life goals, the subjective world of the person is central to the nature of the *problem* and the real *solution,* in the sense of a solvent which frees the person from the bind she is in, lies in strengthening the person's own capacity to assess her situation, determine for herself what needs to be done and finding the inner resources to act upon it. Rather than supplying an answer to the person's difficulties, we seek to supply the key to the problem. This *key,* as Curran puts it, lies in the mental clarification and emotional integration of the person so that her perceptions and values are clarified and her own capacity for rational, responsible self-determination is strengthened (*Understanding,* p. 31).

The Dynamics of Dependency

The Importance of the Self-Concept

Crucial to this is the enhancement of the self-concept of the person. The *self* is the instrumentality of the person in his relationships with the world and how he views the self is central to whether it is a successful instrument in that relationship or not. If the person has a positive view of himself and of his capabilities, he will be much more able to utilize the inner and outer resources available to him in his situation. If his view of himself is poor, then his ability to perceive both what he is capable of doing and what will help him do that will be distorted.

Confidence and trust in the self to be an effective instrument in living is crucial to the development of the mature personality. The main variable, determining whether or not a person is able to realistically and responsibly cope with and work out her own solutions to her difficulties, seems to be the degree to which the situation is experienced to be threatening to the self. Where the self feels very threatened then the person tends to view life with tunnel vision, concentrating narrowly on what she perceives to be the threatening factors. She engages mainly in a self-defensive stance which rigidifies the self — making change and adaptability less possible.

It has been the contention of this paper that the overemphasis on theoretical scientific knowledge concentrated in the hands of experts has contributed to this poor self-image on the part of people. It has led, on the one hand, to the expectation that there is somewhere an answer that will resolve the situation completely and put the person's world right. Because the client does not have this knowledge she feels incompetent to know what to do for the best in the situation she is in. Meeting difficulties in living to which she has no ready answer comes as a severe threat. The tension and fear that results renders her even less effective in coping with the situations. On the other hand, actually giving the person *answers* deepens her own lack of trust in herself; it reaffirms her own incapacity to deal effectively with her situations. This affirmation of her own incompetence can be resisted very strongly, though usually covertly rather than overtly, rendering the advice given ineffective.

The "I"–"Self" Relationship

In the process of successful living the relationship between what Curran refers to as the *I* and the *self* is absolutely basic and fundamental. The *I* is the inner core of self-consciousness which renders the human person transcendent to his experiencing and open to the infinite horizon of fulfillment. Out of this openness he formulates his sense of what that fulfillment is and the ideal self which would realize it for him. As a *self* the person is rooted in the here-and-now, with all his inherited and socially determined limitations. As an *I*, he can only realize his fulfillment through the *self*. He has to determine the *self* to be the vehicle of his striving toward his fulfillment. If he has a positive relationship with the *self* he will be accepting of both its possibilities and its limitations, at the same time formulating and maintaining realistic ideals and goals. He will also be capable of the patience and understanding necessary to enable the *self* to be the instrument of its realization.

This self-structure, however, will be a fluid and changing self capable of adapting itself as necessary to the varied demands and situations it encounters. The *I* will not be identified with a particular self but will be, as Roberto Assagioli points out, able to move appropriately between self-structures, disidentifying from one as it is no longer necessary (see *Psychosynthesis*. New York: Penguin Books, 1965). This is a particularly valuable way of looking at the situation. The transcendent *I,* as Assagioli calls it, is that inner unity of knowing and acting which is the core of human being. It is the original unity of self-consciousness and self-determination which forms the indispensable basis of any sense of continuity.

In itself, though, it is, if we can speak this way, naked. It is never found or experienced without some clothing, the clothing being the particular self-structures that need to be formed to mediate its relationships with the external world. These are constantly changing as it responds to the stimuli in its inner and outer worlds. In childhood generally self-consciousness is weak, the *I* is usually simply a taken-for-granted background and thence the changes required in the self are undertaken without undue stress; indeed, they might be welcomed as the child discovers new potentialities in the self and grows closer to the ideal state of adulthood. In adolescence, however, the child becomes *self* conscious, and the changes that take place are experienced as threatening. The *I* is no longer readily able to identify with any one self and so can come to be experienced as not real, and there can be a constant fear of being overwhelmed and annihilated as a real being. The *I,* out of the sense of threat, then can become identified with one or even several specific self-structures and lose its flexibility. Maintenance of these self-structures then becomes necessary for the continued sense of realness and significance. Maturity is the gradual recovery of the sense of the realness of the *I* and the ability, consciously now, to form flexible self-structures capable of meeting the varying demands of life.

In one who has a positive relationship to the *self* and has come to take its inner core, or the experience of the transcendent *I* for granted in its realness and knows its capacity to form self-structures which are operationally adequate, the difficulties and *problems* of life come to be experienced as challenges. They may be painful and confusing but will not be viewed as ultimately overwhelming. However, the type of person we are considering here, who is in some way desperate for assistance, is usually one who has lost confidence in his *self*. He sees his *self* as inadequate to the task of achieving his goals. His *problems* have become too big for his *self* to handle and, because his *I* has been identified with that *self* he fears in a real way that in losing his *self,* he is in danger of being overwhelmed, of losing his whole being. Looking to the *problems* themselves and offering *answers* may, depending on the problem, temporarily ease the situation but it does not render the *self-structure* more adequate as an instrumentality for living, and indeed may even reinforce its sense of inadequacy.

The *key* to the problematical situation is the strengthening and development of the inner core of the person such that it can take a wider perspective on its self-structure and its possibilities, and be able to change and adapt without fear of being lost. Thereby does the self become a more adequate instrument for the realization of the *I*'s projects.

Resistance to Accepting Advice

From this perspective we can see some of the more subtle reasons why the pressure for advice giving should be resisted as a first approach. Even though a person overtly asks for advice and direction and seems willing to do whatever is suggested by the minister or counselor, his emotional distress and tunnel vision and the need to protect his particular self-structure may prevent him from really hearing and understanding what is being suggested. Furthermore, there is also the real possibility that there will be a subtle resistance in the person precisely to actually doing what is suggested. As Patterson notes,

> every counselor well knows the resistance that develops where direct influence is attempted, and the resistance that often follows the attempt to fulfill a direct request of the client for advice or other help (op. cit., p. 70).

Charles A. Curran has likened this dynamic to that of the swimmer who is in difficulties and screaming for help, yet fights off the lifeguard who comes to rescue him (*Understanding,* p. 16). The person who is desperately holding onto himself in some way lacks the basic capacity to trust another. The person is usually trying to keep control over a situation that seems increasingly chaotic and unmanageable. The desire for control then itself acts as a barrier to the giving over of the self to another's direction. The result is that he will in fact simply discard the advice that is given for the more habitual patterns of responding that he has built up, even when these have been totally ineffectual up until now. Part of this tendency seems to come from the need to hold on in some way to his sense of dignity as an adult. Although the person may come in an overt condition of childish dependency, there can often be a deeper, less conscious rejection of this in himself. To live out the advice would be to own that dependency, and it is this refusal to be totally identified with it which brings about its rejection. To avoid this ownership, then, the person may not directly ignore the advice but rather subtly distort it or in some way misapply it, thereby showing that it was not really relevant or effective. He is thus able to retain something of his own adult control over his life.

However, it might also be sabotaged precisely to safeguard the condition of childish dependency and nonresponsibility. This can be especially true when in some way the *problem* is concerned with some moral issue. There are inherent risks in being personally responsible for what one does. We leave ourselves open to being wrong and of being revealed to others as inadequate and hence we run the risk of experiencing both guilt and shame. We can avoid this by the abrogation of personal responsibility to others, especially to those in authority, and hope instead, as children do, for a sort of magical solution. But, if things do go wrong, it is their fault, not ours.

Benefits and Difficulties of *Key* Modality

The most effective way of responding to people who come asking for advice or answers about their difficulties is, then, not immediately to jump to giving them advice, but to work with them to achieve some internal clarity and to discover their own personal resources for meeting and dealing with their difficulties. This might seem a longer route to take but, given the dynamics of the situation, it is in the long run the quickest and most effective. It activates their own capacities to make sense of and find ways of coping with the difficulties they are in. In their desperation, they may have completely lost touch with these and so shy away from the more difficult but in the long run more beneficial way of personal effort and responsibility. Again, although from a different perspective, the issue is one of trust. The client needs to rediscover a trust in himself and in his capacity to adequately cope with his life and realize the best solutions possible in his circumstances. The counselor mediates this by showing trust. E. Mark Stern and Burt G. Marino are correct when they write:

> Trust begets further trust. With the initial strivings of trust comes the courage to accept the risks inherent in saying yes to the world, to men, to God. A mature sense of trust finally frees man to explore the feeling that he does have a measure of control over the chaotic forces within himself and society. This germ of trust requires much nurturing (Psychotheology. New York: Paulist Press, 1970, p. 70).

This sense of trust is not nurtured by the giving of advice. Indeed advice giving can often radically stand in the way of the development of trust. It reinforces the belief that people indeed cannot come to a personal adequacy but must always rely on others more capable, more knowing than themselves. The incarnate-redemptive approach, mediated by a deep understanding that works with the inner world of the other to bring it to intelligibility and consciousness, however, works to enhance the inner capacities of the other to be self-assessing and self-determining. In dealing with one who wants to come to personal assessments and decisions as to what should be done, the incarnate-redemptive approach is used as a permissive and affirming environment. However, with the type of dependent person we are considering, it meets the clients as a challenge, basically the challenge to become more mature and take control and responsibility for their own lives and decisions.

Personal Responsibility: A Choice for Life or Death

In this we are touching upon a crucial and essential element in human experiencing: the choice between growth and nongrowth, or more starkly, the choice between life and death. Crucial to growth is the ability to act responsibly, to be willing to fully own who we are and what we do. The mature person knows what she is doing and is willing to accept the consequences. In this acting, however, she is aware of and has come to terms with the fact that she may be wrong. Mature persons then accept the risk that their actions might in fact be inadequate and even have negative consequences that they cannot at this point see. They know the risk inherent in altering the situations they are in and yet are willing to accept that risk. The possibility of experiencing both guilt and shame are, hence, inherent factors in the demand to be personally responsible for our behavior. One who chooses life implicitly chooses the possibility that she might be wrong, that further knowledge and experience might show that her response was inadequate. She lays herself open to negative evaluation and rejection, which are of the essence of the experience of guilt and shame.

Those who choose death on the other hand seek to avoid this intrinsic responsibility and the experience of guilt and shame that it might bring. As Maslow rightly puts it, they opt for the security of a known position, for staying where they are. In this opting for security, they are able to avoid the experience of guilt and shame inherent in acting out of one's own assessment of what is needed. Curran would maintain in fact that such people are opting to safeguard their own God-image, a certain invulnerability to moral censure and of revealing themselves as inadequate. They do this by putting responsibility for what they need to do onto another, giving them a God-status of knowledge and competency. It is in fact a choice for death because it is a choice against the inner demands of the dynamism of their own being. It is an alienation from the reality of life. They are living in what we have called an intrinsic transcendental self-contradiction: their choice not to choose for themselves is in fact a choice for which they are responsible. This inner self-contradiction is hidden by defense mechanisms, particularly that of rationalization, through which they are able to blame others if the advice given does not work out or in some way produces effects that are negative. Accepting the role of expert buys into that rationalization and supports it.

A Mechanism of Defense: The Drama Triangle

Being challenged to face this more difficult path can be painful for both counselor and client. In the client it may evoke both guilt and anger: guilt in that the person is being faced with the need to look to himself and his own responsibilities both for and within the situation, and acknowledge the inadequacies of his current perspectives and behaviors; and anger that the other to whom he has granted a superior status and authority over him is not responding in the way he wanted and expected. The client may resort to provoking shame in the counselor by subtly reproaching him for not being the caring, competent minister the client thought him to be. Where this happens a self-perpetuating dynamic can be established which is called the *Drama Triangle*. (Sakubowski and Lange. *The Assertive Option*. Chicago, IL: Research Press Co., 1978, p. 62).

In this the priest begins by accepting the role as rescuer either out of a real sense of compassion for the other's situation or out of the need to avoid the experience of shame in being seen as incompetent or inferior as a minister. Acting out this role, he seeks to find ways of alleviating the other's pain, either by giving advice or by directly taking responsibility for doing certain things for the person. But when the situation does not improve or continues to repeat itself, he then begins to feel less like a rescuer and more like a victim. He begins then to feel angry about the situation and moves to being something of a persecutor, either gently or more severely berating the other either for not doing what was advised or for not taking a more active role in solving his difficulties. But, as the other's helplessness continues, he begins to feel guilty about his harshness and anger and his compassion or pity for the other's helplessness returns, and he reverts once again to being the rescuer. And so the cycle repeats itself, leading to stress and burnout among priests and any in a ministerial role.

Theological Considerations

Pastoral Theology: Rescuer or Enabler?

To help resist this demand and ground a different relationship and expectation, we need to look at the sort of theology that we might be operating out of. Does it encourage this projection or discourage it? Is our God a rescuer God and do we see ourselves as ministers in some way required to mediate this to people? Do we feel guilty if we do not respond in this way? What is God's active relationship to the human predicament? Much of our popular theology in the past has tended to support the view of God as a paternalistic rescuer and alongside him those closely associated with him, the Saints in the heavenly realm and priests and religious in the earthly. The question then is, ought we to look at God in this way and, as ministers, allow ourselves to be interpreted from within this framework? Or does God call us and enable us to achieve a mature independence? That means to be capable of solving our own problems and living with the limitations and difficulties that are intrinsic to the human situation. And, following from this, is our role as ministers rightly one of parent and rescuer, or one of relating to people in a way which challenges and encourages them to an independence and strength that enables them to deal with their own difficulties and limitations?

Covenantal Call to Mature Adulthood

Central to this question is the notion of the covenant and the belief that lies behind it that we are cocreators with God of the kingdom. We have already seen how the world in which we live is not simply there to be discovered but something that we ourselves create. This is true not simply in terms of creating a negative world, the world of sin; but also in terms of extending the kingdom made present among us by Jesus. In Jesus Christ we have been given a real insight into the complex of attitudes and values which will realize the kingdom among us but no answers as to how these are made concrete in any particular set of circumstances. This we have to discover for ourselves through hard thinking and active commitment. In God's work of bringing the world and human life to its fulfillment, then, we are not simply employees but codirectors. God does not merely give us instructions to be followed and answers to problems but has endowed us with the ability to think and decide for ourselves what needs to be done, not apart from him, but in dialogue with him as covenant partners. In this God is parental but in a very positive sense. He relates to us in a way that enables us to grow up to our full stature and maturity. Indeed, this is his whole purpose in creation: Our growth to the fullness of our capacities is his project and he relates to us accordingly. In Jesus Christ he showed himself as the Supreme Enabler, the one who above all makes it possible for us realize our humanity fully. As we have seen He did this primarily through incarnating himself in human life. It is possible to translate the central belief of our faith "the Word became Flesh" into the "I"-"self" categories mentioned before. The Father is the *I* of the whole reality, the Word is the "Ideal," the perfection that reality is oriented to becoming. Creation is God's self. In Jesus, God in his ideal self reached down and integrated himself with his *self* and through his total, accepting, understanding, forgiving relationship with his *self* raised it up to the perfection and fulfillment of the resurrection.

Incarnate–Redemptive Relationship Paradigm

Theologically and psychologically, this is the principle of redemption. This characterized Jesus' own ministry among us. He himself, though he taught people constantly about the way to realize the Kingdom, did not give his hearers any definitive answers to their difficulties; rather, through his own further incarnative relationships with people, through his total, healing presence to them in their inadequacy and need, he sought to evoke an active faith, based on an understanding of who God is, how he related to them, and what he was calling them to be, which would enable them to realize their own potential and deal with their difficulties for themselves. He became angry with the crowds who could not see beyond the miracles he worked to a deeper meaning but simply came to rely on him to solve their problems for them. . . .

> He replied to the crowd, "What an unbelieving lot you are! How long must I remain with you? How long can I endure you? . . . Everything is possible to a man who trusts" (Mark 9:19–23).

Some would see the miracles as evidence that God is a rescuer, but more important than the miracles Jesus did work are the numbers that he did not. There is some evidence too that he gradually moved beyond miracle working as a way of disclosing the Kingdom to people precisely because they could not see beyond them to the meaning they were meant to convey. They got stuck at the level of the act itself and its immediate value to them and could not or would not see them precisely as signs which disclosed who and what he was. In John's account of the miracle of the feeding of the crowds, we read:

> Jesus replied: "In very truth I know that you have not come looking for me because you saw signs, but because you ate the bread and your hunger was satisfied" (Jn 6:26).

It was no part of his ministry to have people simply become dependent on him to solve their problems. He warned sternly against adopting a superior or paternalistic attitude toward those to whom one ministered when he warned the disciples:

> But you are not to be called rabbi for you have only one master and you are all brothers. And do not call anyone on earth father, for you have one Father, and He is in heaven. Nor are you to be called teacher for you have one teacher, the Christ. The greatest among you will be your servant (Mt 23:8–11).

A servant is one who identifies with the life and needs of his master and takes them for his own. Identification is at the core of Incarnation and Redemption. It is this which lies behind the washing of the feet in John's account of the Last Supper.

> If I do not wash you, Jesus replied, then you are not in fellowship with me. . . . Then, if I, your Lord and master, have washed your feet, you also ought to wash one another's feet. I have set you an example; you are to do as I have done for you (Jn 13:8,13).

This process of identification with humanity was completed in the crucifixion and raising of Jesus from the dead. In this, humanity was raised to the fulfillment of its capabilities. This has empowered us with the hope that the final fulfillment of the human task is assured, and that our mistakes, failures, and inadequacies are no final barrier to our participation in that fulfillment. This raises human life out of a sense of futility and encourages us to a full participation in the search to realize the kingdom over ourselves and our world through a recapitulation of the process of Incarnation and Redemption both within our *selves* and between our *selves* in the world community.

Scriptural Perfection and Psychological Maturity

Perfection in the New Testament is the state of the adult as opposed to the child; it is predicated of the fully developed individual in contradistinction to those who are immature. St. Paul specifically calls the Christian life a vocation to mature adulthood, characterized by independence, freedom, responsibility, and love. In 1 Corinthians he relates this maturity, in contrast to the infantile state, to his extended description of charity. Thus he says:

When I was a child I talked like a child, I reasoned like a child. When I became a man, I put childish ways behind me (1 Cor 13:11).

He saw the whole of God's relationship to mankind as being characterized by this dynamic of enabling us to grow to our own full maturity, both as individuals and as a community; Christ was the fulfillment of that work (Eph 4:11–16). This, then, is the call of the Gospel: to enter into that adulthood made possible by the work of Christ and continued in us through the Holy Spirit. Essentially it is the call to love personally with all the risks, uncertainties and inevitable mistakes that that entails. The Vatican Council brought this understanding of the dynamic of God's action in the world into a positive relationship with the increasing desire of the world for those conditions which enhance and develop independence and personal responsibility when it wrote:

In every group or nation, there is an ever increasing number of men and women who are conscious that they themselves are the artisans and the authors of the culture and their community. Throughout the world there is a similar growth in the combined sense of independence and responsibility. Such a development is of paramount importance for the spiritual and moral maturity of the human race (Gaudium et Spes, par. 55).

It is paramount because without a growth in those two characteristics no love is possible, and throughout Chapter 5 of *Lumen Gentium,* the Council specifically links maturity and holiness to the capacity to love and act.

[The Church's] holiness is expressed in multiple ways by those individuals who, in their walk of life, strive for the perfection of charity, and thereby help others to grow (par. 39).

Consequences for Pastoral Practice

Out of this theological reflection we can see that to participate in God's own ministry among us, the primary role of the priest in counseling is not to solve people's problems and thus increase dependency, but, through the mediation of an incarnate-redemptive relationship, to enable them to solve problems for themselves and thereby attain real growth into independence and personal responsibility. Curran writes:

Such growth involves not simply external dependence on others for guidance and decision but the gradual acquiring of an inner capacity to make such judgments oneself (Religious Values, p. 2).

An important part of this process is to enable the person, particularly the overly dependent person, to withdraw the projection of parent and rescuer from the minister and to look for solutions to his difficulties, not simply outside of himself from others, but inwardly to his own capacities and to the resources that God has already provided him with in terms of his own inner nature and of the surrounding life situation and its real, though perhaps limited, possibilities. Through his experience of an incarnate-redemptive relationship with the priest the person is both challenged and enabled to become more incarnate with himself, coming closer to his actual *self* to accept and understand both the strengths, possibilities, and capacities as well as the inadequacies and limitations that make up his reality as it is here and now in this situation. It is a growth into increasing congruity with his own experiential life and hence a greater capacity to work within it.

Given the kinds of people that do come to the minister and the background of dependency out of which often they come, asking the minister to relate to them in this way might seem unrealistic. It would seem to be asking that every request for advice or assistance would turn into a counseling session of some duration. However, such is not the case. With people who have a basic integration and whose difficulties are situational in one way or another, much can be achieved in one session, given the skillful use of counseling. Of course, where skilled long-term psychotherapy is indicated, the minister will seek to refer the person, as soon as possible, to someone who can offer such help and assist the person in entering such a helping relationship. However, although the pastor may think that giving quick advice and encouragement would save himself time and energy, usually this only postpones offering a truly helping process and may even render such help impossible to administer in the future.

11 Limitations in the Helping Relationship
Narcissism and Ministry
Necessity of Recognizing Limits

There are then essential limitations in the use of advice giving in the pastoral relationship. These limitations are not arbitrary but arise both from the very nature of the human situation and from the requirements of the Gospel. Recognition of these limitations is important if we seriously wish to discover what in fact we can do to help another person and further his growth in the Kingdom of God. Recognition of limitations prevents us from going off in false directions and directs us to discover our real strengths as counselors and pastors. It also and most importantly helps us to see precisely how and when advice giving may be helpful. It can help us to use advice giving correctly and to its best advantage.

The recognition of these limitations is important. In order to discover the real benefits of the pastoral relationship, it is essential for both the pastor and the client to discover and accept the limits of what is possible: The client has to learn the limits of what he can expect of the minister, and the minister has to learn the limits of what he can actually do for the person. It is only on the basis of this recognition of the necessary limits involved in the situation that it is possible to discover the positive and effective steps that can be taken to aid the other in the path to growth and fulfillment.

Recognition of Limits and Narcissism

The recognition of our limitations can be a difficult lesson to learn, and perhaps it is in the counseling relationship that one comes up most sharply against that fact. Curran considers that the growth into the realization and acceptance of the essential limitations on our reality is an intrinsic part of growing out of the narcissistic stage of the child to the healthy objectivity of an adult. He terms it the *Therapy of Limits* (see *Counseling and Psychotherapy*). He writes:

> One necessary aspect of the developmental process as a person grows from infancy to adulthood, is, then, a corresponding growth in this sense of, and ability to relate to, limits. . . . This growth away from narcissism can be demonstrated by the way any expert performance, even in sports, finally demands careful conformity to limits, i.e., self-discipline and control. Maturity, in this sense is to the whole of life what conforming to rules is to a sport: a highly developed particular skill (Curran. Counseling and Psychotherapy, pp. 212–13).

Narcissism, as we have seen, results when one simply identifies oneself with her own inner world of ideas and desires: The way we see or imagine ourselves and the world is the way it is and what we want is paramount. Within this world we are omnipotent and can achieve whatever we want. As a pathology it is usually the result of an inability, in early childhood, to come to terms with the limitations of our subjectivity through some experience with the world which is other than us. It is generated through an inability to affect our world in some significant way and so discover our own real agency and significance. In order to hold on to our sense of who we are and our value, we identify our reality with the contents of our minds, with an image of ourselves and resist any questioning from our embodied reality. The continued experience of the limitations and inadequacies of who we are can result in depression if we fail to integrate into our self/world understanding. As Carlo Weber puts it, explaining Eidelburg,

> When this artificial sense of power later confronts an unyielding environment the inadequacy stands in conflict with the power, and the combination of feelings of omnipotence with experienced inadequacy creates a narcissistic depression. The individual needs to think himself responsible, i.e., to have power over another, and failures in such power create the continued shock that there is such a lack of power (Weber. Pastoral Psychology. New York: Sheed and Ward, 1970: p. 110).

Narcissism in Counseling

Though usually not in an extreme form, we can find this dynamic operating in the counseling field. For instance wherever the counselor simply assumes that he understands the world in the same way as the client, and hence can tell the client what can and should be done in it. We said previously that what this usually meant was an assumption that the meaning of the client's world and the values that constitute it are the same as the therapist's. Wherever we simply assume an identity of meaning — worlds between ourselves and another, then inevitably it is the meaning that it has for us that will predominate.

In this we are involved in a fundamental form of narcissism in which, when we look into the other, we, in fact, see ourselves. The advice that we might then give may have validity for us but be quite irrelevant to the world of the client. What we will have missed is the uniqueness of the other person. We have missed the differences in our worlds of meaning and values that is an essential outcome of our ontological subjectivity. It is not that there are not any commonalities; if our worlds were totally unique we could not communicate with one another about them. Psychology, in studying those commonalities, has made an enormous difference in our understanding of ourselves, enabling us to take possession of ourselves in a way never before possible in human history. But psychology remains limited in that it cannot of itself unlock the reality of the unique other to us.

What renders the therapeutic situation narcissistic, then, is where we avoid discriminating the uniqueness of the other. We interpret him out of abstract categories and try to impose our understandings and solutions on him. We might avoid that necessary discrimination for many reasons, but a central and fundamental one is that to discriminate uniqueness is to place ourselves primarily in a learning posture. We have to live the fact that we are in a real sense ignorant as to the unique world and person of the client and what is possible for him in it. We have to give up the role of expert, the one who knows what is going on and what to do about it. There is a fundamental loss of the superior status that attaches to being the expert, which is also a manifestation of the narcissistic impulse. Rather than suffer that, we will seek to assume understanding and competence in the other's world. Where this happens the uniqueness of our world tends to dominate and we may catch some of the commonality but miss the differences, and hence miss the reality of the situation in which the other has to operate. It is the conscious or unconscious refusal to become aware of the differences which increases the tendency to narcissism in counseling, whether that be secular or pastoral.

Beyond Narcissism in Ministry

It may be somewhat startling to think that one of the motivations for being a minister may in fact be an instance of the narcissistic impulse. However, Eugene Kennedy describes well the presence of this impulse in the minister and the challenge to personal growth out of narcissism which the counseling situation can demand of him. He writes:

> It is sometimes surprising for seminarians and priests to discover the selfish alloy that can be part of their efforts to help others. They are disappointed in themselves at first but they come to realize that this knowledge is the beginning of real personal growth. They find, for example, that they too are capable of working with others in order to receive the rewards of gratitude, or to build their own image of themselves as wise men. They find that they often concentrate, not on the person they theoretically hold to be sacred, but on the problem and, as a result, they resort to various artificial approaches and techniques. . . . They tend to handle cases because, on some level of awareness, they feel they have to do something to this individual and send him on his way. They discover that they are very often very subtly trying to remake others in their own image and likeness, rather than giving persons the freedom really to be themselves ("Characteristics of the Counselor," Insight, Winter 1963: p. 43).

Growth from this is achieved only by a radical openness to the uniqueness of the other, with all the limitations on ourselves which that implies. It is a discovery of what it means in fact to be a servant, a minister, and more especially a minister of the Gospel. It is only through the capacity to recognize the differences of the other that I am opened to experience the otherness of God. Enda McDonagh writes:

> As human beings are created in the image of God and are called by Jesus to be sons and daughters of the Father, their human otherness reflects and participates in the Divine otherness, making them in their differentiation from one another focusses of recognition and reverence. . . . Failure to recognize and reverence divine and human otherness expresses a tendency, readily indulged, to use God and other people as furnishings in one's own world of which the ultimate reality will be mere projection of the self in power or wealth or pleasure ("The Holy Spirit and Human Identity" Irish Theological Quarterly, 49(1), 1982: p. 47).

Intrinsic Limitations: Recapitulation

The more we give ourselves to this discrimination of others in all their uniqueness the more we will begin to realize the limitations involved in our assisting them. In the first place we will become aware of the limitation of actually being able to catch the uniqueness. Of its very nature, uniqueness cannot be categorized, it can only be pointed to. All concepts are to a lesser or greater degree abstract, that is, they have to drop the differences in order to convey the commonalities. Otherwise communication is impossible. So even the best understanding of another is only approximate. The second limitation that is revealed out of this is that it is only the one who is actually present to that uniqueness by nature, that is the individual himself, who can know how best to move forward in it. This is not an intellectual progress but what Curran calls a know-feel process, or what we referred to previously as operational knowledge. Gendlin calls it the *felt-sense* (*Focusing*. Everest House, 1978).

The fact then that it is only the individual herself who is in a position to discriminate the *felt-sense* of the next step forward means that the counselor is intrinsically limited in what he can do to further the process of growth or action from the outside. To seek to impose a program of action stemming from an ideal scheme of what is most desirable is to run the risk of being a barrier to that discrimination. Theologically, it is to prevent the discernment of the will of God for the person and a hindrance to the action of the Holy Spirit operating in the person's growth.

The Narcissistic Society and Ontological Limitations

To talk of realizing and accepting our limitations goes against the grain today. There is in our society a very definite narcissistic trend which Alexander Lowen has caught well when he says:

> What stands out today is the tendency to regard limits as unnecessary restrictions on human potential. Business is conducted as if there were no limits to economic growth, and even in science we encounter the idea that we can overcome death, that is, transform nature to our image. Power, performing and productivity have become the dominant values, displacing such old-fashioned virtues as dignity, integrity, and self-respect (Narcissism. New York: Collier Books, 1983, p. 11).

The prevailing attitude tends to be that limitations are somehow evil and should never be tolerated. It issues in a sort of defiant energetic attempt to overcome them. In the United States this would seem to have certain historical roots which Barratt has commented on thus:

> The American has not yet assimilated psychologically the disappearance of his own geographical frontiers, his spiritual horizon is still the limitless play of human possibilities, and as yet he has not lived through the crucial experience of human finitude (The Irrational Man, p. 10).

Distinction: Ontological and Ontic Limitations

There is a sense, of course, in which it is true that limitations are there to be overcome or transcended. The weakness of this perspective is that it fails to distinguish between ontological limitations which are intrinsic to human relationships as such and which can never be transcended since they belong to the essential nature of human beings and what the existentialists would call ontical limitations, i.e., limitations imposed by the way things in the world are related at the moment. These latter are being continually overcome as we increasingly discover what those relationships are and the different combinations that can be achieved. This constitutes the process of human growth and development in all its manifestations. This overcoming of ontical limitations is in principle at least infinite. However, that progress in whatever field will always be subject to the ontological limitations because these belong intrinsically to the nature of the beings which are developing.

Result of the Failure to Distinguish

The failure to distinguish between these two modes of limitations leads to an unthinking extension of the latter to the whole of reality. Humanistic psychology, especially in terms of its promotion of transcendence, has fed into this: one should never accept limitations upon one's self-realization. It has so tended to emphasize the individual character of the human person that it has in many of its forms simply become a selfish pursuit of human growth *experiences.* This is essentially narcissistic and forgets the intrinsically communal dimension of the human person and the limits on one's self-realization as an individual that this imposes. This has rightly led to the charge by some authors that humanistic psychology issues essentially in a narcissistic self-worship in which one becomes indifferent to, or tries to avoid, the inevitable limitations involved in being a part of the human community while yet feeding off its benefits (e.g., Vitz. *Psychology as Religion.* Grand Rapids: Eerdmans, 1977). Others have made the same charge and in fairness to proponents of this school there have been serious attempts to rectify the deficiency.

Science too, in the extraordinary advances it has made in recent years and in the technological marvels it has spawned, lends itself to the notion that humankind is unlimited in what it can achieve; it is simply a matter of finding the right technique. Psychology in its desire to be considered in the same light as science has likewise been infected by this, and it has issued in a plethora of techniques for overcoming a whole variety of human problems, each new technique claiming to be definitive. This reduces the complexities of personal life to the level of technological efficiency. This tendency is fed by the prevalent need which dominates much of our culture to be relevant, to be effective, to be able to offer a product that works. The words *effective* and *fast* are constants in the advertising of *self-help* psychology.

This reductionism leads to a feeling of Godlike dominance, of absolute control and power, in which everything can be manipulated to create the ideal world. Within this framework the expert becomes the sort of mediator and dispensor of this power and control. The almost Godlike control that we have established over nature is then transferred to the human level where it is expected to be equally effective. This is sometimes called the sin of objectivism, where human beings are viewed under the same categories as those which apply to physical reality and are then seen as fixed entities, ruled by laws of behavior which can be studied and correlated. Relationships, then, become a matter of knowing the right thing to do or say which will manipulate the other into achieving the right end.

The existentialists have rightly pointed to the essentially dehumanizing effects of this attitude. It is not that human beings and human life do not have a dimension that is objectified. In many ways there are predictable patterns operating in human reality, both individual and communal, but they have through our intrinsic capacity of self-reflection and self-determination been relativized. We can become conscious of our world and ourselves as distinct and transcendent to it and so able to change its meaning and structure. It is this essential inner freedom which enables the individual to ultimately escape control or determination by another. Hence, patterns of manipulation will operate only as long as they are not reflected upon and raised to consciousness. Once they are so raised to awareness, we are faced with the necessity of choosing to continue in them or to change them. If the latter, then the patterns are altered and the reality that is being studied changes. Then the patterns of manipulation that operated in the past will no longer be effective, and others will have to be devised.

Narcissism and the Pastoral Counselor

Here again whether a pastoral counselor adopts this approach to ministry so that he or she is primarily concerned to say or do the right thing to achieve what is seen as the desirable goal for the other will depend on the sort of theology he or she operates out of. Does the counselor see the end to be achieved as the attainment of certain well-defined attitudinal and behavioral patterns which he or she would identify as ideal, or does the counselor wish to see the person grow in his or her capacity to be more self-directing and independent, more capable of deciding for herself what she can or ought to do? If the former, then, the counselor is likely to be most involved in discovering the right buttons to press, the right way of presenting things, the most effective advice to give. But if the latter, then the counselor needs to find another way of influencing the other, one which will further that end of greater self-evaluation and determination. To involve oneself in manipulative patterns of responding would be in contradiction to the end the counselor wishes to achieve.

We have already established that it is the latter which is the central end of Christian Faith and therefore the one which should be espoused by pastoral ministers. This is not always an end which we have kept sight of; the Church has often fallen, unfortunately, into a pastoral approach that seeks control over the individual and ways of forming him to fit into predetermined behavior patterns. It has in fact been practically, if not theoretically, behavioristic in its approach. This, as we have seen, came out of a fundamental belief that the individual, because of sin, could not be trusted, and that he needed the social control of the Church if he were to be morally good or socially acceptable. Guilt was one of the major tools for achieving this, and where congregations gave the priest the authority to work this way, to a large extent this method was very successful in maintaining social control.

That people today, as we mentioned before, are less susceptible to this sort of control is something to be welcomed and encouraged. It makes possible the realization of the kingdom among us in a new and radical way. We are, to use Curran's expression, entering *the age of the person,* in which the Church is becoming less like an impersonal city in which authoritarianism is paramount and obedience the primary virtue and more like a community in which each person can find an environment in which his dignity and freedom are enhanced. This is opening up the possibility of a new experience of God, one which comes to a living experience of the mystery of the Trinity, of God as himself a vibrant community of distinct persons. The more we can reduce our tendency to adopt a

Godlike posture over others, the more we can be open together to the experience of the true God among us. It is only as we can gradually accept, realize, and live within our limitations as creatures that the face of God can become clearer to us.

Theological Perspectives

The Holy Spirit and the Recognition of Limitations

An essential ingredient in this experience of God is the fact that he is through his Spirit immanent in his creation, working in and through us to bring us to the perfection of his life. A willingness and capacity to recognize our limitations is also, then, the only way of realizing the ultimate dependency of each one of us on the power and love of God operative among us, revealed in Jesus Christ and continually mediated to us through the Holy Spirit. We can actually be open to experiencing that power operating in our lives. The spiritual program of recovery in Alcoholics Anonymous, which is highly successful in one of the most difficult of problem areas, is based entirely upon this dynamic. To really believe in the Holy Spirit is to recognize and live in the belief that the well-being of each person is primarily the responsibility and concern of God and that through his Holy Spirit he is operative already in the other's life for his salvation in accordance with his uniqueness and in a way that is prior to and more foundational than any help that I might be able to offer. This faith in God operative in the other's life can be realized only through a faith in the other to manage their lives for themselves. Only by trusting in this capacity in others can we actualize our trust in the God who is operating in them, just as according to St. John we can show our love for God only through our love for others (1 Jn 4:20).

The Experience of Powerlessness and Counselor Status

In pastoral work, then, we join with God in his task, but we do not try to take it over. Too often our advice giving is an expression, not of faith in the God who is operative in the lives of each of us, but an abrogation of that position to ourselves. When we do that we act as if the other's well-being or salvation is somehow totally our responsibility. We, then, are responsible for either coming up with the right answer or manipulating the other into doing what we think is the right thing for them. Overreliance on advice giving then can be an expression of a real lack of faith in God and a subtle identification of ourselves with his role.

To be open to a real faith in God and experience his power in our lives, we need to first come to experience the limits of our own power over others. St. Paul himself came to realize the importance of the experience of powerlessness in experiencing the power of God in his ministry. When he pleaded with the Lord to take away a particular weakness in him that he felt was hindering his ministry, he heard the Lord saying to him:

> "My grace is sufficient for you, for my power is made perfect in weakness." Paul then concluded that "Therefore I will boast all the more gladly about my weaknesses, so that Christ's power may rest on me" (2 Cor 12:8–9).

If we take as the guiding light of our ministry that essentially we are there to serve the growth and development of the other into his or her own maturity as a self-aware, self-determining individual, capable of formulating the meaning of the world and acting responsibly in it, then our ministry must be founded on the awareness and acceptance of powerlessness over the other.

Power Over vs. Power For

Of all the modern authors in counseling psychology the one who in recent years has made the most powerful plea for an acceptance of this on the part of counselors is Carl Rogers (*On Personal Power*. New York: Delacorte Press, 1977). His whole work is in fact a plea for the counselor to be willing to give up power over the client so as to be able to discover a power for the person. It is this which has made his work so highly relevant to pastoral counseling and in one way or another influenced it so strongly in recent years. The sense of the community was that in so many ways he has discovered real behavioral correlates to the perspectives of the Gospel, particularly that which has emerged so strongly since Vatican II of respect for and promotion of personal freedom and responsibility. We find this reflected in this quotation from Louis Monden's now classic work *Sin, Liberty, and the Law*. It is worth quoting him at length on this:

> Man suffers so much from his helplessness precisely because in him it conflicts with another reality. That other reality, which alone can render the helplessness conscious as helplessness, can only be a creative freedom. In quite a number of insane people, suffering lacks this moral character, since they are no longer aware of their helplessness and their distress. Psychotherapy, on the other hand, becomes possible only through a steady appeal to the implicitly present creative liberty. Whether consciously used or resulting spontaneously from the circumstances, it is ultimately only a technique which gives the option of freedom the possibility of growing creatively through, and emerging from, the network of determinisms.
>
> In Freudian psychoanalysis this appeal to freedom remains largely implicit. It is somewhat more explicit in the Jungian process of individuation. In more recent schools, such as the existential analysis of Frankl, the therapeutic praxis of Binswanger, Matussek and von Gebsattel, and even more in the non-directive therapy of Carl Rogers, an effort is made to enter into dialog with deepest creative freedom (New York: Sheed and Ward, 1965, p. 33).

Revolutionary Aspects of the Understanding Process

Rogers, in seeing that this approach aimed precisely toward the empowerment of the client to a creative freedom, recognized that, despite the democratic ideals that theoretically stand behind all therapeutic practice, this would still be a revolutionary concept in psychotherapy and one which is very threatening to many counselors (p. 16). It hits directly at their professional status as doctors of the soul after the model of doctors of the body, experts in the control and prediction of the processes which bring mental and physical health. It is interesting to note that it is increasingly being realized within the medical profession itself that the doctor is not in control of the forces of health; rather, he assists the body to heal itself by removing blockages to that healing. He is not the master of the situation but a servant. This is the call that Rogers' has been making to the psychotherapeutic community: to realize and act as servants of another's process, not as its master.

In the same sense that this can be threatening to the professional counselor, it can also threaten the minister or priest; it hits directly at his sense of competency and his status as an expert. To give up control of the other is to court a real loss of prestige and status, and, to the extent that he is identified with these, a real loss of being. And if there is anything upon which the minister or priest has to try to build his reputation, it is on being an effective helper to those in difficulty and distress. Very often our success is gauged by how the client leaves us emotionally. Does he feel better or worse? If through our ministry the person has not achieved some emotional relief, we automatically feel that it is we who have failed. In this we have effectively taken over responsibility for the way the other is feeling and their improvement then becomes our responsibility. We have succumbed to the model of master rather than that of servant. This leads directly to the problems of countertransference that Freud pointed out as intrinsic to the therapeutic process as then understood.

This fear of lack of success and corresponding loss of prestige can make it very difficult for a priest or minister to look at the real limitations on his power (to change another's condition or situation) imposed upon him both by the nature of the human reality and by the Gospel, and to take these limitations into consideration. But if our ministry is to be fruitful it is essential to be able and willing to do this. Only then does it become possible for us to discover our actual strengths and what is really possible in helping others. It is not a matter of doing nothing but a matter of being realistic, of discovering what really is possible.

The Importance of Counseling

The first thing that we now know is possible, and to this we are indebted to Rogers, is that there is a fundamental process of relating to another which does empower the other to grow and develop toward increasing self-consciousness and self-determination. This obviates the dangers of narcissistic countertransference and in doing so enables us to understand how the helping process can incorporate the educative and guidance dimensions in a way which enables them to be truly growth producing and not growth inhibiting.

In the way we have described it, however, we have moved somewhat beyond Rogers' position, though building firmly upon it. Following the work and research of Charles A. Curran, we have talked about our work as a process of *understanding* and have linked it, not simply to an acceptance of the client and a reflection back of what was said, but as a way of truly understanding what was meant. Out of a deeply committed relationship characterized by faith and trust in the client, it reaches to the inner intentionality of the client and articulates something of the values that are being conveyed in and through the client's communication and which are the core of his or her uniqueness. It is in and through the recognition of his or her value investments that the client is able to reach a deeper, more objective understanding of who the client is, what he or she is seeking, and what needs to be modified.

As an art and a skill which aims, first of all, at creating an environment in which the client can gradually gain the confidence to explore his own inner world and behaviors and begin to formulate a better understanding of his situation and what it requires, counseling can be a powerful instrument in helping the person to clarify and understand his own inner world in all its uniqueness. It empowers the person's own rational reflective processes, freeing up their own dynamism to be self-determining. A detailed explanation as to how this skill operates and how to achieve competence in it does not belong here, but, as we have seen, its basic core consists in the capacity to be incarnational, to leave one's own world behind and enter into the world of another and to be able to articulate it in a way that the person comes to ever deeper levels of understanding about himself and his situation. It reaches to draw out and clarify the actual meaning structures that the person is operating out of and so makes it possible for him to assess and evaluate them and if necessary to formulate more adequate under-standings and goals. It recapitulates on the psychological level what God has done for the human race in Jesus Christ.

Counseling and the Giving of Advice

Egan, like many others in the field, would see the counseling process in it empathic dimensions as a way of creating a trusting environment in which the person will be open to the suggestions and guidance of the counselor (*The Skilled Helper*). One might disagree with him on this as being a subtle manipulation of the client and see with Curran that empathy is at the heart of the relationship and of paramount value in and of itself and not just as an instrument for the attainment of some ulterior end (*Counseling and Psychotherapy: the Pursuit of Values*. East Dubuque, Ill.: Counseling-Learning Institute). But, if a person does really experience and appreciate in the counselor a respect for his own freedom of self-evaluation and determination and begin to realize these dimensions in his life, then it is undoubtedly true that he or she will become more able to benefit from other more direct input from the counselor.

This might include offering the person alternative ways of viewing his or her situation both internally and externally and of tackling more directly cognitive distortions and ineffective behavior that the counselor perceives. Or it may be the suggestion of factors in the situation that the person is not clearly alluding to but which the counselor, as a detached observer, thinks the client able to per-ceive.

In all of this the counselor would be primarily working out of what the client himself has disclosed to him or her. Our insights may be sounder if we have a real and personal knowledge of the person's background and situation. For a pastor this may often be the case. It might also on occasion be necessary to challenge the client in various ways. Confrontation within the right environment can be enormously powerful in helping a person clarify and realize what he or she is doing and why. But the counselor needs to own his own subjectivity in doing so, making clear the freedom of the other to accept or reject what is said. He or she also needs to be continually sensitive to the response of the client to the suggestions made and able to enter into responses and articulate suggestions in an understanding way.

Finally, there is advice giving, the actual suggestion of alternative or new ways of behaving in order to realize some goal. The ability to do this is governed by the factors already mentioned: (1) that the counselor be sure that he does have expertise in the area in question; (2) that the counselor is able to share the goals and values of the client in that area; and (3) that he or she is confident that the client is able and willing to take responsibility for the consequences of acting on suggestions. For all these conditions to be fulfilled, advice giving is more normally something one would do only after considerable dialogue with the client. Everett Shostrom, however, says that, if it is used as a first approach, then

> . . . *it is most appropriate when it is known in advance that the contact will be short and where a relatively inconsequential life decision must be made quickly. The counselor recognizes that this is a superficial, intellectualized approach which generally does not affect basic attitudes. If used sparingly and cautiously on normal people with situational problems and with minor decisions to be made, little risk is involved. Normal people generally are capable of evaluating suggestions and rejecting them when not acceptable (op. cit., p. 270).*

It is most appropriate, however, when the person has already come to a certain clarity about himself or herself and his or her situation and is able to weigh the advice for himself or herself and relate it to his or her own individual circumstances with a certain discrimination. Where, through the counseling process, the person has come to realize and accept the primary responsibility for assessing and deciding what can and ought to be done, then he or she is in the position of making the best and most judicious use of the suggestions. Advice in fact can be really assimilated and applied in a fruitful way only by someone who has the ability to understand what is being said and how it might apply in his or her circumstances. The key is the capacity and willingness of the person to be responsible for his or her own behavior. Suggestions as to the best way forward might then aid a person in his independent evaluation and perhaps increase his ability to act more effectively than previously. It gives him other options to weigh, other avenues he can explore, and different possible ways of construing his situation and its possibilities. Such advice or guidance should be offered to the person not in any dogmatic or coercive fashion but in humility and tentativeness, with full recognition that in the final analysis it is the client who must bear the consequences for any behavior he adopts. Care, too, needs to be taken that the client understands that this is accepted and respected by the counselor and that noncompliance with the advice would not bar the person from returning for further exploration.

Conclusion

As I said at the beginning, this book was not written primarily to address the problem of possible lawsuits arising out of the giving of advice. Nevertheless, I think that the guidelines that have emerged here concerning the limitations of advice giving and its proper use will be helpful in obviating the possible danger of such legal action. The existence of such legal actions should reinforce our awareness of the dangers and difficulties involved in a too-ready use of advice giving in our pastoral practice and reinforce our need to master our counseling skills in dialogue with God as covenant partners. In this, God is parental but in a very positive sense. He relates to us in a way that enables us to grow into our fullness, not preventing us from making mistakes but creating the environment which enables us to learn from them. It is this creative environment which we seek to create in our ministry, too.